"Scholarship of law in the 21st century demands openness to diversity, attention to ethics, methodological reflectiveness, and above all an ability to reimagine our legal worlds in new ways. Ann Genovese meets these challenges with her highly imaginative and self-reflective book. *Feminist Jurisography* offers readers an entirely fresh approach to the writing of law as a writing of life. Throughout, the need to experiment with writing, with life, and with ideas is emphasised and the result is a highly engaging account of feminist legal writing as a practice as well as of the writer's journey with and experiences of a vast, sometimes eclectic, and always fascinating oeuvre."

Margaret Davies, *Flinders University, Australia.*

"*Feminist Jurisography* is a wonderfully radical, innovative, and imaginative text. It explores the relationship between feminism, law, history and writing in an intensely personal manner that has implications for all of us. In tracing the emergence and obligations of the feminist jurisographer, Genovese suggests an intellectual approach for the future."

Ann Curthoys, *University of Sydney, Australia.*

"A powerful and refreshingly original approach to reading and writing about law. Grounded in the analysis of key feminist texts, such as de Beauvoir's *The Second Sex*, *Feminist Jurisography* heralds a novel way of making sense of the world from a feminist perspective."

Margaret Thornton, *Emerita Professor, Australian National University.*

Feminist Jurisography

This book offers a jurisprudential meditation on and methodological performance of how feminist and legal thought come into relation. This book is about the conduct of one's scholarship and why it requires examination.

Across six essays, the book reintroduces official and unofficial jurisprudence writing of the late 20th century to show how disciplinary methods were transformed, and how relations between people and place, and between law and humanities, were transferred from the periphery to the centre of contemporary scholarship. To demonstrate this story, *Feminist Jurisography* experiments with genre, style, and form to historicise the relationship of a feminist jurisprudent to her own sources, methods, and interlocutors; and remind that it was feminist intellectuals from 1949 onwards who altered conducts of interdisciplinary scholarship in ways that are underacknowledged today. It exemplifies why naming a practice for yourself is an acknowledgment of relations of difference, collaboration, and inheritance, but also a performance of the feminist tradition of intellectual self-assertion that the book explores.

The book will be a useful resource for scholars and students of law and humanities, feminism, and history, and of value to a general audience interested in feminist ideas. The book will benefit contemporary conversations about the history and status of feminist contributions to these fields.

Ann Genovese is Professor at Melbourne Law School, University of Melbourne, Australia.

Feminist Jurisography

Law, History, Writing

Ann Genovese

Routledge
Taylor & Francis Group
LONDON AND NEW YORK

Designed cover image: *La gioia del risveglio (Emma Baeri's table, Catania)*

First published 2023
by Routledge
4 Park Square, Milton Park, Abingdon, Oxon OX14 4RN

and by Routledge
605 Third Avenue, New York, NY 10158

Routledge is an imprint of the Taylor & Francis Group, an informa business

A Glasshouse book

British Library Cataloguing-in-Publication Data
A catalogue record for this book is available from the British Library

ISBN: 978-1-138-61860-2 (hbk)
ISBN: 978-1-032-42043-1 (pbk)
ISBN: 978-0-429-46113-2 (ebk)

DOI: 10.4324/9780429461132

Typeset in Bembo
by Apex CoVantage, LLC

Contents

Acknowledgments

I pay my respects to the custodians and Elders – past, present, future – of the Wurundjeri peoples of the Kulin nation, on whose land much of this book was written. I also pay my respects to the custodians and Elders – past, present, future – of the Meintangk people, on whose land the book was finished. I wish to convey to all my sincere gratitude for your hospitality.

I thank Taylor and Francis for permission to use aspects of the following published essays in Chapters One, Two, Three and Four:

Ann Genovese (2013) 'Inheriting and Inhabiting the Pleasures and Duties of Our Own Existence: *The Second Sex* and Feminist Jurisprudence' *Australian Feminist Law Journal* 38/1: 41–57 DOI:10.1080/13200968.2013.10854482.

Ann Genovese (2014) 'On Australian feminist tradition: three notes on conduct, inheritance and the relations of historiography and jurisprudence' *Journal of Australian Studies* 38/4: 430–444 DOI:10.1080/14443058.2014.954137.

Ann Genovese and Shaun McVeigh (2015) 'Nineteen eighty three: a jurisographic report on *Commonwealth v Tasmania*' *Griffith Law Review* 24/1: 68–88 DOI:10.1080/10383441.2015.1022891.

I thank the publishers and editors of the journal *Law Text Culture* for permission to use aspects of the following essay in Chapter Three:

Ann Genovese (2016) 'About Libraries: A Jurisographer's Notes on Lives Lived With Law (in London and Sydney)' *Law Text Culture* 20/1: 33–65 DOI:10.1080/13200968.2013.10854482.

I thank the Australian Research Council, whose funding of a Postdoctoral Fellowship in 2006 enabled me to begin the work that transformed itself slowly into *Feminist Jurisography*. I also thank Colin Perrin for his belief that the book was worth publishing, and his patience waiting for the worst of 2020–2021 to be over for the manuscript to be delivered. I also want to thank all the editorial team at Routledge, in particular Naomi Round Cahalin, for their hard work and assistance.

I would like to thank all my wonderful students, from whom I have learned so much during the long period of researching and writing this book. I am particularly indebted to my current and former PhD students, and the scholars who have worked alongside me as tutors in my subjects, all of whom have been important interlocutors, and always my imagined audience. Three former students (now doing incredible work in their own projects and fields) were generous enough to agree to be my research assistants during the long haul. Erica Millar, Claire Oppermann, Cinzia Pellicciotta: your excellent skills, attitude, and good humour at the three different stages of this book made starting, continuing, and finishing a pleasure.

I would also like to thank the friends and colleagues whose generous invitations (both official and unofficial) to discuss this often-hidden project over the past ten years provided much-needed intellectual camaraderie. The conversations taught me a lot, and undoubtedly improved my argument, and my spirits. Thanks to: Emma Baeri, Jenny Beard, Elena Caruso, Eddie Cubillo, Margaret Davies, Adriana Di Stefano, John Docker, Shaunnagh Dorsett, Maria Drakopoulou, Debolina Dutta, Julie Evans, the late Virginia Fraser, Rosemary Hunter, Marett Leiboff, Alex Martinis Roe, Crystal McKinnon, Mark McMillan, Jenny Morgan, Linda Mulcahy, Connal Parsley, Kim Rubenstein, Kristen Rundle, Margaret Thornton, Christopher Tomlins, Karin Van Marle, Scott Veitch, and Kevin Walton.

The following friends are also integral to how I have lived with this project, and contributed in countless ways: Theodora Beatty, Andrew Burrow, Anne Davies, Julie Evans, Susy Gee, Jennifer Lade, Alexander MacDonald, Livingstone McVeigh, Bess Meredith, Karin Riederer, Peter Rush, Maureen Tehan, Alison Young, and Charlie Young. Thank you all for the solidarity, hospitality, patience, fun, and support.

Two people have read every word and walked every step of this project with me, Ann Curthoys and Shaun McVeigh. Without your friendship and faith there would be no book at all. Thank you.

Finally, I would like to dedicate this book to my family, with my love and admiration. Mary Genovese, John Genovese, Paul Ronfeldt, Joe Genovese Ronfeldt, and Sam Genovese Ronfeldt: *vi ringrazio, per tutto*.

Ann Genovese, May 2022

Essay 1

Feminist Jurisography (Introductory Notes)

An Introduction: Jurisography

Simone de Beauvoir, in 1949, posed a question: 'How, in the feminine condition, can a human being accomplish herself?'[1] In this book, I reflect upon the inheritance of this question, to examine what it means to become the author of your own knowledge and experience. The six essays that form the book have been written and rewritten over the course of more than a decade, and are practical examples of how I have been working alongside different disciplinary traditions. In my writing I have not set out to replicate, excuse, or critique these traditions. Instead, I have tried to reimagine them, drawing on their practices to make visible the conditions of living with law in my own time and place. In one view, then, these essays are personal exercises that draw from my training as feminist, historian, and jurisprudent in Australia. They can be read as explorations in how to take sufficient care of the methods, styles, and genres which belong to all three traditions of which I am a beneficiary. In a more general view, the essays offer a short history of the conditions in which written accounts of feminism and jurisprudence came into relationship in the second half of the 20th century. My premise, in either view, is that the method, technique, and argument deployed in feminist and jurisprudential writing is not separate from the scholarly and personal experiences of the writer.

Placing method, technique, and argument into overt relationship (and front and centre in this formal part of my Introduction) is to emphasise how activities of writing help me think about the jurisprudence and feminism that I live with every day. This includes being clear how my practices are not necessarily interchangeable with yours. It is not my intention, I would stress before you generously begin reading, to foreclose others' experiences of becoming responsible for their knowledge, or to suggest there is ever one preferable account written about that knowledge. On the contrary, what I want to do in the essays collected in this book is demonstrate a simple point: how any scholar comes into relationship with their own projects is a subject that requires technical attention by them, and conscious acknowledgement of their own situation and

DOI: 10.4324/9780429461132-1

obligations. I think this is a crucial prerequisite for being able to enter responsible public relationship with accounts of other knowledges. That many accounts of feminist traditions (including my own) are still not yet in full institutional view is, I think, a condition of our own scholarly times and a problem. That they might become so is an overtly political consideration, also specific to our times, and one that has caused me to persevere in finishing my own project in the form it now takes.

From this starting point, it is important to pay regard to expectations you might have about a feminist/jurisprudence book, so I do not disappoint before I even begin. The essays presented here are not necessarily concerned with settling the accounts of feminist legal theory, telling a history of feminist lawyers or women at law schools, or giving a reformist tale of a particular subject matter. Neither are they animated by an impulse to complicate the tropes and taxonomies of feminist legal praxis; nor to challenge perspective, revision, or 'context' in schools of jurisprudence, or historiography. All those projects are central to contemporary scholarly work, and the scholarly worlds in which I live, and I am grateful for any opportunity to enter dialogue with them. I observe, however, that although each of those projects can be written in multiple traditions (including the socio-legal, the critical, the poetic, or the biographical), they do not always overtly address how methods deployed are not only useful to tell a story, but in fact also carry the story themselves. This includes being attentive to how histories of method and technique are integral to the distinctiveness of located jurisprudence (in my case, in Australia). I hope to attend to these matters in the essays that follow. But I hope my main contribution to scholarly conversation will be the demonstration of a practice – *jurisography* – that I have named to achieve these ambitions.

Jurisography is the outcome of collaborations I have done over the past ten years with jurisprudents Shaun McVeigh and Peter Rush. Naming a practice, and inventing a persona to do the work, is not intended as a convenient self-promotion of a rule-based template for jurisprudence writing, nor a programmatic formula for writing histories that include jurisprudential texts. Rather, it is a recommendation to give a public jurisprudential shape to the conduct of life tradition, an ethos of engagement concerned with what it means to inherit, and write about, different sets of duties that are part of living a disciplinary life. I will elaborate and explain more about this tradition in the notes that follow. For now, I would observe that the jurisographer's key public duty is to take care of the many forms and sources of writing of jurisprudence the individual jurisographer inherits, noting these won't simply be derived from jurists, judges, and jurisprudents. The jurisographer's duties, we also suggest, include cultivating an openness about one's own choice and use of sources, and being clear what technical (as well as aesthetic or performative) work form, style, and genre do in those sources. For feminist jurisographers, and this is my chief concern, these duties extend to cultivating methods of acknowledgment, reintroduction, and reimagination (terms of art I will demonstrate as we move along). The point is to make visible how fragmentary unofficial sources and forms have conditioned both the conduct of everyday lives lived with law, and the experience of what it means to assert oneself as a knowledge holder who may not be the usual academic suspect.[2]

In that spirit, this first essay – now the formalities are out of the way – deploys a genre that is itself fragmentary. I have chosen to write my introductory remarks as a series of notes. The note is central to feminist histories of writing shaped by limited opportunities (writing done in snatched or divided time, 'proceeding by twists and turns').[3] That has been my own experience in producing this book, so it seemed a fitting way to start. It should go without saying (but never does) that writing oneself into disciplinary frame as feminist has been strange and difficult, and for many includes a refusal of the assumed completeness of standard form hypothesising. So instead of further monographic exposition on my intentions (the monograph being a genre not readily available for dissemination of women's knowledge until scandalously recently),[4] I offer some notes on disciplinary self-formation (and self-preservation) as a scholar. I hope these notes explain why I named the persona of the feminist jurisographer, and how taking up that persona shapes the essays you are about to read on law, history, feminism, and writing.

Note One – The Conduct of Life Tradition

Jurisography is a self-invented practice that worries about jurisprudence writing and belongs to a tradition of conduct. To explain how and why those two things join, I need to take a step back, and start with what philosophers have meant for centuries when they write from this tradition.

The tradition of conduct is concerned with asking the question: 'How should I conduct a life?'[5] It exists as a rival tradition to that of critique, where the philosopher's questioning of the world operates at a distance, intentionally or not, from the philosopher's own self, temporality, and location. From the Greeks onwards, philosophy within the tradition of conduct is not a discourse to be mastered, but a type of 'know-how', as philosopher Pierre Hadot reminds, in order 'to change [one's] way of living and seeing the world'.[6] In order to care for the conduct of a life in this way, the philosopher is understood to be continuously engaged in activity. One of these is writing. The writing of philosophy is understood to be a series of *spiritual exercises* through which a scholar offers training, to themselves and those who learn from them, in how to form a disciplinary life. This is not a relentlessly positive activity about self-fulfilment realised through *writing it all down*. What matters in that writing is to hone arguments specific to a public role, and to remind that choosing the forms and expressions of writing when inhabiting that role can come at a cost. It is also to demonstrate that there are possibilities for innovation, change, or relationship, occasioned because you are writing as a philosopher who is conscious of how you live in the world. The act of writing is therefore always experienced by the philosopher, in this tradition, as relational, although this may not be expressly stated. These relations run in several directions: between the philosopher and their philosophy, between the writing of the philosopher and those that follow them (a question of inheritance), and importantly, but often undervalued, between the philosopher and their collaborators (or as Hadot puts it, with those 'whom [they] share temporal space, and intellectual conversation').[7]

To understand writing as a relational practice in these ways requires methods sufficient, or at least responsive, to the question asked. This applies as much to the writing of philosophy as to the writing of history, jurisprudence, or feminism which draws from this tradition of conduct. An important aspect is self-awareness that a person takes up a persona consciously to do their disciplinary work and fulfill their public obligations. This means that when in pursuit of the question 'how should I live' and how that might be written, the 'I' is not directed to an authoring of self, or disclosing an authentic self, through writing. Writing in this tradition is not Romantic nor confessional. It is not about identity. Instead, the 'I' attaches to the ethos of the persona – be it philosopher, historian, jurisprudent, or, as we shall see, feminist.

The duties to self and others that attach to different personae in this tradition are not identical, and these differences are important. For the historian, for example, the duty in the writing of history (historiography) invokes responsibility neither to simply communicate nor assert a narrative of the past, but 'to form and train' the historian to care for a life through an examination of their inheritances. This involves a specific attitude toward time. Hadot, for example, argues that it is the realities of one's own experience that contour how the past is addressed. This suggests a relation between past and present that must always be reimagined and relocated, as the exercise of its writing 'presents a continuous act, permanent and identical with life itself, that must be renewed at every instant'.[8] Being very clear about that temporal relation is therefore part of a training in which a person takes up their role as historian and enters into a 'mode of existing-in-the world'.[9] Writing history in these terms is an exercise in ethos that shows the historian exactly how they are responsible for what they inherit (be it as narrative, source, or technique). French philosopher and historian Michel Foucault of course addresses this question in his later work, and his ethical *poesies* is what most historians identify as the exemplar of this tradition.[10] In his lectures at the Collège de France in 1982–1983, and his history of sexuality, Foucault argues that understanding how to conduct a life ethically infers attention be given to the 'arts of living', or self-fashioning. This includes a concern with the practices of writing histories of the present in which the writer addresses the conditions of their own time. Foucault directed himself to explain and perform that task – through the question of male desire – by referencing back the classical Greek world, and delineating the differences between histories of representation, and those of knowledge and experience.[11] As he explained to his audience in Paris on 5 January 1983, he wanted 'to bring about a shift from the contents of knowledge, to forms of knowledge';[12] and a shift from subject identity to formation. 'Instead of referring to a theory of the subject', Foucault argued, 'it seemed to me that one should try to analyse the different forms by which the individual is led to constitute him or herself as subject'; a subject (or disciplinary expositor) who then had carriage of 'discursive forms of veridiction'.[13]

Jurisprudents who align with this tradition of conduct ask similar questions, directed toward how to live with law. Yet these jurisprudents, although not taking up the persona of historian, are careful to pay attention to what they too inherit, and how it informs the shape and obligation of the care and practice of law in their own time. By also returning to the Greeks and showing their continued presence through the 17th century to our own times, jurisprudent Peter Goodrich, for one important example, reminds that the tradition of 'knowledge of oneself and care of oneself' produces a 'materialisation of thought', that 'entail[s] decisions that ground a life' — decisions which include those made with, in and about law.[14] For Goodrich, the obligations of the jurisprudent who understands law as a way of life are to pay attention to 'the relationships that law engenders and the practices it supports'.[15] Thinking with conduct thus has its own genealogies that can be re-joined to the critical use of history in law. As an activity, this involves showing that history is not only an object to reframe, reform, or revolutionise law, nor only a technique to abet and complicate law's critical projects. It is also a practice of writing law's inheritance that trains the jurisprudent to understand how to take care of the conduct of their law.

Note Two – Office and Persona

But is all this explanation satisfactory if one is also a feminist, and taking care of feminist knowledge and practices? In these accounts so far, the arts and duties of writing are oriented toward shaping the realm of men. From Aristotle onwards, writing in the conduct of life tradition has expressed 'an exemplary human experience'[16] to prepare a man for 'institutionalised social office' as priest, mayor or monarch, as well as the 'more elusive offices of the intellect ' such as those of poet, jurisprudent, or historian.[17] In his work, Shaun McVeigh has reanimated the duties and virtues of scholarly office bearing (an old but consistent language and way of thinking in law).[18] He has considered the forms of conduct that might be adequate to contemporary practices of jurisprudential life in public, and understood as lawful relations, particularly in Australia. Thinking about office and associated duties is of course central to Shaun and my jurisographic collaboration too, but it is important to be clear how I have a distinct legacy when I take up and reimagine disciplinary roles.

It is, for instance, an historical fact that women's experience of office-holding *per se* has been predicated on forms of exclusion and demarcation, based on sex.[19] It is also a fact that such injurious demarcation is distinctive to Western traditions. In Australia, leading Indigenous feminist jurisprudents and scholars have patiently demonstrated how Indigenous men and women have separate but not subordinate responsibilities to law. This is a distinction that is rarely understood positively by settler colonial law and jurisprudence but is central to Indigenous jurisprudence, and extends to both women and men holding positions as law holders of Indigenous nations, in the past and present.[20] The Western tradition (the one in which I am trained, and for which I am responsible in the encounter with Indigenous jurisprudence, especially on this question of the conduct between men's and women's law) stands in stark contrast. Although women have long occupied clearly (and legally) defined social roles with specific duties and skills, performed in the home or church (for example, as nuns or midwives, as much as mothers or wives), these roles did not attach as exalted 'offices' to the realm of the State (the realm of men). They have instead been historically devalued, mythologised, and stripped of any innate creativity or agency.[21] At the same time, however, the art of self-fashioning that is practiced by the intellectual personae, each with their distinct and distinctive 'skills or virtues', has nevertheless been accomplished by many women, and for a very long time. Although a more difficult register for women than men until very recently (writing out of office, at the edges of kitchen or café tables, sometimes with male *nom de plumes*), to assert oneself as writer or poet (and often as philosopher and historian too, through that writing) does have exalted feminist forebears.[22] Thinkers and writers as diverse as Christine De Pizan, George Eliot, and Virginia Woolf[23] have been exemplary in practicing personae that show there is a difference between expressing oneself through one's art, and the art of fashioning a self through activity, which involves acceptance of the responsibilities that attach to the performance of that activity in a life. There is, however, one very particular exemplar who is guiding my project. Simone de Beauvoir, in *The Second Sex* in 1949, showed for the first time what it meant to inhabit an intellectual persona *as woman*. She made explicit that her duty as writer was to pay attention to the experience of woman's life lived in relation with man, and in and with institutions, and to understand how it conditions the present in which she writes.[24] Although this may seem almost identical to the duty of a historian as exemplified by Foucault in the 1980s (and I note as an aside that Foucault inherits from Beauvoir, rather than the other way around),[25] persona and personal experience are not necessarily separated in the same way.

Note Three – Inheritance

The Second Sex has been a seminal text for Western feminist disciplinary self-determination since it was written.[26] Australian feminist philosopher Moira Gatens has argued that in Beauvoir's famous assertion that 'One is not born but rather becomes a woman' can be found '[t]he backbone of contemporary western feminist thought . . . *The Second Sex* allowed its readers to collectively construct an imaginary that became a feminist imaginary'.[27] As one of the readers who has inherited this text, Beauvoir's work and example anchor all my essays in *Feminist Jurisography*. In each of them, an aspect of the story I will tell is about how that work and example have influenced feminist thought and writing practices, and how that influence has changed over time. As part of these introductory notes, I therefore need to examine what Beauvoir accomplished, and explain what I mean by 'inheritance', to shape what I want to say in my own project.

'Inheritance' is a commonplace trope in feminist work, and clearly understood as an active performance, not simply an organisational flourish in a text. This performance can be about building a relationship that gives succour and solidarity.[28] But it can also be about intergenerational rejection, as political urgencies change how a text is accepted.[29] The point is that inheritance of a source, for each feminist writer, is unique to her own formation and situation. In one sense, then, '*The Second Sex* [had] an ordinary fate', as the French feminist philosopher Michèle Le Dœuff notes, '*habent sua fait libri*, books have their own destiny and the most usual of these is to be fragmented — we'll take this, and not that, says posterity'.[30]

The Second Sex was written in 1949 and translated (not without controversy) into English in 1953. It became famous very quickly for an intimacy in style, and an openness about sex, as well as having quite a lot to say about existential thought. By the early 1970s, *The Second Sex* retained some of its jolt of recognition,[31] but readers no longer spoke 'fluent existentialis[m]'[32] as they once might have. One result was that Beauvoir's innovations in genre, and originality of intent, became divorced from the intellectual world in which *The Second Sex* was conceived and written.[33] (This is perhaps not unusual for any book, even one that sold 22,000 copies in France and was prohibited by the Vatican in its first week of public life, and has been reprinted and republished and translated countless times since).[34] Further, Beauvoir was adamant that *The Second Sex* was not a manifesto for collective action,[35] nor happiness,[36] so the desires of readers, over time, that might be seeking solely those forms of guidance from their feminist canon would result in fragmentation of the text, and less careful attention paid to her form and argument. More significantly, Beauvoir has long been the subject of a feminist abjection by some critics because of her relationship with Jean-Paul Sartre. One result is that *The Second Sex* has been misinterpreted as speaking from or through his work.[37] *The Second Sex*, however, is defiantly Beauvoir's own, as Le Dœuff first argued in 1980,[38] and has done so since then, alongside many other outstanding feminist scholars. Toril Moi, Karen Vingtes, Margaret A. Simons, Emily Grosholz, and Claude Imbert remind that what can be taken up, and when, as an inheritance, is already a mediated relationship, through text but also intellectual companionship and apprenticeship. The major contributions of these intellectual translators and interlocutors of Beauvoir (including those located here in Australia, who we will soon meet) was to demonstrate how the existential project of 1940s Paris was transformed precisely because Beauvoir wrote through her own experience. Such intellectual advocacy has aided the legacy of *The Second Sex*, but also insisted that inheritance is a conscious activity that includes reintroduction rather than redescription of thought[39] to guide those that read and follow in their own present situations. In this way, *The Second Sex* is increasingly understood as both a textual foundation for many feminist knowledges,[40] but also for intellectual history and contemporary philosophy *per se*.[41] This is of course what Beauvoir was arguing for all along, and in part demonstrates why *The Second Sex* remains relevant: experience and assertion of knowledge for men and women are distinct but not set apart, and this fact must be confronted with clarity and without sentimentality, to see how each exists in relationship of complicity, with the other.

Note Four – *The Second Sex* as Training Manual

To explore this idea, I want to think with the text closely in two ways. The first is to understand how Beauvoir's project in *The Second Sex* works as a set of technical exercises, but also as exercises in the assertion of an ethos, for herself, and for her readers.[42] The second is to begin the work of my own book, which is to situate that training into an Australian feminist tradition.

Beauvoir published *The Second Sex* when she was 41 years old, and already a publicly known intellectual.[43] Although 'excluded from the elite education of her male contemporaries' she was 'nevertheless at the Sorbonne studying philosophy alongside them'.[44] Beauvoir became one of the first generation of professionally trained women philosophers in France (with Simone Weil), yet one who did not work or teach within the university. She was also, famously, not writing in isolation, but in conversation with her contemporaries and friends: Sartre, Camus, Lacan, Merleau-Ponty, and others.[45] Theirs was a studied art of living. Writing and ideas structured how lives were conducted, although this was not as ascetic as it sounds. As has been documented by many, the writing of philosophical thought directed to being in the world was not disassociated from pleasure (the arts of conversation, café life, and the adventures of desire).[46] It was also politically charged, and not without competition. Beauvoir and her contemporaries challenged what responsible action for a human being might look like as a response to their own experiences after Occupation and war's end. Central to the practices that emerged as existentialism (and absurdism) was a '"French-style" German phenomenology' that experimented with relationship/duality and responsibility/complicity.[47] Intellectual milieus are never disassociated (which is one of Pierre Hadot's points about philosophers living their philosophy), and the work produced by these friends and writers bears close scrutiny of interrelationship. As Le Dœuff notes wryly, 'someone does a seminar at the College de France [on Self and Other] and we are stuck in it for fifty years at least. Lacan, Levinas, Lévi-Strauss, Simone de Beauvoir and a few others all took their bearings from it, directly or indirectly'.[48] (It is also worth reflecting on our own experiences in scholarly worlds, to be clear-sighted about how certain provocations may well be politically of their time, and intellectually *à la mode*, but some works and some authors have different fates to others).

Situating Beauvoir into her world, however, helps explain some of her work's central innovations. It is useful, for example, to remember that in 1947 Beauvoir had published *The Ethics of Ambiguity*, where she rehearsed her ideas about how to live with the immense contradictions of a world in reformulation. *The Ethics of Ambiguity* has an abstracted narrator, who speaks from and to the philosophical realm as if that, ironically, remains unambiguous. For example, Beauvoir writes:

> 'But the present is not a potential past; it is the moment of choice and action. . . . One cannot justify all that is by asserting that everything may equally be the object of contemplations: since man never contemplates: he does'.[49]

The tone of *The Second Sex* just two years later is startlingly different. Beauvoir is no longer standing aside. For example, in the Introduction to *The Second Sex* she notes frankly and conspiratorially:

> 'I used to get annoyed in abstract discussions to hear men tell me "you think such and such a thing because you're a woman". But I know my only defence is to answer, "I think it because it's true" thereby eliminating my subjectivity; it was out of the question to answer "And you think the contrary because you are a man", because it is understood that being man is not a particularity, a man is in his right by virtue of being man [. . .].[50]

Beauvoir seeks to understand not only the social question of why men 'have no doubt'[51] (although that is her lived starting point, and remains, in my view, an excellent question to ask). Rather, she wants to interrogate how answers and explanations given to demarcations of 'man' and 'woman' exist in life, but also in knowledge, as 'an absolute vertical that defines the oblique'.[52] This provocation and insight is of course commonplace (and made complex) today, but was not in 1949. Beauvoir argues that 'Enlightenment philosophy, rationalism or nominalism', and the changing views of 'biological and social sciences' (including Marx, and Freud)[53] collectively make the 'irritating' claim that 'women are, among human beings, merely those who are arbitrarily designated women'.[54] The 'justifications' on offer for why sex is designated in this way are written by men ('both judge and party')[55] and are 'only too clearly dictated by their own interest'.[56] Beauvoir is careful not to suggest an essential and 'eternal' feminine as a response. This is not surprising for a scholar writing in Paris, the year after the Universal Declaration of Human Rights was adopted. She takes as certainty that 'woman like man is a human being'; her point, instead, is to be clear how 'such an assertion is abstract'.[57] What is missing, Beauvoir argues, is an address to these same designations of sex from the vantage point of those who live with the 'concrete' conditions such designations perpetuate.[58] It is from this point that Beauvoir invites her reader to think about 'the problem' from their own experience of walking around in the world:

> '[A]nyone can see clearly see that humanity is split into two categories of individuals with manifestly different clothes, faces, bodies, smiles, movements and interests, and occupations; these differences are perhaps superficial; perhaps they are destined to disappear. What is certain is that for the moment they exist in a strikingly obvious way. . . . If the female function is not enough to define women, and if we also reject the explanation of the "eternal feminine", but if we accept, even temporarily that there are women on earth, we then have to ask: "what is a woman?"'[59]

It is what Beauvoir writes next that I want to underline, italicise, and bold:

> 'Merely stating the problem suggests an immediate answer to me. It is significant that I pose it'.[60]

This, I think, is her declaration of intent. It elucidates a method for her project: 'How, in the feminine condition, can a human being accomplish herself?'[61] Beauvoir's 'I' is not the self-conscious 'I' of memoirs, or the hidden 'I' of novels, that have shaped the feminist tradition that has come before her; nor is it an attitude that enables self-reflection for its own sake. 'I pose it' announces a training, for herself and others, in how to live as woman, where intellectual persona and personal experience are not separated, but exist in relation to each other. To show the conduct of life *as* relational in these ways offers something explicit and original to the disciplines in which Beauvoir worked and lived as philosopher, and as writer.

Note Five – Responsibility and Complicity (Existentialism, c.1949)

To explore what I mean by 'persona and the personal being drawn into relation' (a central organising concept for my own essays) I want to spend a little time thinking about the existential project of 1940s Paris. As noted, existentialism is not such a familiar language these days, but to see how *The Second Sex* engaged with its own tradition is important to a project like mine. There are many ways to say 'I am responsible' (or complicit) with a disciplinary practice or set of ideas when discussing your own work. I want to make transparent how Beauvoir confronted that question. I also want to show how in doing so, she provided a practical guide to readdress but not reject a relationship with philosophy (and by application, other disciplines too).

The core problematic of existentialism is an ethical question of conduct, posed in a particular way. If it is irresponsible to refuse to recognise oneself as a free subject, how is it possible to live an authentic life? The subject self for existentialists is not captive to external determinations that produce inevitable consequences on and for a life. As such, the subject's choices about their existence – how they practice the art of their own living – is directed always to realisation of their liberation as a human being. It involves self-questioning, and robust 'rearticulation of boundaries and norms' as they relate to the self, but also in relation to and with others.[62] This ethic in one sense refuses political engagements. For Jean-Paul Sartre (in *Being and Nothingness*, 1943) it is for example 'senseless to dream of complaining, since nothing alien to us has decided for us what we feel, what we live, what we are. . . . Isn't it myself who decides the coefficient of the adversity of things?'[63] The existent self thus aims always to 'transcend' the 'immanence' of the 'facticity' of the material world, and denies 'the efficacy of social or historical determinations'.[64] Oppression – the usual double to liberation – therefore has at its heart a void in the existential project; it cannot be 'thematisized'.[65] The self, and how the self might conduct relations with others, exists outside any institutional rule, or its determinate powers; as such, it can always be transformed.

Beauvoir works with the same problematic, but this 'leads to opposite consequences'[66] in *The Second Sex*, because woman's experience of her situation – which she must acknowledge responsibly in her own ethical projects – is formed by an exteriority *she did not fully choose*. Woman, like any human being, seeks autonomy, but 'in a world where men force her to assume herself as Other'.[67] As Beauvoir explains: 'no man would consent to being a woman but all want there to be women'.[68] Her point, made repeatedly in *The Second Sex*, is that the male existential 'project' is to give meaning, or value, to 'life'. Life itself, its reality, is forced instead to be represented by woman through her body – by blood, sex, birth, death. Her existence is therefore, for men, as an immanent Other that reminds him of what he cannot transcend. The way Beauvoir interprets the relation of men with women's bodies in this way enables her to 'ground an ontological-carnal hierarchy of "the masculine" and "the feminine"'.[69] This relation is what Beauvoir argues produces men's horror of women, and presupposes the use of force against them.[70] It also enables the myths and meanings within which both sexes experience life: it is this Self/Other relation that grounds her claim that woman is not born, but made. Beauvoir thus 'transforms' existentialism by orienting it toward a world where institutions and cultural practices perpetuate woman's Otherness. Woman cannot deny her exteriority, as the male existential subject has done (but perhaps should not). As Beauvoir explains:

> 'Woman's drama lies in this conflict between the fundamental claim of every subject, which always posits itself as essential, and the demands of a situation that constitutes her as inessential'.[71]

In this way, Beauvoir places the problem of freedom expressly into relation with a lucid description of how experience of a life is formed. She argues repeatedly for women to take responsibility for reading their 'situation', 'condition', or 'exteriority', with clarity, and often discomfort. This is not to reify or celebrate 'women's experience' as an essence, but to demonstrate that in paying attention to how women's condition is constantly reinvented, and lived, it can be changed.[72]

Beauvoir makes this connection between liberation and agency to insist that conduct of a life is chosen. Throughout the text, she is resolute about women taking responsibility for all the messy dimensions that form their experience, and thus shape their ways of being in the world. Importantly for my own interest in inventing and reinventing roles, Beauvoir organises her thought in *The Second Sex* (as she also does in *The Ethics of Ambiguity*) around female lived personae: the mother, wife, lover, narcissist, 'Independent woman'.[73] In each instance, she is clear-sighted about how a woman as subject can be complicit in her subjection. Beauvoir offered, then, in 1949, a feminism in which there is no exculpation of the self through structures and institutions or ideologies exterior to oneself, although she insists that we read these as dangerous and often seductive realities that require change. She makes the point that despite many educated, independent (French) women achieving concrete means to live an authentic life, it is possible to accept one's subordination and refuse responsibility for one's freedom by continuing (or neglecting) to see oppression in more convenient or conventional terms, such as duty, custom, obligation, security, or exceptionalism in relation to other women.[74] Beauvoir is tough as regards the situation and subject position 'woman' acting as an accomplice with 'man' and the material and cultural means by which her subjection is 'made'.[75] But it is important to recognise that for Beauvoir if 'woman' is to move toward liberation, towards the conditions of her own independence, this emancipation is not a separation. Her agency is a complicit act with the institutions and knowledge 'man' perpetuates in his unceded experience. As she concludes:

> 'To emancipate woman is to refuse to enclose her in the relations she sustains with man, but not to deny them; while she posits herself for herself, she will nonetheless continue to exist for him as well: recognizing each other as subject, each will remain an other for the other; reciprocity in their relations will not do away with the miracles that the division of human beings into two separate categories engenders: desire, possession, love, dreams, adventure'.[76]

Note Six – History and Experience

It is one thing to focus on Beauvoir's philosophical 'moves', for want of a better word, for their own sake. But I am not a philosopher, and the inheritance I want to draw from *The Second Sex* as an ethics is how Beauvoir undertakes her craft to make her intervention, and how she worked to 'accomplish herself' in the process. This is not only because *The Second Sex* is a writing project about knowledge that comes from Beauvoir's life, but because of the step she takes to understand how her experience of that life is situated for, and in, the here and now. This includes an address to the past and present that I have been taught as part of an Australian feminist tradition that follows on from Beauvoir and informs the crafting and content of *Feminist Jurisography*.

I think it is useful, before I directly describe that content, to be explicit about what I draw from Beauvoir's intervention into history writing and the centrality of experience. Although this inevitably slows down the action a little, this first essay is an important exercise in the ethos I am trying to train myself to perform in these essays as a whole: an acknowledgment, a giving of technical attention to what is learned, and how things might be done.

The Second Sex is divided into two books. Book One ('Facts and Myths'), is rarely read (aside from the Introduction), while Book Two ('Lived Experience') is the part with all the quotable quotes, and the direct discussion about sex and liberation. Sheila Rowbotham (a ground-breaking feminist historian) has observed:

> '*The Second Sex* shattered taboos in its negative portrayal of marriage, its courageous defence of contraception and abortion, its references to women taking young lovers. These all provoked comment and criticism, but most disturbing to the defenders of the status quo was the mix of sex and philosophy. A woman theorising in sensuous language broke all the rules of containment. Beauvoir contrived to embed her theme of the woman defined by others and yet struggling for her existential freedom in the structure of the book and in her mode of communication. She merged female and male zones, and this combination disturbed as much as what she actually said'.[77]

Book Two is what made publishers Knopf feel inclined to have it translated into English in 1953, thinking it was akin to the Kinsey Report (which Beauvoir had in fact read),[78] and sensing it was something that 'all Smith [College] girls' would want to read[79] (which in fact was right, as it turned out). What I think is important to observe is how the two parts work together.

Beauvoir describes the aims of her project as 'an attempt at lucidity . . . to take stock of the current state'.[80] In unfolding the concrete conditions of the 'current state', Beauvoir includes a longer history of how woman's ambiguous choices are derived. The conditions of the present Beauvoir describes are clearly her own (Paris, 1949), and as a consequence she does not reify an essential experience of 'woman' as it developed over time. The historical past, as she herself states, 'cannot be considered as defining an eternal truth'. Her experiential viewpoint in this way is distinctive to other feminist historiographical accounts of how experience can be a dangerous form of historical evidence (most famously, as argued for by Joan W Scott).[81] For Beauvoir, experience shapes the conduct of the writer, and the exploration for others of what and how her own present is embodied and located. Beauvoir's attitude to her own life, the fact that her experience grounds her consideration of the relational ontology she develops in *The Second Sex*, thus avoids the dangers of historical reconstruction of experience that Scott (and others since her) warns against. She is not reclaiming or seeking to essentially explain, or bury, the experience of others' oppression. As Rowbotham has pointed out, 'in the history section of the book [Beauvoir] is completely aware of differences in degree of subordination', in particular as regards race, and 'space to manoeuvre, leeway to live your life, ideas of entitlement emerge from such distinctions'.[82] Beauvoir is adamant that a writer cannot avoid partiality approaching the conditions of the present (this is what she must take responsibility for, in fact) and that any account she writes cannot be teleological. She insists, then, that an account of the present's lived dimensions cannot be written if in doing so the writer seeks to exculpate their embeddedness in it. As she explains:

> '[E]ven the way of asking the questions, of adopting perspectives, presupposes hierarchies of interests . . . every so-called objective description is set against an ethical background. Instead of trying to conceal those principles that are more or less explicitly implied, we would be better off stating them from the start; then it would not be necessary to specify on each page the meaning given to the words "superior", "inferior", "better", "worse", "progress", "regression" and so on'.[83]

This interrogation of the past for the present is necessary to understand materiality and the choices women make in accepting their freedom, *for the now*.[84] History in *The Second Sex*, and *The Second Sex* as historiography, operate to perform the problematic of Beauvoir's ethical project. Beauvoir writes neither to transform nor reclaim women or their experiences but 'to merely translate . . . a situation that is showing itself to be historical precisely in that it is in the process of changing'.[85]

Note Seven – Writing (Genre and Sources)

The last aspect I want to draw out of *The Second Sex* is about writing. If Beauvoir's purpose is to understand how to form a life that does not refuse the conditions of existence, the mode of becoming she addresses as writer is not divisible from her activity of writing. Beauvoir of course wrote memoirs that expressly explored her life,[86] and as philosopher Karen Vintges has argued, these 'autobiographical works . . . should be seen in the framework of her ethical theory . . . conceived of as a self-technique in a moral sense. [Alongside her] diaries and letters [they] were a means for her to question her own conduct and to shape herself as an ethical subject.'[87] This experiential viewpoint also appears in Beauvoir's novels, such as *The Mandarins* (1954).[88] As philosopher and literary theorist Elenore Holveck has argued, Beauvoir was explicit about how she wrote in various forms as technical and spiritual exercises.[89] For Beauvoir, the act of writing in different genres rendered her 'lived and felt experiences' into a form that could ground her otherwise abstract thought.[90] Beauvoir was adamant that her ethical philosophy as expressed in *The Second Sex* were 'essays', belonging to a literary genre, rather than the traditional form of philosophy writing.[91] The act of writing in these different genres aided Beauvoir to reimagine her disciplinary training, her conduct of life as a philosopher. The purpose of *The Second Sex* is different from Beauvoir's previous 'philosophy' writing (as we have seen), and it is useful to consider her 'I pose it' assertion in the context of her own writing life. *The Second Sex* was in fact written it as a preparation for *Memoirs of a Dutiful Daughter* (1958). As she later reflected: 'Wanting to talk about myself I became aware that to do so I should first have to describe the condition of woman in general'.[92] Beauvoir offered no polemic or 'theory' for any political movement, or any bounded, moralising feminist analysis, in doing so. The project, the exercise, was clear: 'writing about myself is the most appropriate way of talking to others about themselves', so they could be clear-sighted about their own restraints and institutional relationships, and forms of agency.[93]

This question of how women write philosophy through other genres as a way of asserting the specificity of their persona has been considered by both Michèle Le Dœuff and Moira Gatens.[94] Both argue that in understanding how writers like Beauvoir (and George Eliot) appreciated the forms and inheritances of their own traditions, and the choices made in the self-expression of their ideas and experiences of those traditions, it is possible to 'stress the experimental and embodied nature of [their] art [and how it holds] as a philosophical practice'.[95] In this way, *The Second Sex* performs its project. It is about writing the self as a practice, as a training manual for herself, and others, in how to hold an ethical tension between 'the fundamental claim of every subject, which always posits itself as essential, and the demands of a situation that constitutes [woman] as inessential'.[96]

Beauvoir made plain that this 'drama'[97] requires acknowledgment and attention to sources. The epigraph to *The Second Sex* is a quote from 17th-century French philosopher François Poulain de la Barre (a quote Beauvoir uses twice, and must have had double significance for her, as Poulain de la Barre was a man): 'Everything that has been written by men about women should be vowed with suspicion, because they are both judge and party'.[98] The sources Beauvoir uses in *The Second Sex* include official medical, scientific, anthropological, and psychoanalytic accounts about women's lives and desires, in order to be sceptical of their authors' intentions. She also technically reintroduces philosophical tracts or laws that presupposed official knowledge (men's knowledge) as neutral, or also unexperienced.[99] At the same time, Beauvoir mediates the past and present of woman's condition through alternate sources. Diary (Sophia Tolstoy, Marie

Bashkirtseff's *I am the most interesting Book of All*), essays and memoirs (Virginia Woolf), fiction (George Eliot, Louisa May Alcott, Katherine Mansfield), and philosophical tracts too (Christine de Pizan, Olympia de Gouges, Mary Wollstonecraft) become a means through which the expression of women's condition, and their exclusion from official or institutional record or public account, can be found.[100] Holveck, commenting on Beauvoir's approach to her materials, makes it plain: 'Before a woman can decide what kind of life she wants to live, she must grapple with forms of knowledge and understanding and institutionalised forms of that knowledge and understanding – about her'.[101] And Beauvoir says herself 'then only – with so much understood – shall we be able to comprehend the problems of women, the heirs of a burdensome past, who are striving to build a new future' and who 'aspire to full membership in the human race'.[102]

The use of such sources as conduits to, and expressions of, women's *knowledge* (not only as evidence for institutional accounting) was unorthodox and original in 1949, and holds its importance today. When juxtaposed against official sources that show how (male) knowledge assumes its own abstraction, Beauvoir produces work that is intimate, and yet designed to disturb. Sources are in this way a matter of experience for which Beauvoir, as writer, is obligated to take responsibility. To do otherwise refuses the potential agency of woman as human being to liberate herself, and to reimagine her existence and the work she can then do within the institutional practices and structures that are not separate to her experience of a life. Beauvoir offers, then, a training in which the selection and organisation of sources for writing the present are a way of authoring one's own experiences and their affiliations. This an activity I hope to demonstrate in *Feminist Jurisography*.

Note Eight – Reimagining Practices: In Australia

Beauvoir's address to knowledge has been described by Le Dœuff as a '*métis*': an art of craftiness with and toward the *techne* or practices in which she has been trained. Beauvoir, as we have seen, 'seize[d] the opportunity' to reintroduce herself to her discipline, and by placing abstract conventions into relationship with context and particularity she 'undermine[d] the structure'. It was this mastery of experience (as the Greeks argued) that 'enabled one to move in an unknown world'.[103] *The Second Sex* in particular, for the reasons I have been discussing, has had a profound influence on humanities scholars who are also feminists, as they joined unknown institutional worlds of their own. It is also perhaps worth noting (returning as we are for a moment to the Ancient philosophers and the example that everyday crafts and activities give purpose and duty to an office or persona) how *métis* is displaced in Greek philosophy as *phronesis*, a practical wisdom, or in Latin as the virtue of *prudence*, a careful consideration of experiential self-discipline in the comportment of one's obligations.[104] The extent it was possible for such a craft, understood as feminist experiential wisdom, to enter a relationship with *jurisprudence*, is of course where I am heading in these essays. To do so, I want now to turn to how Beauvoir's example entered intellectual feminist life.

Making visible how feminists came to inhabit humanistic disciplinary personae is a story that I tell in textual detail in this book, particularly in Essays Four and Five.[105] My focus, however, is not generalised, but an exemplification that speaks to my own training and inheritance in Australia. Michèle Le Dœuff, in considering Beauvoir's legacy in general terms, has emphasised:

> 'If we make the link between thinking philosophically and self-assertion through thought . . . then 'thinking philosophically' and 'being a feminist' appear one and the same: a desire to judge by and for oneself, which may manifest itself in relation to different questions'.[106]

Le Dœuff's point is that Beauvoir's own projects cannot be transposed. They must be continually reinvented to meet the conditions of a writer's own situation. Australian philosopher Christine Battersby has paid careful attention to the ways in which that self-assertion has manifested distinctively in Australian philosophy as something translocated between Europe and Australia, something 'inter-continental', and also directly responsive to the lived conditions in the here and now.[107] In Australia, for scholars with institutional status regardless of discipline, this has included, and includes, an awareness of obligation to observe, work in collaboration, and take responsibility for the lived experience of settler colonial violence.[108] Feminists writing in this tradition, because they work with relationality, embodiment, and experience, rather than discourse, the linguistic, or the analytical, have demonstrated sustained openness to confront and address their complicity with settler colonial projects.[109] Battersby argues (and I agree) that an identifiable, affiliated Australian feminist tradition becomes visible through this scholarship. This tradition, Battersby explains apropos philosophers, is 'anti-essentialist in tone and motivation, but it is by no means anti-philosophical or anti-rationalist'. 'Instead', she argues, 'it involves a reconfiguration of philosophy and reason [or knowledge] itself',[110] in order to think 'beyond boundaries – including the boundaries of the sayable and imaginable'. It also, I think, involves being clear as to how the traditions of conduct (and knowledge) in which the feminist practitioner writes are themselves open to continual reimagination, as an act of inheritance and of responsiveness, through the content and form of their activities.[111]

As a consequence, and as Moira Gatens shows in her own work, the Australian feminist intellectual project that works within the conduct of life tradition has been to understand 'the need to know how we became what we are, not in order to live what we have become as our "truth" but rather as our conditions of possibility for that which we may become'.[112] This is neither a utopian, nor an abstract, project. The most important lesson because of this inheritance that I would emphasise is understanding there is need to work alongside a tradition – including that of feminism itself – to reimagine practices adequate to write and show the conditions of one's own time and place. This trains us to think robustly for ourselves, to practice our own projects with responsibility, and an eye to our own complicity (in the register Beauvoir offers, and as she demonstrates).

I am a beneficiary of this tradition. I have been taught the techniques of reintroduction and acknowledgment, delineated in these notes, and through my personal and textual relationships with the writers whose work shapes and gives content to the essays to follow. But to take up my training to address the conduct and experience of law in life – how *jurisprudence* has been both asserted and accounted for – has required practices of reimagination of my own. This project, understood and invented through conversation and collaboration with Shaun McVeigh and Peter Rush, is of course what we have called jurisography. The duties that attach to the persona of jurisographer, as observed earlier in these notes, are tethered to the conduct of life tradition, and in many ways join together the duties of the historian and jurisprudent (as practised within that tradition). We named the practice to be very clear that we each bear different duties to our different intellectual forebears, and our different institutional experiences. But what brings our work into relationship is an obligation to take care of jurisprudence, with careful consideration of our agency, and acknowledgment of our complicity with the law we live with and inherit.

From this starting point, the obligation in this book (noting I have other projects, with different forms of address to the relation of laws in Australia) is to show that what I know, and how I learned to come into relationship with jurisprudence, is not severable from my self-formation as a feminist. To tell that story and assert the practices that are attached to a tradition of feminist knowledge – how to conduct thought and life relationally – is central to this book.

Note Nine – Feminist Jurisography

My first note in this Introduction declared my intention for these essays, and the notes that have followed have been offered as exercises to explain and demonstrate their sites of engagement, and my duties as a feminist jurisographer. This final note is more prosaic, a description of what is to follow.

The essays in this book (as you might have suspected by now) will not follow a traditional structure or style, nor undertake a singular, exhaustive historical or jurisprudential enquiry. What they do explore is the conduct of relations: between feminist personae and jurisprudential office holders; between abstracted and experiential knowledges; and, allegorically (and to give textual definition to my story), between men and women in Australia as a subject of and for law. I address these accounts and experiences by interleaving persons, places, events. I do so at different times (each essay wends its way through materials produced, respectively, in the 1950s, 1960s, 1970s, and 1980s); in place (moving between Sydney and London, Melbourne and Sydney, France and Australia, and finally Italy and Australia); and with different genres and idioms. Each essay emphasises something specific (be it status and condition; sources and institutions; methods and techniques; disciplinary persona and personal experience). Each essay, I also must admit, is not addressed to the same imagined reader. My task is to write between and join disciplines, and different readers will not have identical relationships to what I place into view (and want to say) about historiography, feminism, or jurisprudence. Writing these essays is, then, also an exercise in the conduct of relationship, for myself, and a demonstration of what a feminist jurisographer might look like, and request to think, beyond disciplinary demarcation.

So, by way of conclusion, I offer three things to draw through the following essays (noting too that each could also be read on its own and gives its own account).

First, I hope you can trace through a history of jurisprudence, in Australia, addressed through techniques and methods, and note how and when jurisprudence came into relation with other disciplines. My contention is not to critique or complicate the different challenges to positivism, which held law and legal writing apart from the societies in which it was experienced. Rather, it is to pay close attention to how jurisprudents within the university (those with official responsibility to care for law's dissemination), from mid-century, wrote about that challenge; and to see how they opened up law to other ways of accounting for its legal and social experience in the process. This story will be told through the expected official sources: law journals, lectures, monographs, and orations. My key interlocutors are the famous jurisprudent Julius Stone (in Essay Two, and in Essay Four); British sociologist Norman MacKenzie (author of the influential *Women in Australia* (1962) in Essay Three); and the jurisprudents Costas Douzinas, Ronnie Warrington, and Shaun McVeigh (authors of the genre-bending introduction for contemporary law and humanities scholarship, *Postmodern Jurisprudence: The Law of Text in the Texts of Law* (1991) in Essay Five).[113]

Second, I hope to show what knowledges, and what experiences, were hidden, subsumed, or not recognised, despite these jurisprudential interventions and innovations. Of course my central challenge is the accounting for, and of, women's experience, and an emergent and assertive tradition of interdisciplinary feminist knowledge, with its own distinctive conducts of practice and engagement. Again, I would remind that this activity is not synonymous with a feminist critique. It is simply to notice how jurisprudential thought, perhaps ironically, and despite attention to these questions, continued for the most part to conduct its engagements as unapologetically and persistently abstracted (and male). By following a story of 'law in relation' for jurisprudence, it becomes possible to make observations about when, how, and with what techniques and methods, the experience of women as more than objects of research came into view. It also enables me to pose the reverse question: how, and in what circumstances (and with what costs) the assertion of feminist knowledge became desired, plundered, or occluded by entering relationship with institutional jurisprudential writing and method.

My commitment, my own project as jurisographer, is to ask of jurisprudence writing what Beauvoir taught herself to ask of philosophy writing. As Le Dœuff has noted of the philosophical enterprise (and I think it holds for legal institutional life, research, and writing too) 'feminist knowledge' is too easily recast simplistically as 'women's way of knowing'. It is often lazily predicated on 'an affectionate, attentive rapport with the objects of knowledge' (women 'studying' women, a simple transfer of untethered experience); a technical classification of exceptional women's achievement as 'honorary great men'; or 'an involvement typical of the closest emotional relationship' (as intellectual wife, mistress, or fiancée, a question I return to in Essay Five). If feminist knowledges are asserted in and of themselves (to paraphrase Beauvoir), as carrying an intellectual tradition of their own that nevertheless exists in disciplinary relationship, their fate is often 'erasure entirely from the discussion'.[114]

My duty, and intention, in these essays is to make that experience of feminist knowledge visible as a conduct of relations in and of law. It is undeniable that women have for a very long time written of their experience of living with law, inside and outside of institutions (but often told through non-'scholarly' genres and sources, including fiction, letters, magazine editorials, and tracts, as well as books). I place these accounts in a dialogic relationship with the official writings of institutional jurisprudents in each essay. My chosen exemplary feminist texts also reflect the changing circumstances of publication opportunity. My key interlocutors in Essay Two, which addresses the 1950s, are the journalists and novelists who reported and commented in magazines and novels on the same questions of *de jure* relations between men and women as jurisprudents, but to distinctly different audiences. In Essay Three, I place into conversation with *Women in Australia* (1962) the letters, circulars, and notices of the organisations of the actual women of Australia whom Norman MacKenzie sought to engage as survey subjects for the book (and who were not entirely sanguine about the assumptions or the process). In Essay Four, I reflect on (now classic) feminist texts, such as *Woman's Estate* (1971) by Juliet Mitchell. Mitchell, like others, followed Beauvoir's example to disturb and energise the institutional positioning of feminist intellectual personae, and I ask how her book might (or might not) have subverted accounts of jurisprudence. In Essay Five, I think with *The Pirate's Fiancée: Feminism, reading, postmodernism* (1988), by the significant Australian feminist intellectual, writer, and cultural critic, Meaghan Morris. Morris is important for my project in ways that may not seem obvious, for it must be acknowledged that by the late 1980s the intellectual persona 'feminist legal scholar' had asserted herself into the institutional world of the modern law school. But for my own story, Morris lets me make important things visible about my own training and self-formation. *The Pirate's Fiancée* offered a guide in how to read the texts of 'the post' (like Douzinas et al) in a way that joined them to existing disciplinary feminist projects in Australia. I read both these texts as training manuals that showed how to do my own work as a feminist 'law and humanities scholar' in Australia in the early 1990s, and the essay contemplates why this was important to naming the practice of jurisography today.

Essays Two to Five, then, are not limited to a description or exegesis of all these texts 'in context', but to an exploration of how what they espouse becomes known technically and intellectually by different personae. But Essay Six is more openly personal. I have written it in fragments, to reflect my own situation, over a long period in taking up diverse scholarly duties, inside and outside of institutions, and with the restraints and pleasures of my life, and my personal commitments to others. As the central question of my book is 'how does a feminist jurisprudent come to know herself?', the final essay I hope will offer a performance of what can best be described in the Italian feminist tradition as *affidamento* (the practices of feminist inheritance through women's writing, usually outside proscribed institutional convention, and based on recognition, reliance, trust, and invention). It is this consideration of what it means to be 'the one who knows and writes' that will conclude *Feminist Jurisography*.

Notes

1 Beauvoir 2011: 17.
2 See Genovese 2013, 2014, 2016; Genovese & McVeigh 2015; Docker & Genovese 2016; McVeigh 2016. The practice has now been taken up by others. See, for example, Leiboff 2016; Goodrich 2021.
3 Le Dœuff 1991: 3.
4 Le Dœuff 1991: 2–3; Gatens 2007.
5 The formulation used here is drawn from Hadot 1995: 264–274, 2004: 253. I have borrowed from my own work to undertake this explanation; see Genovese 2013. There are, of course, other routes to make conducts of life relevant to feminist practice. To preempt my argument in later chapters, see: Butler 2005; Gatens 1996a; Cavarero 2000; Lorde 2018.
6 Hadot 1995: 274.
7 Hadot 1995: 275.
8 Hadot 1995: 268.
9 Hadot 1995: 265.
10 Foucault 2011, 1992.
11 Foucault 2011: 1–39.
12 Foucault 2011: 4.
13 Foucault 2011: 4–5. I return to this point in Essay Five, *Feminist Jurisography*.
14 Goodrich 2004: 500.
15 Goodrich 2004: 501.
16 Hadot 2004: 261.
17 Condren 2006: 67.
18 McVeigh 2016; Minson 1985.
19 This is an historical fact, but for two examples pertaining to law and philosophy, see Thornton 1996; Le Dœuff 2003: 217–221.
20 For three diverse examples of this point: Langton 1996; Watson 2014; Moreton-Robinson 2013.
21 This point is made clearly by Beauvoir herself in Beauvoir 2011: 71–125. For an example of consideration of women's occupation of intellectual personae, see Beauvoir 2011: 724, and throughout *The Second Sex*.
22 Gatens 2008.

23 Woolf 2001; Green & Broad 2006; Gatens 2009.
24 For elaboration on Beauvoir's practices of writing, see Vintges 1996; Le Dœuff 1991; Gatens 2007.
25 Vintges 1999: 138. I return to this point in Essay Five, *Feminist Jurisography*: 96–97.
26 I am conscious there are other traditions to follow; see Moreton-Robinson 2013. The account given in this essay is to join to a lineage I directly inherit.
27 Gatens 1996b, quoted in Bulbeck 1999: 10; Le Dœuff 1991: 56. I return to the question of reception in Australia in the 1970s in Essay Four, *Feminist Jurisography*. Note there are traceable routes to contemporary thought on gender, race, and sexuality that are not present in the 1949 text. See, for example, Altman 2007; Parker & van Leeuwen 2018.
28 For different contemporary examples, see Ahmed 2017: 19; Halley & Parker 2011. For discussion of other modes of inheritance, see Essay Six, *Feminist Jurisography*.
29 For an excellent analysis of this point in Australia, see Henderson 2006 and my commentary in Genovese 2012.
30 Le Dœuff 1991: 56 makes the point that the arrangement of *The Second Sex* into two distinct parts contributed to this problem.
31 Two prominent recent examples are in prefaces to the US and UK editions of the new English translations: see Thurman 2011; Rowbotham 2010.
32 Le Dœuff 1991: 56.
33 The feminist accusations against Beauvoir are also reflective of the philosophical and political temper of the times in which they were written. For examples of summary and commentary of this point, see Imbert 2004; Moi 2008: 198–232; Simons & Benjamin 1979.
34 Moi 2010; Thurman 2011; Rowbotham 2010. The sales figures are from Moi 2010.
35 Simons & Benjamin 1979: 16.
36 As Beauvoir 2011: 740–741 argues in *The Second Sex*, women's agency is grounded in the problem of freedom, not the promise of happiness. This has been read, or misread, as a negativity, or an abjection; see Wilson 2004: 90–91. The examination of happiness as category is also taken up by Ahmed 2010.
37 See, for example, Moi 2008: 145–167; 198–232; Chanter 2000; Fishwick 2002.
38 Le Dœuff 1980, 1991, 2004.
39 Le Dœuff 1991: 106–107.
40 See, for example, Butler 1986; 2007; Lorde 2018.
41 I return to this point in Essay Five, *Feminist Jurisography*.
42 Vintges 1999; and for a literal significance of this training: Portuges 1985.
43 See Imbert 2004; Beauvoir 1975.
44 Rowbotham 2010: xiii.
45 See Imbert 2004; Grosholz 2004: x.
46 See Beauvoir's own descriptions in her autobiographies, in particular Beauvoir 1965. The lifestyles of the Sartre-Beauvoir milieu are also well described in the popular biographies of Bair 1990; Rowley 2007.
47 Le Dœuff 1991: 107.
48 Le Dœuff 1991: 107.
49 Beauvoir 2000: 76.
50 Beauvoir 2011: 5.
51 Beauvoir 2011: 10.
52 Beauvoir 2011: 5.
53 Beauvoir 2011: 4.
54 Beauvoir 2011: 4.
55 Beauvoir 2011: 10.
56 Beauvoir 2011: 10.

57 Beauvoir 2011: 4.
58 Beauvoir 2011: 4.
59 Beauvoir 2011: 4–5.
60 Beauvoir 2011: 5.
61 Beauvoir 2011: 17.
62 Garber, Hanssen & Walkowitz 2000: viii—xii: 'ethics is a process of formation and self-questioning that continually rearticulates boundaries, norms, selves, and "others"'.
63 Sartre quoted in Le Dœuff 1980: 280.
64 Le Dœuff 1980: 280.
65 Le Dœuff 1980: 280.
66 Le Dœuff 1980: 279.
67 Le Dœuff 1980: 278.
68 Beauvoir 2011: 161.
69 Le Dœuff 1980.
70 For example, Beauvoir 2011: 176–180.
71 Beauvoir 2011: 11.
72 Beauvoir 2011: 762.
73 Beauvoir 2011: 439–664, for example as mother, wife, lover, 'Independent woman' as described in Part Two, Volume Two 'Situation'.
74 Beauvoir 2011: 723. These are named as 'justifications' used by 'the woman in love', 'the narcissist', and 'the mystic' in Part Three, Volume Two 'Justifications'.
75 Beauvoir 2011: 759
76 Beauvoir 2011: 756.
77 Rowbotham 2010: xi.
78 Beauvoir 2011: 5; Glazer 2004; Rowbotham 2010: xi.
79 Glazer 2004.
80 Beauvoir 2011: 11.
81 Scott 1991.
82 Rowbotham 2010: xii.
83 Beauvoir 2011: 11.
84 Le Dœuff 1980: 284. As Beauvoir (2011: 761) writes: 'it would be impossible to keep women from being what she was *made*, and she will always trail this past behind her; if the weight of this past is not accurately measured, it is obvious that her destiny is not fixed in eternity'.
85 Beauvoir 2011: 750.
86 Beauvoir 1963, 1965, 1975, 1993.
87 Vintges 1999: 136.
88 The reaction between novel and other genres discussed in Gobeil 1965; Curthoys 2000.
89 Holveck 2002: 31. The examples are from Holveck 2002: 91–109; Holveck 2002: 131–150.
90 Simons & Benjamin 1979: 338–339. Simons has been a consistent and important interlocutor of Beauvoir's work for an Anglophone audience: see also Simons 2006 and Simons 2010.
91 Simons & Benjamin 1979: 338–339.
92 Vintges 1996: 119.
93 Vintges 1996: 119.
94 Le Dœuff 1991; Gatens 2007.
95 Gatens 2007: 30.
96 Beauvoir 2011: 11.
97 Beauvoir 2011: 11.
98 Beauvoir 2011: v, 10.

99 In Book One of *The Second Sex*, in all three parts ('Destiny', 'History', and 'Myths') Beauvoir undertakes her practices of reintroduction with reference to St Thomas Aquinas, Genesis, Aristotle, Kierkegaard, Marx, Freud, DH Lawrence, and Stendhal, among others.
100 Beauvoir 2011.
101 Holveck 2002: 115.
102 Holveck 2002: 155; quoting from Beauvoir 1953: xxxvi.
103 Le Dœuff 1991: 106.
104 Le Dœuff 1991: 106–107.
105 I return to this point in Essay Four and Essay Five, *Feminist Jurisography*.
106 Le Dœuff 1991: 29.
107 Battersby 2000.
108 Battersby 2000: 5.
109 Genovese 2014.
110 Battersby 2000: 5.
111 See Gatens 1996a; Walker 2016.
112 Gatens 1996a: 77.
113 See Essay Two, Essay Three, Essay Four, Essay Five, *Feminist Jurisography*.
114 Le Dœuff 2003: xiii.

References

Ahmed S 2010 *The Promise of Happiness* Duke University Press Durham.

Ahmed S 2017 *Living a Feminist Life* Duke University Press Durham.

Altman M 2007 'Simone de Beauvoir and Lesbian Lived Experience' *Feminist Studies* 33/1: 207–232 DOI:10.2307/20459130.

Bair D 1990 *Simone de Beauvoir: A Biography* Jonathan Cape London.

Battersby C 2000 'Learning to Think Intercontinentally: Finding Australian Routes' *Hypatia* 15/2: 1–17 DOI:10.2979/HYP.2000.15.2.1.

Beauvoir S de 1953 *The Second Sex* Trans H M Parshley Jonathan Cape London (first published 1949).

Beauvoir S de 1963 *Memoirs of a Dutiful Daughter* Trans J Kirkup Penguin Books Harmondsworth (first published 1958).

Beauvoir S de 1965 *The Prime of Life* Trans P Green Penguin Books Harmondsworth (first published 1960).

Beauvoir S de 1975 *Force of Circumstance* Trans R Howard Penguin Harmondsworth (first published 1963).

Beauvoir S de 1993 *All Said and Done* Trans P O'Brian Paragon House New York (first published 1972).

Beauvoir S de 2000 *The Ethics of Ambiguity* Trans B Frechtman Citadel Press New York (first published 1948).

Beauvoir S de 2010 *The Second Sex* Trans C Borde and S Malovany-Chevallier Vintage London (first published 1949).

Beauvoir S de 2011 *The Second Sex* Trans C Borde and S Malovany-Chevallier Vintage New York (first published 1949).

Bulbeck C 1999 'Simone de Beauvoir and generations of feminists' *Hecate* 25/2: 5–21.

Butler J 1986 'Sex and Gender in Simone de Beauvoir's *Second Sex*' *Yale French Studies* 72: 35–49 DOI:10.2307/2930225.

Butler J 2005 *Giving an Account of oneself* Fordham University Press New York.

Butler J 2007 *Gender Trouble: Feminism and the Subversion of Identity* Routledge New York (first published 1990).

Cavarero A 2000 *Relating Narratives: Storytelling and Selfhood* Trans P A Kottman Routledge London and New York (first published 1997).

Chanter T 2000 'Abjection and Ambiguity: Simone de Beauvoir's Legacy' *Journal of Speculative Philosophy* 14/2: 138–155 DOI:10.1353/jsp.2000.0013.

Condren C 2006 'The *Persona* of the philosopher and the rhetorics of office in early modern England' in C Condren, S Gaukroger and I Hunter eds 2006 *The Philosopher in Early Modern Europe: The Nature of a Contested Identity* Cambridge University Press Cambridge and New York 2006: 66–89.

Curthoys A 2000 'Adventures of Feminism: Simone de Beauvoir's Autobiographies, Women's Liberation, and Self-Fashioning' *Feminist Review* 64/1: 3–18 DOI:10.1080/014177800338927.

Docker J and Genovese A 2016 'Places Lived: An Ego-Histoiriste and Jurisographer Discuss Living with Law in Sydney' *Law Text Culture* 20/1: 14–17 <http://ro.uow.edu.au/ltc/vol20/iss1/2>.

Fishwick S 2002 *The Body in the Work of Simone de Beauvoir* Peter Lang Oxford and New York.

Foucault M 1992 *The Use of Pleasure: The History of Sexuality: Volume 2* Trans R Hurley Penguin Books London (first published 1984).

Foucault M 2011 *The Government of Self and Others: Lectures at the College de France, 1982–1983* Ed F Gros Trans G Burchell Palgrave Macmillan New York (first published 2008).

Garber M, Hanssen B and Walkowitz R L 2000 'Introduction: The Turn to Ethics' in M Garber, B Hanssen and R L Walkowitz eds 2000 *The Turn to Ethics* Routledge New York (1st edn): viii–xii.

Gatens M 1996a *Imaginary Bodies: Ethics, Power and Corporeality* Routledge London and New York.

Gatens M 1996b 'Keynote Address' *Sixth Australian Women's Studies Association Conference* 27–29 November Perth.

Gatens M 2007 'The "Disciplined Imagination": Literature as "Experimental" Philosophy' *Australian Feminist Studies* 22/52: 25–34 DOI:10.1080/08164640601145020.

Gatens M 2008 'Re-Coupling Gender and Genre' *Angelaki* 13/2: 1–3 DOI:10.1080/08164649.2013.876664.

Gatens M 2009 'The Art and Philosophy of George Eliot' *Philosophy and Literature* 33/1: 73–90 DOI:10.1353/phl.0.0037.

Genovese A 2012 'Writing the Past as Politics: Some reflections on Historiography and Margaret Henderson' *Lilith* 17–18: 132–138.

Genovese A 2013 'Inheriting and Inhabiting the Pleasures and Duties of Our Own Existence: *The Second Sex* and Feminist Jurisprudence' *Australian Feminist Law Journal* 38/1: 41–57 DOI:10.1080/13200968.2013.10854482.

Genovese A 2014 'On Australian feminist tradition: three notes on conduct, inheritance and the relations of historiography and jurisprudence' *Journal of Australian Studies* 38/4: 430–444 DOI:10.1080/14443058.2014.954137.

Genovese A 2016 'About Libraries: A Jurisographer's Notes on Lives Lived With Law (in London and Sydney)' *Law Text Culture* 20/1: 33–65 DOI:10.1080/13200968.2013.10854482.

Genovese A and McVeigh S 2015 'Nineteen eighty three: A jurisographic report on *Commonwealth v Tasmania*' *Griffith Law Review* 24/1: 68–88 DOI:10.1080/10383441.2015.1022891.

Glazer S 2004 'Lost in Translation' *The New York Times Book Review* 22 August: 13.

Gobeil M 1965 'Simone de Beauvoir, The Art of Fiction No. 35' *Paris Review* 34.

Goodrich P 2004 'Satirical Legal Studies: From the Legists to the Lizard' *Michigan Law Review* 103/3: 397–517 DOI:10.2307/4141929.

Goodrich P 2021 *Advanced Introduction to Law and Literature* Edward Elgar Publishing Cheltenham.

Green K and Broad J 2006 'Fictions of a feminine philosophical *persona*: Christine de Pizan, Margaret Cavendish and *Philosophia* Lost' in C Condren, S Gaukroger and I Hunter eds 2006 *The Philosopher in Early Modern Europe: The Nature of a Contested Identity* Cambridge University Press Cambridge and New York: 229–253.

Grosholz E R 2004 'Editor's Preface' in E R Grosholz ed 2004 *The Legacy of Simone de Beauvoir* Clarendon Press Oxford and New York: vii–xxxii.

Hadot P 1995 *Philosophy as a Way of Life: Spiritual Exercises from Socrates to Foucault* Ed A I Davidson Trans M Chase Blackwell Publishing Malden (first published 1981).

Hadot P 2004 *What Is Ancient Philosophy?* Trans M Chase Belknap Press Cambridge (first published 1995).

Halley J and Parker A 2011 'Introduction' in J Halley and A Parker eds 2011 *After Sex? On Writing Since Queer Theory* Duke University Press Durham and London.

Henderson M 2006 *Marking Feminist Times: Remembering the Longest Revolution in Australia* Peter Lang Bern.

Holveck E 2002 *Simone de Beauvoir's Philosophy of Lived Experience: Literature and Metaphysics* Rowman & Littlefield Lanham.

Imbert C 2004 'Simone de Beauvoir: A Woman Philosopher in the Context of Her Generation' in E R Grosholz ed 2004 *The Legacy of Simone de Beauvoir* Clarendon Press Oxford and New York: 3–21.

Langton M 1996 'The Hindmarsh Island Bridge Affair: How Aboriginal Women's Religion Became an Administrable Affair' *Australian Feminist Studies* 11/24: 211–217 DOI:10.1080/08164649.1996.9994819.

Le Dœuff M 1980 'Simone de Beauvoir and Existentialism' *Feminist Studies* 6/2: 277–289 DOI:10.2307/3177742.

Le Dœuff M 1991 *Hipparchia's Choice: An Essay Concerning Women, Philosophy, etc.* Trans T Selous Blackwell Oxford (first published 1989).

Le Dœuff M 2003 *The Sex of Knowing* Trans K Hamer and L Code Routledge London and New York.

Le Dœuff M 2004 'Towards a Friendly, Transatlantic Critique of *The Second Sex*' in E R Grosholz ed 2004 *The Legacy of Simone de Beauvoir* Clarendon Press Oxford and New York: 22–36.

Leiboff M 2016 'Theatricalising Law in Three, 1929–1939 (Brisbane)' *Law Text Culture* 20/1: 93–135.

Lorde A 2018 *The Master's Tools Will Never Dismantle the Master's House* Penguin London (first published 1984).

McVeigh S 2016 'Jurisprudent of London: Arts of Association' *Law Text Culture* 20/1: 189–215 DOI:10.2139/ssrn.3169144.

Minson J 1985 *Genealogies of Morals: Nietzsche, Foucault, Donzelot and the Eccentricity of Ethics* St Martin's Press New York.

Moi T 2008 *Simone de Beauvoir: The Making of an Intellectual Woman* Oxford University Press Oxford and New York (2nd edn).

Moi T 2010 'The Adulteress Wife' *London Review of Books* 32/3 DOI:10.1093/oso/9780190608811.003.0006.

Moreton-Robinson A 2013 'Towards an Australian Indigenous Women's Standpoint Theory: A Methodological Tool' *Australian Feminist Studies* 28/78: 331–347 DOI:10.1080/08164649.2013.876664.

Parker E A and van Leeuwen A eds 2018 *Differences: Rereading Beauvoir and Irigaray* Oxford University Press New York.

Portuges C E 1985 'Simone de Beauvoir: Feminist As Teacher' *Dalhousie French Studies* 9: 107–116.

Rowbotham S 2010 'Foreword' in Beauvoir 2010: ix–xix.

Rowley H 2007 *Tête-a-Tête: The Lives and Loves of Simone de Beauvoir & Jean-Paul Sartre* Vintage London.

Scott J W 1991 'The Evidence of Experience' *Critical Enquiry* 17/4: 773–797.

Simons M A 2006 *The Philosophy of Simone de Beauvoir: Critical Essays* Indiana University Press Bloomington.

Simons M A 2010 'Confronting an Impasse: Reflections on the Past and Future of Beauvoir Scholarship' *Hypatia* 25/4: 909–926 DOI:10.1111/j.1527-2001.2010.01132.x.

Simons M A and Benjamin J 1979 'Simone de Beauvoir: An Interview' *Feminist Studies* 5/2: 330–345 DOI:10.2307/3177599.

Thornton M 1996 *Dissonance and Distrust: Women in the Legal Profession* Oxford University Press Melbourne.

Thurman J 2011 'Introduction' in Beauvoir 2011: ix–xvi.

Vintges K 1996 *Philosophy as Passion: The Thinking of Simone de Beauvoir* Indiana University Press Bloomington.

Vintges K 1999 'Simone de Beauvoir: A Feminist Thinker for Our Times' *Hypatia* 14/4: 133–144 DOI:10.1111/j.1527-2001.1999.tb01257.x.

Walker M B 2016 *Slow Philosophy: Reading Against the Institution* Bloomsbury Academic London and New York.

Watson I 2014 'First Nations Stories, Grandmother's Law: Too Many Stories to Tell' in H Douglas, F Bartlett, T Luker and R Hunter eds 2014 *Australian Feminist Judgements: Righting and Rewriting Law* Hart Publishing Oxford: 46–53.

Wilson C 2004 'Simone de Beauvoir and Human Dignity' in E R Grosholz ed 2004 *The Legacy of Simone de Beauvoir* Clarendon Press Oxford and New York: 90–114.

Woolf V 2001 'Three Guineas' in V Woolf ed 2001 *A Room of One's Own and Three Guineas* Vintage London (first published 1938).

Essay 2

On Personal Relations, 1949 (A Jurisographical Report)

On Personal Relations

The essays in this book aim to demonstrate a history of the conduct of relations between feminist knowledge and jurisprudential knowledge. My project has a dual purpose, or at least two points of view. One is about authorising the self as writer through a series of technical exercises. This is an important feminist tradition that affiliates the scholar to her sources, her training, and her place. In my own case, as one trained in history and jurisprudence, I name that practice as jurisography. The other is to give an example of feminist jurisography, the first of five for those reading these essays in order as a book.

There are several reasons that I have chosen to set this first example in 1949 and call it 'On Personal Relations'. Simone de Beauvoir's *The Second Sex* was first published in 1949, and as I described in my Introduction, Beauvoir's work and example anchors *Feminist Jurisography*. In each essay, I consider how Beauvoir influenced the public arrival of feminist disciplinary personae, and how that influence has changed over time. In this essay, I begin my historical retelling by treating *The Second Sex* as an unofficial work of feminist jurisprudence. In 1949 there was of course no such public office as a 'feminist jurisprudent', a university-based scholar or public advocate charged with obligations of challenging the differential understanding of woman as subject of law in the language of law. That did not mean that women were silent about how the conditions of their lives were legally circumscribed. In *The Second Sex*, Beauvoir questions woman's legal status from the standpoint of her conditions for living, using different role-based examples. Following one of her examples – 'the married woman' – opens historical examination of how similar concerns with law's creation of social and sexual roles were treated by others in the late 1940s and early 1950s. The other reason for naming this essay 'On Personal Relations, 1949' is to make plain exactly what that expression meant, as a subject for law. Seventy years ago, 'personal relations', for lawyers, was the name given to an aspect of private (matrimonial) law, domestic and international, that concerned itself with status relations between 'husband' and 'wife', the organisation of marriage and divorce, or what we might now consider as

DOI: 10.4324/9780429461132-2

family law. The older meaning is important to understand, because it carries provocations that remain unresolved but should still matter to jurisprudents and feminists alike today. For example, is there a difference between a legal person and woman as a person? And whose task is it to ask that question, and challenge the answers law provides?

I noted in the Introduction to this book that jurisography is concerned, amongst other things, with taking sufficient care of both unofficial and official sources of jurisprudence writing, and being explicit about the work that method, style, and genre does in those sources. This extends to my own writing, and my own choice of genre. For example, I wrote the first instalment of this book as a series of notes, to introduce my relationship to a feminist tradition, and to draw out how I have conducted my writing about it (on the edge of my kitchen table, between other kinds of obligations). This second instalment is organised more prosaically as a report. A report is not a narrative history, nor a theoretical analysis. It is necessarily limited in scope and ambition by its form: part record or chronicle, and part commentary on style and genre.[1] The jurisographic report attends to how a particular question – in this case, the conduct of personal relations – was presented inside and outside of formal jurisprudence writing at a precise time, and in a particular place. The selection of sources for a report is therefore necessarily partial and located. In a feminist jurisographic report, those sources are also arranged to enable a reader to see if, or when, accounts of jurisprudence that attend to women's experience and knowledge can enter relationship with those that do not. In this report, my examples are a feminist book, a jurisprudence book, a law handbook, a novel, a magazine article, and a law journal article. All are examples of writing about law in life and the life of law, in a slice of time, 1949–1955, and most are Australian. My examples also present conducts of life to inhabit: the office of the jurisprudent inside the court and university, and the persona of the writer in the offices of women's magazines, or in her own home. By writing these texts into relationship in this report, I can start to examine how feminist traditions of writing acted as an intervention, an invitation, and sometimes a riposte, to those with responsibilities to law. In this way, one ambition of my report is to suggest questions that law and humanities, and feminist, scholars might pose to 1949, as well as revivify how the ethos and methods of 1949 foreshadow the work we do today.

The Second Sex (Paris, 1949)

In 1949, the world was coming to terms with the aftermath of total war. People questioned the ambiguous experience of loss, freedom, and disruption. The post-war epoch made particular demands of scholars and intellectuals, and they experimented with techniques to question the conduct of the self and the condition of being human, in a world exposed as in transition, and asking to be remade. For some, those techniques reflected ethical problems about action and agency, and relationship and responsibility. There are many examples of public writers who helped reorient thought to the conditions of life during this period in that vein: George Orwell, Hannah Arendt, Jean-Paul Sartre, Simone de Beauvoir, Albert Camus; as well as many examples of jurisprudents dislocated by war who challenged the enclosure of legal thought.[2] But it is Beauvoir, in *The Second Sex* (1949), who writes of these concerns, revolutionarily, from the perspective of a self who is a woman.

I introduced Beauvoir's innovations and achievements in the first essay in this book. Two bear repeating because they foreground how *The Second Sex*, as a text of 1949, can be read as an unofficial, and provocative, account of jurisprudence. In *The Second Sex*, Beauvoir's major achievement is to demonstrate how knowledge and its material 'forms and customs' are organised relationally between 'man' and 'woman', but for the benefit of man, and in a way that oppresses woman. She is cast as an Other to his Self. Her major innovation was to write that account in a particular way: as an *essay*, a genre and style that was unmistakably immediate and intimate. In doing so, Beauvoir opened up what might otherwise have been relegated to a philosophical problem – is woman reduced to her legal status – to a public readership deeply interested in learning how desire was a form of agency, and how it might be compatible with being 'a wife'.[3] In her treatment of philosophical issues as personal and sexual relations, Beauvoir's 'nerve is manifest, her meaning unambiguous'. For as philosopher Michèle Le Dœuff notes rightly, '[i]n 1949 it took courage to say that pleasure is a good in itself and that it is to be found outside of institutions'.[4]

In the Introduction to *The Second Sex*, Beauvoir explains how law and other institutions are complicit in woman's relegation to secondary status in her own life. She writes, persuasively: '[l]awmakers, priests, philosophers, writers, and scholars have gone to great lengths to prove that women's subordinate condition was willed in heaven and profitable on earth'.[5] Beauvoir then demonstrates the consequences of male office holders' sustained efforts throughout the 700 or so pages of *The Second Sex*. Beauvoir's point is to remind the reader that she should be vigilant. Legal thought and practice assign woman a status, but woman is also complicit with the contradictions such status creates. Beauvoir's point is that status (a legal concept) and condition (lived experience of assigned status) are neither in mutual operation, nor separate. Nor can they be trusted as stable categories. Status and condition often work against each other, Beauvoir argues, to create differential relations for women, with men and with institutions, which are not fixed in time.[6] The experience of living with law is also not the same between women, as it depends on the role each inhabits in her own situation. Beauvoir's examples include the 'Independent Woman' (the status of a woman with access to the public realm) and the 'Married Woman' (the status of a woman living within the institution of marriage). She crafts these personae technically, to organise her argument, but also to make the point that such roles are not hierarchical.[7] What is required, in either case, is attention to how an opposition between law and custom creates the material ambiguities for a woman's particular situation. As Beauvoir writes and warns: 'abstract rights . . . have never been sufficient to guarantee women a concrete hold on the world'.[8]

'The Married Woman', a chapter in Book Two of *the Second Sex*, offers the best example for this report. Beauvoir argues that 'from a feminist point of view'[9] women in 1949, despite the upheavals of war, continued to suffer from the historic, institutional conditions of marriage. She observed:

> 'The period we are living through is still a period of transition. Only a part of the female population participates in production, and those same women belong to a society where ancient structures and values still survive. Modern marriage can be understood only in light of the past it perpetuates'.[10]

Beauvoir argues that a 'married woman' should not expect her experience of relationships with men to be transformed, and herself to be liberated, even if lawmakers 'reform' the discriminatory effects of the civil law of marriage. As she argues:

> '[t]hat the civil code [in France] erased "obedience" from [a woman's] duties changes nothing in her situation; her situation is based on . . . the very structure of her conjugal community. . . . The successes and failures of her conjugal life have much more importance for her than for the man: he is . . . a producer before being a husband; she is above all, and often exclusively, a "wife"'.[11]

This is not an endorsement. But Beauvoir does not go on to critique the oppression of 'the wife' as other political thinkers, such as John Stuart and Harriet Taylor Mill, had done. Beauvoir is not in intellectual dispute with the Mills (who she cites with admiration), or feminist reformers in her own time.[12] She differs in what must be given priority. For Beauvoir, it is never enough to 'reform law' as something abstract and attenuated, if that reform does not respond to the dramas and conflicts of everyday life by those living inside the institution.[13] 'The Married Woman' is therefore a persona that infers contradiction but agency, unlike 'The Wife' who is purely a legal status attached to 'The Husband'. For Beauvoir, it is 'The Married Woman' whose experiences are unaddressed, for she experiences marriage intimately, and not only as a sanctioned legal institution. 'Modern marriage', in this view, is not to be left on trust to those legislators and thinkers who perpetuate its 'ancient structures and values' and refuse woman's experience of its forms ('man only took possession of that which he already possessed; he put law into harmony with reality').[14] It is instead the existent relations between man and woman that demand primary scrutiny, Beauvoir argues, as they are open to change by an assertion of woman's own actions and desires. She insists that for the conditions of freedom for both man and woman to be realised in marriage (as well as outside), that both sexes recast and understand their 'drama' of personal relations as ethical and sexually experienced, not simply a question of law. As Beauvoir concludes, in language bold enough to have her book sanctioned at the time of its publication:

> 'To emancipate woman is to refuse to enclose her in the relations she sustains with man, but not to deny them . . . reciprocity in their relations will not do away with the miracles that the division of human beings into two separate categories engenders: desire, possession, love, dreams, adventure'.[15]

The Outline of Law in Australia (Sydney, 1955)

The Second Sex was translated into English in 1953, and it was circulated in Australia as early as 1955.[16] ('We appreciated very much the gift from conference members of a copy of "The Second Sex" by a French Woman, Simone de Beauvoir', reported the League of Women Voters after their Triennial Conference in Adelaide). Although intriguing to imagine the League's discussion of *The Second Sex*, I am not suggesting Beauvoir's ideas immediately influenced a rival way to address marital relations in Australia. On the contrary, the 'forms and customs' of status that Beauvoir challenged were asserted in contemporaneous Australian legal writing as the *status quo*.

Outline of Law in Australia (1955), by John Baalman, 'Barrister-at law', legal scholar, and 'Examiner of Titles in the NSW Department of Registrar General', offers an example. It was written for legal practitioners, law students, and 'members of the community . . . who regard some knowledge of the rules which regulate their daily conduct as a sheer cultural necessity'.[17] *Outline of Law in Australia* ('*Outline of Law*') was the first 'introduction to law' text of its kind in Australia, and updated regularly between 1947–1979.[18] Baalman's textbook is not organised through practice areas, but through legal categories that belong to the common law, including a chapter on 'Personal Relations'.[19] Although the chapter carries within it the law on divorce and marriage, Baalman does not write as we might today of litigants in contest, nor does he describe this as 'family law' or 'divorce law' (these were yet to come), or propose any reform.[20] Baalman states law as it is, and as it had been for some time. When Baalman writes of 'human affairs', for example, he is reminding his readers how law relegates embodied people into classes – assigns them status – to which differential rights and duties accrue as a result. As Baalman notes, this occurs 'quite independently of the wishes of the individual' and often 'in spite of his wishes'.[21] Status, in Baalman's professional opinion, was not a category to expose (as it was for Beauvoir). It was instead a device of personal jurisdiction to put into practice.[22]

Any readers trained at the sandstone law schools of the era would have been well versed in the concept of status through their study of eminent jurists such as Sir Henry Maine and RH Graveson.[23] They knew that legal status emanated through Roman Law's distinction between living people and their legal *persona*,[24] and they would have been proficient in using status to organise the legal person's action in relation to others, and with institutions. This is because, as a matter of law, status determines what duties the legal person must perform, what lawful assertions by others they must suffer, what obligations and conduct they must carry, and in what courts and on what bases they can bring actions.

These techniques of personal jurisdiction were, of course, well understood in relation to the status of wife (as Baalman restates, and updates). The ceremony of marriage is a technical arrangement in law, in which a status *relation* is legally acquired. 'Man' and 'woman' become 'husband and wife', and obligations and duties accrue to each other consequentially. Their personal relations are regulated 'by laws over which they have no control' (be it coverture, or consortium), although these are experienced differentially for husband and wife. For example, both parties had a right to consortium: 'the sum total of companionship, love, affection, comfort, mutual services, and sexual intercourse'.[25] The husband, for his part, acquired a common law right for action for damages against a legal person who occasions the loss of his consortium: a woman on marriage is his sexual and domestic possession. His wife, on the other hand, did not. Marriage transformed a woman's personal status, but left a man's intact. Her legal personality was subsumed in his.[26] Blackstone's famous maxim was not yet completely past its use by date for the everyday practice of law in 1955:

> 'By marriage, the husband and wife are one person in law: that is, the very being or legal existence of the woman is suspended during the marriage, or at least is incorporated and consolidated into that of the husband; under whose wing, protection, and cover, she performs everything'.[27]

Beauvoir excoriated the same status relation in *The Second Sex*:

> 'In marrying, the woman . . . becomes [the man's] other "half" . . . she breaks with her past more or less brutally, she is annexed to her husband's universe; she gives him her person: she owes him her virginity and strict fidelity . . . she perpetuates the immutable species, she ensures the even rhythm of the days and the permanence of the home . . . she is given no direct grasp on the future, nor on the universe; she goes beyond herself toward the group only through her husband as a mouthpiece'.[28]

In either view, the legal repercussions for 'the wife' if they sought to dissolve the union were different to that of 'the husband'. To provide one example, the unified status of husband and wife meant that his domicile became hers. Domicile is a practice that attaches a person to a place, and the laws of that place. Domicile therefore lets a person know to which body of laws, and to which courts, they are subject. By the early 1950s, domicile was not an arcane legal term in Australia, or other common law countries. As I will soon report, domicile assumed expansive proportions as a challenging conflict of law problem for male jurists, as many of the marriages formed between men and women because of movement and global war sought forums for dissolution at war's end. As a legal question, a person's domicile could be changed through stated intention. But this was not a legal possibility for a wife, or persona of other lesser capacity, according to law. As Baalman explained:

> 'Every person is presumed to have what the law calls his domicile, a status which is determined by the country in which he makes his home. An adult person (not being a married woman or a lunatic) can change his domicile at will'.[29]

'The wife' was therefore subject to the laws of her husband's place, regardless of whether or not those laws were to her disadvantage, and regardless of whether those laws differed from her own place of origin. She had what was legally understood as a 'dependent domicile', and she had no way to be heard by law.

Come in Spinner (Sydney, 1951)

A legal text which reduced a married woman to less than an adult person, regardless of whether that was the state of the law of the time, would not pass without comment (or protest) today. The feminist legal jurisprudent now formally exists, and she could scrutinise law's supposedly abstract and immutable technicalities, in the expected forms and forums available to the university scholar. It would be spurious to suggest, however, that there was no legal writing by women about status (or domicile) at this time. By the early 1950s, some Australian women had succeeded at both Law School and the Matrimonial Causes Bar, and some (like the pioneering barrister, Joan Rosanove) wrote about the law of personal relations, in the same idiom as Baalman.[30] More prominent in this period – in profile, number, and action – were the established women's political organisations who challenged the function of status as a barrier to public participation as a political cause. Groups such as the League of Women Voters and the Union of Australian Women are foundational to feminist political traditions in Australia;[31] I will return to writing by some of these political reformers in Essay Three.[32] What is relevant to observe here, however, is their 'self-abnegating' attitude. As Australian feminist historian Marilyn Lake has argued, these groups were 'determinedly anti-sexual in their politics, philosophy, and platforms'.[33] Such restraint, or refusal, removed complexities of lived experience from these courageous campaigners' tireless efforts to reform the pernicious effects of the laws of personal jurisdiction. Such restraint also placed these established political groups apart from Beauvoir's forthright discussion of sex as a challenge to the institutional viewpoint of 'conjugal relations' in *The Second Sex*.

By the early 1950s in Australia (as elsewhere) there were, however, other accounts, that did bring the rules of status and desire into a reckoning. Publishing in popular genres, many professional women writers had different duties (and freedoms) to those of the lawyer, or the political campaigner, and their work foreshadowed the joining of the 'personal and political' that comes to dominate the liberation of women's knowledge in the 1970s (as we shall see in Essay Four).[34] For the purposes of this report, I want to consider two examples. The first is the best-selling novel *Come in Spinner*, by writers Florence James and Dymphna Cusack, published in 1951.[35] The second is a series of articles on 'Divorce', in the *Australian Woman's Weekly* ('*The Weekly*') by journalist Zélie McLeod, also published in 1951.[36] Novels like *Come in Spinner*, and magazines like *The Weekly*, are well-observed in Australian feminist literary criticism and history as important examples of women's differentiated experience of a society and culture, in life and art, in time and place. The excellent scholarship of Susan Sheridan, for a leading example, has carefully reintroduced these texts to an Australian literary canon, and traditions of feminism. Sheridan's work makes it possible to comprehend an era of Australian women's writing as expressive of a desire by an individual with skills and talents to write herself, and her situation, into view. This includes a careful, scholarly interrogation of translocation and compromise, opportunity and opportunity cost, for the writers, and for their work.[37] *The Weekly*, in particular, should be understood in this regard as more than patterns and recipes. (I mention this explicitly, as it has been my own experience in delivering versions of this report to legal academics that *The Weekly* is reduced, in question time, in exactly those terms). *The Weekly*'s editor in the 1950s, Esmé Fenston, commissioned columns, fiction, reports, and other features that responded to contemporary questions that affected their readers.[38] Fenston provided a forum, but also income, for serious writers – novelists, poets, political journalists, diarists – who fought to have their work published, commissioned, and paid for in the male-dominated literary journals and newspapers of the day. This was not without calculated risk. Many women wrote under alternative names, or in different styles, for as Sheridan notes: '[w]omen's magazines did not even count as proper journalism, far less as real writing. Yet the magazines' pages could provide a meeting ground for women writers and their readers, in the days before the advent of literary festivals and public readings'.[39]

Dymphna Cusack and Florence James both came of age as individual writers through that tradition. *Come in Spinner*, their jointly written novel, is rightly known in the Australian canon as the most accurate contemporaneous capture of the conditions of women on the home front in Australia during the Second World War. It won the Sydney *Daily Telegraph* novel competition in 1948, but was subject to prurient editorialising, and 'markedly abridged on sexual grounds'.[40] When *Come in Spinner* was finally released in 1951, however, it was a best seller.[41] The novel is set in Sydney, and explores the working, family, and romantic lives of the employees of the Marie Antoinette Beauty Salon, part of the glamorous (fictional) Hotel South Pacific. Through three main characters – Deb, Guinea, and Claire – the authors explore the complexities of how women navigated social convention, class, work, their own need for personal fulfilment, and the burdens and opportunities of their personal relations with men. The renowned Australian author (Stella) Miles Franklin (she of the groundbreaking and ironically titled *My Brilliant Career* (1901)) reviewed the book in 1951 for the literary journal *Meanjin*, and noted explicitly:

> 'Dymphna Cusack and Florence James have seized a handful of time when the Americans were here in force and our cities a passion parade of warriors – native and imported – gaudily pursuing their leave . . . it is an uncompromising overall exposure of woman's situation in the existing economic system, and particularly during wartime'.[42]

This situatedness mattered to Cusack and James. They were part of a circle of Australian women writers who had lived and worked overseas but were 'fired with . . . the burning conviction' that they needed to write about their own country, and about their own experience.[43] In this, they were influenced by the example of Miles Franklin herself, who had argued that 'an unsung country does not fully exist nor enjoy adequate exchange in the inner life'.[44] In 1944, James' husband was with the RAAF and stationed in London, and she had just given up her wartime job to return home. Cusack, for health reasons, had left her teaching post.[45] With their 'three small girls, aged between nine and seven' they 'set up temporary housekeeping'[46] in the Blue Mountains outside Sydney (a tourist destination, and also a retreat for artists and writers). Away from the threats of the war in the Pacific, which were real and immediate, they began to work on a project together. Between the rituals of their everyday life they wrote, in friendship and collaboration, about their own situation, just as Beauvoir was writing about hers in Paris. The point was, as James remarked, later, 'Why not write about the women's world we knew? We would keep within the range of our own and our friends' experiences. We would tell the Sydney story as we knew it, pulling no punches'.[47] James and Cusack described the sexual license American servicemen took with young Australian women, the pain and illegality of abortion, the complexity of marriage to absent men, sexuality, adultery, and the vexed question of independence.

Cusack and James' characters, in many respects, also mirrored the personae Beauvoir used to exemplify her arguments in *The Second Sex*. For example, the book's 'Married Woman', Deb, is contemplating an affair and a divorce. Her husband, a member of the Allied forces, is serving overseas, and in order for her to work, her child is in the care of relatives. Deb's suitor is a wealthy Australian man: older, not in uniform, whose solicitous attention promises a different life. In a frank exchange with her friend Dr Dallas McIntyre (the book's

'Independent Woman', professional, single, in charge of her own affairs, in all senses), Deb explains the reality of most women's lives:

> '[W]hat is there for the average woman if she doesn't get married? Only an underpaid job and a back room in some cheap boarding house. And anyway most women are romantic and if you give them their choice they'd rather have love than a career any day of the week . . . '.[48]

Dallas, for her part, disagrees (as she might). To live a life of her own involves refusing the conventions, restraints, and also opportunities imposed by becoming a wife:

> 'Whichever way [women] turn, most of them are caught. It doesn't matter whether they are driven by love or lust; they're the ones who fall in. If I had a daughter . . . as I won't, because society says unless I'm prepared to tie myself up to some man legally, I have no right to bear a child – but if I did have a daughter, I'd teach her very early that the only real salvation for women is work . . .'.[49]

In 1948, this was radical. For the purposes of this report, what I want to observe in this limited exchange is the 'drama' (in Beauvoir's sense) of being caught between the conditions of life and desire, and the structures and limitation of a status that reduces woman to a situation that conflicts with her own emancipation. Dallas and Deb are of course fictional, but they articulate keen observations by their creators, who lived these experiences themselves; they took up the duty of the novelist to represent the world that women knew. The title chosen by James and Cusack – *Come in Spinner* – is thus apt, and candid. It is Australian slang of its time, the call made in Two-Up (a coin toss gambling game), and its meaning infers deception, the moment when the players 'realise the status of the truths about themselves'.[50]

The Australian Women's Weekly (Sydney, 1951)

If Cusack and James' novel reflected the 'status of the truths' about personal relations for a post-war readership, Zélie McLeod's four-part reporting for *The Weekly*, in early 1951, explained the consequences. The sexual and romantic adventures that many women and men experienced during the war, as explored in *Come in Spinner*, often resulted in marriage as a souvenir, or a necessity. At war's end, these marriages felt to many 'like a fit of temporary insanity'.[51] For many women and men, both those who had sought extramarital sexual experience during the war, as well as those who had not, the mundanity of domestic life at war's end was a difficult adjustment, and divorce rates soared.[52] The emphasis by McLeod in her series on 'Divorce' was, unsurprisingly, on women's personal experience of married life in this time of transition. As one source told her:

> 'My husband couldn't seem to settle down after the war. . . . We lived in a small flat. He was a salesman in a department store. I worked as a typist. . . . He just liked going out all the time. We used to quarrel about going out, and he started to go out by himself. Then I found out he was going around with someone else, and I decided the best thing was to break our marriage up'.[53]

For many women, however, the choice to end the marriage was not theirs. And what is important to observe for this report is the care taken by McLeod to explain exactly how the law worked in these circumstances, for a readership who would have had little or no formal legal experience.[54] For example, the most common reported ground for divorce, taken from 1949 statistics, was desertion. And it was that fact, McLeod explained, which raised the problem of domicile, and exposed a potential unfairness for at least one of the parties (as we have already seen): the wife. In Australia each state – or jurisdiction – had its own divorce laws. Despite the potential for the Commonwealth to legislate a uniform law on divorce, and despite increased attention to the complexity separate state-based legislative schemes caused, it remained the case that in 1951 each state differed as regards how and in what circumstances desertion (or for that matter adultery, or any other ground for divorce) could be argued before a court.[55] These differences meant that laws organising divorce could therefore be applied and asserted differentially, between states, and against applicants and respondents, depending on where an application was filed and heard. Such differences were consequently not benign. Not only was it difficult to unravel which law applied, and in which forum, but the legal reasons why one jurisdiction was preferred to another had significant ramifications as to relief. The point made in *The Weekly*, however, was not that these were merely unfair divorce procedures. It was to inform their female readership of what they perhaps already knew, from their own lives, or suspected from those of their neighbours and friends and family: that it was '[w]omen, particularly', who experienced this jurisdictional tangle as 'a grave disadvantage'. This was because of the techniques of law – of domicile, jurisdiction – as much as the state's legislation that embedded and performed those techniques, something that Zélie McLeod intimated when she wrote:

> 'Jurisdiction in divorce depends on domicile, and the law accepts the place of domicile as the State which the husband recognises as his home state. . . . The whole intricate ramifications of questions of domicile difficulties in divorce suits are too complex to go into here, but this issue often puts difficulties in the way of a woman getting a divorce from her husband if he has set up his domicile in a State other than the one in which the wife lives'.[56]

But exactly how, and why, law continued to accept those 'intricate ramifications' was hard to explain. Although personal relations between men and women were increasingly discussed in Australia in terms of desire and liberation as a counter to obligation (as *Come in Spinner* indicated), the problem was that 'personal relations' meant something precise and technical in law, as we have seen, that carried an opposite effect. It would have been difficult for those who were subject to law, ordinary readers of the *Women's Weekly*, to understand that it was this precise legal formulation – 'personal relations' – that in fact perpetuated the 'grave disadvantage' experienced by their daughters, sisters, or themselves in divorce.

The Province and Function of Law (Sydney, 1946)

By contrast, what was difficult for the legal fraternity to conceptualise was that women's experience could of itself be considered a material 'problem' worthy of recognition by jurisprudence *per se*. The conventional approach to jurisprudence as taught at the Universities, in 1950s Australia, was formal and positivist.[57] However, there were some jurisprudents who challenged the boundaries of their own discipline to write about how law might conduct itself in a world in transition. The exemplar in Australia, and important to my project of making visible how jurisprudence come into relation with other ways of knowing, was Julius Stone.

Stone's monumental *The Province and Function of Law* (1946) (*The Province*) was written at this precise moment when, as he described, 'the study of law' started to be seen as 'a social instrument', that required, resultantly, 'an inquiry into the effects of the interaction of law and human behaviour', and 'what effects men ought to achieve through law'.[58] The book was produced early in Stone's tenure as Challis Chair in International Law and Jurisprudence at the University of Sydney.[59] The appointment in 1941 of Stone – English, Jewish, and American educated – was controversial, and not the finest hour in the annals of Australian university administration. These events have been forthrightly recorded, often by the many beneficiaries (and custodians) of Stone's teaching over his long career.[60] Feminist jurisprudent Margaret Thornton, for one example, describes Stone's appointment as clouded by 'anti-Semitism, mingled with anti-intellectualism and personal animus', that 'contributed to the bizarre history of separation between the Department of Jurisprudence and International Law, and the Department of Law [at the University of Sydney]'.[61] Stone's own relations with institutions and scholarship, his personal journey from an intellectual outsider to a world renowned, and nationally revered, figure in jurisprudential thought, is a story I will follow, in part, in other essays in this book. At this point, I would just observe that in our own time, although rarely read (maybe not a surprise at 793 pages), *The Province* is, however, acknowledged as foundation for an orthodoxy: understood as part of the 'gift of realism' that set in motion, through those who it trained, the maturation of a responsive, and cosmopolitan, Australian jurisprudence.[62] In its own time, *The Province* was purposively and boldly assertive,[63] and I want to examine *The Province* as a synthesis of Stone's intellectual ambition for a decidedly modern jurisprudence.

The project of modernity for Stone's jurisprudence, in as much as it can be limited by its origins in this report, emanated from two traditions. One was the sociological insight about power and institutions offered by Harold Laski and others in England, at the London School of Economics, which came to form a strong undercurrent in the *Modern Law Review* from its foundation in 1937.[64] The other tradition were the propositions drawn from American Realism, especially Roscoe Pound at Harvard (who taught and supported Stone in his earliest endeavours).[65] These propositions were that the social and the legal were interactive, as well as active upon each other, and that law as a corpus of thought needed to attend to distinctions between 'paper formulae' and 'social reality'.[66]

Stone argued in *The Province* that he was responding to a 'clash between actual social trends and accepted ideas', and this required a different response in and from law, a 'new threat to the monopoly held by analytical jurisprudence'.[67] Analytical jurisprudence, a story perhaps most famously told by the British jurist John Austin in his *Province of Jurisprudence Determined* (1832), centralised law's own techniques and forms at the expense, Stone and others argued, of considering its relation to thought, institutions, and practices outside law's territorial domain. The influential English jurist HLA Hart noted critically in 1953, in an article on the nature and status of British Jurisprudence (which he extended, in an acceptable gesture of the 1950s towards the Dominions, and to Stone at Sydney University), that the treatment of fact by analytical jurisprudence occasioned a 'vicious abstraction'. As a consequence, 'the major purpose of twentieth century jurisprudence', a duty shared amongst this fraternity of jurists, was to take their discipline 'out of the Austinian rut'.[68]

In *The Province*, Stone explained how that might be done. Stone was interested in how other disciplines – sociology, psychology, and other empirically and human-based social sciences – increasingly discussed the function of law in shaping social conditions. What 'ought to be' in the sphere of law, Stone argued, must be based on a prior or concurrent assessment of 'the concrete situations in which it is sought to realise the idea'.[69] What social science practice offered to law was insight into how to shape 'the fact of actual ethical attitudes of real people'.[70] For Stone, the challenge was to think more broadly about other disciplines as domains that could, and should, be explored. 'Jurisprudence', Stone wrote, 'is first of all the examination of law in light of other disciplines'.[71]

But it is important to pause and remember that what we might consider as 'law in relation' today ('law and humanities' or 'socio legal studies') was not exactly as expansively drawn in 1946. For example, from the title page onwards, Stone's 'law in relation' project extends, rather than displaces, Austin's dominance.[72] The purpose of other disciplines for Stone was material, to provide 'a mass of data' that 'displayed law behaviour in society'.[73] The preferred techniques by which this data was produced were derived from sociology, empirically based anthropology, or political science. Stone was sceptical towards disciplines influenced by Marxist thought, as Indian jurisprudent Upendra Baxi (another former student) has noted.[74] Social science data, on the other hand, was ultimately not about interests but a form of fact, which jurists could evaluate and determine, and legislators could codify. The point was that law maintained its authoritative voice. Facts about the human and social condition of 'the spirit of the times' were important, Stone explained, but had a limit: 'facts albeit scientifically ascertained are of themselves of no avail; for they do not evaluate themselves . . . [that] task is only begun when the facts have been gathered, organised and interpreted'.[75] (In other words, when they have become intelligible to law and its institutions). Evaluation remained the task, Stone argued, of 'jurists', of 'wide enough vision to survey some part of [modern disciplines'] vast territory'.[76] Modern jurisprudence, for Stone, was therefore concerned with 'not merely formulating desirable rules on paper but of ascertaining by what means such rules can be made effective in the existing conditions of social life'.[77] Stone's point was that the task of the jurisprudent remained constant: to assert control over which 'existing conditions' (and whose) could be recognised by, and in, law. Thus, although there was a 'nexus' between jurisprudence and the 'main problems of the present age',[78] any 'reflections' on such problems must be arranged by law 'under its own categories'.[79]

The Australian Law Journal (Sydney, 1951)

The Province was of its time in aspects of reception as much as scholarship. In the 1940s and 1950s, the academic and legal world was homosocial. Jurisprudents reviewed each other's books, attended each other's universities, wrote about their ideas in personal letters, and nominated each other for prizes. Thinking about jurisprudence, and the experience of thinking as male jurists, were activities that existed in relation to each other.[80] These activities, and this mode of enclosure, of course still occurs today (for men and women), but it is the small scale and intimacy of this period which bears closer observation. Pointing this out may seem redundant in the spirit of our own scholarly times, but it is an important part of my project to make plain that studying connections between men of law (then, or now) reveals just as much, if not more, about how jurisprudential knowledge is sexed, as it does about how it is translocated. To demonstrate how jurisprudents engaged in the personal relations of law, and also responded to the 'social problems' entangling the law of personal relations, I want to make some observations of an event held in Sydney in August 1951. The event was the Seventh Australian Legal Convention, organised by the Law Council of Australia to mark the Federation Jubilee, 50 years of legal relations under the Constitution. It was covered expansively by the *Australian*

Law Journal. The *Australian Law Journal* ('ALJ') is not only the oldest ongoing legal journal in Australia (first published in 1927), but in 1951 was also one of the very few local periodicals available to the Australian legal profession, and important in the Commonwealth common law world.[81] In observing the ALJ coverage, I want to draw out two things. The first are matters of emphasis in presentation; the second are techniques of modern jurisprudential thinking in performance.

Style and scale dominated how the Convention was presented to the Journal's readership. They learned that 1,500 members of the Australian legal profession[82] were joined by '55 Empire judges' (including the Chief Justices of Canada, India, and South Africa), Presidents of the Law Societies and Bar Associations of these and 'other Dominion nations'; members of the American Bar; and jurists from all over Australia and the world.[83] These jurists included the Dean of Harvard Law School, Erwin N Griswold, who was one of very few guests invited to address the gathering. The editor of the *Australian Law Journal* commented that that such a congregation was 'the greatest and most representative collection of legal talent which Australia has ever seen'; which 'from a legal viewpoint' created 'an event without rival in the history of this continent'.[84] The activities of 'the world's great legal men' were documented in the style of the social pages. Readers were given front row seats at an exhausting round of excursions, dinners, and cocktail parties (including one at Stone's home), and learned who attended, how they were attired, and what they consumed.[85] The opening ceremony at the Sydney Town Hall was the showpiece, in all coverage. The 'vivid plumage' of the 'legal eagles' was reported in intricate detail: Lord Jowett, as the Lord Chancellor, 'The Keeper of the King's Conscience',[86] appeared in 'his 1,000 pound gold embroidered black silk gown of office'. The 32 judges of the Australian State Supreme Courts, also in the procession, wore 'full vivid crimson robes with ermine-edged capes and white ermine cuffs'. They were 'outshone' by the Chief Justice of the High Court, Sir John Latham, and the six other High Court judges, attired in 'black silk gowns with lace ruffles, knee breeches, silver buckle shoes', in 'full bottomed wigs', and 'each carrying as a matter of tradition, a black silk tricorn'.[87]

By today's standards, the populist attention given to the Convention in legal and other publications at the time is idiosyncratic. However, in 1951, the Commonwealth still had political and legal meaning, and Australia was still in thrall to her British foundations.[88] In those terms, the appearance of undisputed stars of British Justice in Sydney was treated as a benediction for Australian law and lawyers. When reading the unbridled self-congratulation of the Convention coverage now, I find it hard not to think of *Three Guineas* (1938), and Virginia Woolf's excoriation of an imagined parade of these figures of the House of Lords and Oxford. '[T]o express worth of any kind', she wrote 'whether intellectual or moral, by wearing pieces of metal, or ribbon, coloured hoods or gowns, is a barbarity which deserves . . . ridicule'. 'Any woman', she added, 'who advertised her motherhood by a tuft of horsehair on the left shoulder would scarcely, you will agree, be a venerable object'.[89]

For the purposes of this report, however, the principal insight to draw is the ascription of meaning given to the conduct of personal relations:

> 'The late afternoon party at Royal Sydney Golf Club was attended by over 1000 people . . . The harbour trip on the Show Boat, the visits to the Blue Mountains and the golf, tennis and bowls tournaments also went a long way in bringing together members of the profession and creating enduring friendships'.[90]

As the Convention was 'naturally not concerned with any precise legislative project, but the exchange of ideas on subjects of fundamental importance';[91] the 'firsthand contacts with leaders of thought from overseas' thus provided opportunity for Australian lawyers, and opportunity for 'vitalising effects' on their legal thought.[92]

Erwin N Griswold, Dean of Harvard Law School, and friend of the newly established Challis Professor of Jurisprudence and International Law at University Sydney, Julius Stone, brought this alternative 'vitalising effect' to the Convention platform.[93] Griswold's speech, 'Divorce Jurisdiction and Recognition of Divorce Decrees: A Comparative Study', was published in full in the ALJ.[94] In the context of a gathering with a diverse national and international audience, the prominence given to the topic – domicile – reiterates its prestige as a pressing modern problem to solve.[95]

Griswold's text began by asking the Sydney Town Hall audience to consider that 'the great problem of law' for the modern age, what it 'must face up to', is 'the merger of antithesis, the synthesis of opposites', of law and its outside.[96] It is one thing, Griswold argued, to recognise law may well have a relationship with society. It is quite another to assert that law be responsive as a consequence. The assertion that law consider its function in the contemporary world required an active approach. The one that Griswold favoured was 'compromise', between law's 'fictions' and fact. Griswold argued that jurisprudential attentiveness to the way judges interpret fact enabled modern law to address the problems of material life. But, like Stone, Griswold made plain that this could only occur once those problems had become recognisable to law.

In the specific context of Griswold's paper, of course, the particular 'problem' was divorce, which had become 'acute during the war' with 'the crossing of states, territories, borders' when marriages formed between women and 'soldiers of foreign countries' broke down.[97] Griswold explained to his audience: '[w]e [are] immediately confronted with the fact that here is a social problem' that law needs to solve.[98] He delineated that it was often unclear, as a simple matter of conflict of laws, which national (or state) jurisdiction prevailed to authorise the dissolution of the marriage. It also became confusing, legally, as to how different forums in different countries could recognise divorce authorised in a different place. Griswold noted that domicile made these private international law questions into 'problems of rest and motion, stability and change',[99] and even more complex. Like *The Weekly's* consideration of the same phenomena, Griswold centralised the fact that the return of a husband to their domicile of choice or origin had unique implications for the wife. Regardless of whether she remained in her country or state of birth, her status as wife, and her inability to assert herself as a legal person for the purpose of divorce proceedings, created extra-legal difficulties. *The Weekly*, as noted, sought to understand how this was experienced as a 'grave disadvantage', and asked that question of women themselves. Griswold, unsurprisingly, returned domicile immediately to law, but did so in a way that asked the lawyers present to cleave their use and expectations of categories and devices like domicile away from accepted traditions. In the United States, for example, married women 'had always', at common law, had a separate domicile to their husband, 'simply depending on the fact' of where they resided. Griswold suggested – somewhat pointedly to his audience of Commonwealth common lawyers – that the American rejection of the inherited British evisceration of a wife's status to that of her husband for the purposes of marriage and divorce law was an artefact of how his country's national history and jurisprudence related to each other:

> '[The USA is a] young country, with rather numerous and relatively small states, and a considerable freedom and volume of moving about. We were also in the beginnings of a strong development towards the equality of women and a recognition of that equality in our laws'.[100]

Griswold reminded his audience, however, that in both the UK and in Australia, the state had passed legislation that 'confected' residence as a solution to the problem of unitary domicile to cope with the difficulties of war-time marriage and its unhappy consequences. This legislative 'confection' worked in a similar way to the US common law. It altered the 'fiction of the wife's domicile',[101] the effect of which was 'to extend to the wife the opportunity to obtain a divorce in the State where she resides, at least where the husband remains domiciled somewhere in Australia'.[102] This legislative sleight of hand, giving a wife separate domicile based on where *she* lived, did not of course change her status in British, and Commonwealth, common law. Her personhood remained sublimated.[103] But Dean Griswold argued that this did not matter very much. As he gently chided the Commonwealth lawyers at the Sydney Town Hall:

> 'Domicile did not come from Mount Sinai . . . if the legislative authority wants to give the wife a separate domicile for divorce, no reason is perceived why it cannot do so. Moreover . . . it makes no difference whether the true operation of these statutes is in terms of domicile or residence'.[104]

From his perspective, domicile of the wife in any form – unitary, or based on the fact of residence – was important to consider *only* because it was an incidental hurdle to the real problems that doctrinal law – and modern jurisprudence – had to manage. This problem was, as noted, how to deal with social movement of populations, exposed because of the hasty formation of unsatisfactory and unsatisfying marriages in the heat of war. Doctrinally, this meant the law of divorce now needed to share ideas and practices across national borders. The goal then became changing the common law recognition of another's forum and authority, attending to the difficulties enveloped jurisdictionally in the doctrine of *res judicata* – not, as it were, attending to, or recognising, how a woman managed to live institutionally, with law, and within marriage, in a place as a *de jure* wife.

Coda: In Place and Out of Office

By way of conclusion on conducts of jurisprudential life, circa 1949, I want to think about the tension that presents itself in Griswold's address. In reading Griswold's speech now, what is visible (behind the complicated doctrinal exegesis) is how divorce was a question that modern jurisprudents considered intellectually and technically amenable to permeation between 'the social' and 'law'. I want to emphasise, however, what this advancement in jurisprudential knowledge could still not comprehend. What was unrecognisable to the best legal minds of the day was how any woman experienced social existence, and that this was a consequence of her status as a dependent and lesser legal person. As noted in my report, written expression of feminist thought was present in Australian intellectual life at this time, and recognisable as an assertion of woman's experience and knowledge. It was produced by women taking up the duties of writers, journalists, essayists, but written out of office (or at least outside of the institutions of university or court that authorised the content and form of jurisprudential and legal thought). It is not a surprise that official jurisprudence, and male university jurisprudents, circa 1949, had little interest in women writing of their social experience. Nor is it a revelation that they had little inclination, as a consequence, to find innovative techniques to draw the assertions of women's lived experience of law into relationship with their own. It is, nevertheless, a disjuncture that I think is worth drawing into direct view.

What Griswold and his friends did recognise as 'the social', in contrast, were the places people lived, and how they moved between places. This was, perhaps, because place is a question that law already has techniques to manage: it is capable of redescription as a problem of territorial jurisdiction.[105] In this way, the doctrinal solutions that Griswold and many others proffered are both of their time, and unsurprising. The case made for reform to the law of divorce was through extra territorial recognition as a matter of private international law, or, in Australia, for uniform law as a project of Federalism. These legal reform projects were of course successful (a story that other scholars have told very well, in different idioms and with different ambitions to mine).[106] For my own project, I would simply observe a transition. Jurisdiction as a device of law that had organised the relations of men and women for centuries moved, from person to place. The older ideas of law that organised personal relations – domicile, status, legal personality – could not meet, it appeared, the demands of the contemporary post-war world. Personhood – woman's personhood, and its denial in law – was thus of little consequence, or made little difference, to the social problem that Griswold suggested territorial jurisdiction could enliven.

The centralisation of territory was not isolated to legal doctrinal reform. Territorial expansion also became a preoccupation of 'law in relation', as modern jurisprudential thought aspired to have control of the empirical data produced by other disciplines. Julius Stone, for example, borrowed a 'striking metaphor' from Harold Laski's *A Grammar of Politics* (1925) to reiterate his argument about law's function, and its relation to society. Jurisprudence, Stone explained, should be the 'eye of the law', giving lawyers their 'insight into the environment of which it is the expression and the relating of law to the spirit of the times'.[107] A problem with jurisprudence's disciplinary voyeurism, I would suggest, is that it treats the social environment and its expression as something that lawyers can master and possess. This movement becomes difficult to see, over time. Stone's teaching, for example, embeds in the collective normative practices of Australian law and its institutions.[108] It becomes an orthodoxy, affixed to certain methods and attitudes, and with preferential treatment given to certain forms of disciplinary practice outside of law that make it difficult for heterodox knowledge holders and their practices to be seen and heard.

My report's mid-century examples of relationship problems – *de jure* and otherwise – can be understood in one view as a product of institutionalised sexual hierarchy, and indifference, that marked the spirit of the times. But I want to note that this failure of jurisprudential and feminist knowledge to meet then also represents a problem of authorisation that endures now. Who writes about the experience of law, and the very mundane question of where that writing takes place (at the kitchen table rather than for the Convention podium) informs jurisprudential methods as much as what is written about, and how it is transmitted. My argument in all my essays in this book is that these topics need explicit attention, and self-acknowledgment, by custodians of law and legal writing to gain full 'insight into the environment of which [jurisprudence] is the expression'. From that viewpoint, my activity of reporting on personal relations circa 1949, trying not to gloss, misremember, or give weight more than is due, is something of course made available through some of the engagements that come after 1949.[109] But it is also an assertion that the disjuncture, and the character of the relations between feminist and jurisprudential knowledge, require explicit attention as a story of method and ethos. It is that story that is to be continued in my next instalment of *Feminist Jurisography*.

Notes

1 A report is a genre I have experimented with before to address different questions about the conduct of jurisprudence as jurisography: Genovese & McVeigh 2015.
2 See Bartie 2019.
3 See Essay One, *Feminist Jurisography*: 14–16.
4 Le Dœuff 1991: 113.
5 Beauvoir 2011: 11.
6 Genovese 2013: 51–53.
7 Beauvoir 2011: 439–664, for example as mother, wife, lover, 'Independent woman', as described in Part Two, Volume Two 'Situation'.
8 Beauvoir 2011: 152. She reminds her readers this ambiguity carries particular weight and warning in 1949, one year after the UN Declaration of Human Rights: Beauvoir 2011: 15.
9 Beauvoir 2011: 439.
10 Beauvoir 2011: 439.
11 Beauvoir 2011: 485.
12 Beauvoir 2011: 139–152.
13 Beauvoir 2011: 11.
14 Beauvoir 2011: 88.
15 Beauvoir 2011: 766.
16 'Annual Report' *League of Women Voters of South Australia* 1955.
17 Baalman 1955: iv.
18 See reviews of the book by Barcs 1947; Hambly 1969.
19 Baalman 1955: 75–105.
20 See for these two points, respectively: Halley 2011; Finlay 2005.
21 Baalman 1955: 75.
22 See Dorsett & McVeigh 2012: 81–84.
23 Star 1992: 17.
24 Dorsett & McVeigh 2012: 81–84; Maine 1912: 182 as quoted in Graveson 1941: 261.
25 Baalman 1955: 98.
26 Baalman 1955: 98.
27 Blackstone 1893: 279.
28 Beauvoir 2011: 442–443.
29 Baalman 1955: 90.
30 See Rubenstein 2016; Rosanove 1954.
31 Simic 2007.
32 See Essay Three, *Feminist Jurisography*: 57–69.
33 Lake 1999: 198–199.
34 I return to this general point in Essay Four, *Feminist Jurisography*.
35 Cusack & James 1994.
36 McLeod 1951a, 1951b.
37 Sheridan 2012; Sheridan et al 2001; North 1990, 2001.
38 Lawson 1996; Sheridan 2012: 195.
39 Sheridan 2012: 195.
40 James 1994: v.
41 Moore 2012: 161.
42 Franklin 1951.
43 James 1994: vii.
44 Franklin 1951 quoted by James 1994: vii.
45 James 1994: vi.
46 James 1994: vi.

47 James 1994: viii.
48 Cusack & James 1994: 329.
49 Cusack & James 1994: 329.
50 Mauger & Hartley 1985: 118.
51 Bongiorno 2012: 199.
52 McLeod 1951a. McLeod 1951a: 20 reported: 'in 1930 about one in every 500 Australian married couples got divorced. Now the divorce rate is about one in every 245 married couples'. See too: Featherstone 2013.
53 McLeod 1951a: 21.
54 Organised feminist political activity during this period was very much focused on altering (and recognising) the status of women as a formal political (rather than legal) question, including unifying and simplifying divorce laws: see Lake 1999: 191–213.
55 For an overview of the technicalities of divorce law during this period, see Finlay 2005.
56 McLeod 1951b: 20.
57 Star 1992: 83–84.
58 Stone 1950: 387.
59 Star 1992: 81–97.
60 Star 1992: 56–67; Goldring 1985; Kirby 2012; Thornton 1995.
61 Thornton 1995: 136.
62 Johns 2010.
63 Star 1992: 81–97; Hutchinson 2010.
64 W 1987.
65 Star 1992: 28–32.
66 Stone 1950: 387; and favorably and expansively reviewed by, see Pound 1948.
67 Stone 1950: 11.
68 Stone 1950: 15, quoting the Constitutional scholar Jennings 1938: 35, an article written during the latter's time at London School of Economics. For general exemplification of this point, see Hart 1953: 359.
69 Stone 1950: 386.
70 Stone 1950: 386.
71 Stone 1950: 386.
72 Allan Hutchison makes a similar argument in Hutchinson 2010.
73 Stone 1950: 387.
74 Baxi 2010: 78.
75 Stone 1950: 23.
76 Stone 1950: 15.
77 Stone 1950: 409.
78 Stone 1950: 35.
79 Stone 1950: 30.
80 See, for examples of personal relations story of this generation of jurisprudents from biographies, Star 1992; Lacey 2004. For a contemporary take, and reflection, see Goodrich 2003; Baxi 2010: 74–77, on the benefits and obligations of creating juristic fellowship.
81 Kirby 2007.
82 Bowen & Else-Mitchell 1951; 'Distinguished guests for big law conference' *The Australian Women's Weekly* 1951.
83 'World's great legal men were there' *The Argus* 1951.
84 Bowen & Else-Mitchell 1951: 234.
85 'Party for law visitors' *The Sydney Morning Herald* 1951; 'Their Honors concurred. . .' *The Argus* 1951.
86 'Impressions Of Sydney Law Convention' *Border Watch* 1951.
87 'World's great legal men were there' *The Argus* 1951.

88 Bongiorno 2013.
89 Woolf 2001: 119. I thank John Docker for this reference.
90 Bowen & Else-Mitchell 1951: 235.
91 'Jubilee visits a stimulus' *The Advertiser* 1951.
92 Bowen & Else-Mitchell 1951: 235.
93 Star 1992: 117.
94 Griswold 1951.
95 To give a flavour of some of these sources: Kahn-Freund 1952; Graveson 1950; Sawer 1953.
96 Griswold 1951: 240.
97 Griswold 1951: 250.
98 Griswold 1951: 268.
99 Griswold 1951: 248, quoting from Cardozo 1928.
100 Griswold 1951: 255.
101 Griswold 1951: 252.
102 Griswold 1951: 255.
103 Griswold 1951: 268.
104 Griswold 1951: 252.
105 Griswold 1951: 249, 256.
106 For example, Finlay 2005.
107 Stone 1950: 25.
108 See, for example, Irving, Mowbray & Walton 2010.
109 Genovese & McVeigh 2015.

References

Baalman J 1955 *Outline of Law in Australia* The Law Book Co. of Australasia Sydney (2nd edn).

Bartie S 2019 *Free Hands and Minds: Pioneering Australian Legal Scholars* Hart Publishing Oxford and London.

Baxi U 2010 'Revisiting Social Dimensions of Law and Justice in a Post-Human Era' in Irving et al 2010: 69–86.

Beauvoir S de 2011 *The Second Sex* Trans C Borde and S Malovany-Chevallier Vintage New York (first published 1949).

Blackstone W 1893 *Commentaries on the Laws of England in Four Books, Volume 1 – Books I & II* J. B. Lippincott & Co. Philadelphia (first published 1765–69).

Bongiorno F 2012 *The Sex Lives of Australians: A History* Black Inc. Collingwood.

Bongiorno F 2013 'Herbert Vere Evatt and British Justice: The Communist Party Referendum of 1951' *Australian Historical Studies* 44/1: 54–70 DOI:10.1080/1031461X.2012.760634.

Bowen N H and Else-Mitchell R 1951 'Seventh Legal Convention of the Law Council of Australia' *The Australian Law Journal* 25/5: 233–384.

Cardozo B N 1928 *The Paradoxes of Legal Science* Columbia University Press New York.

Cusack D and James F 1994 *Come in Spinner* Angus & Robertson Pymble and Glenfield (first published 1951).

Dorsett S and McVeigh S 2012 *Jurisdiction* Routledge Abingdon and New York.

Featherstone L 2013 '"The one single primary cause": divorce, the family, and heterosexual pleasure in postwar Australia' *Journal of Australian Studies* 37/3: 349–363 DOI:10.1080/14443058.2013.815256.

Finlay H 2005 *To Have But Not to Hold: A History of Attitudes to Marriage and Divorce in Australia 1858–1975* Federation Press Annandale.

Franklin M 1951 'Come in Spinner (Book Review)' *Meanjin* 10/1: 81–82.

Genovese A 2013 'Inheriting and Inhabiting the Pleasures and Duties of Our Own Existence: *The Second Sex* and Feminist Jurisprudence' *Australian Feminist Law Journal* 38/1: 41–57 DOI:10.1080/13200968.2013.10854482.

Genovese A and McVeigh S 2015 'Nineteen eighty three: A jurisographic report on *Commonwealth v Tasmania*' *Griffith Law Review* 24/1: 68–88 DOI:10.1080/10383441.2015.1022891.

Goldring J 1985 'Julius Stone and the Study of Law and Society in Australia' *Australian Journal of Law & Society* 2/2: 4–10.

Goodrich P 2003 'Laws of Friendship' *Law & Literature* 15/1: 23–52 DOI:10.1525/lal.2003.15.1.23.

Graveson R H 1941 'The Movement from Status to Contract' *The Modern Law Review* 4/4: 261–272.

Graveson R H 1950 'Capacity to Acquire a Domicile' *The International Law Quarterly* 3/2: 149–163.

Griswold E N 1951 'Divorce Jurisdiction and Recognition of Divorce Decrees: A Comparative Study' *The Australian Law Journal* 25: 248–266.

Halley J 2011 'What Is Family Law?: A Genealogy Part II' *Yale Journal of Law & the Humanities* 23/2: 189–294.

Hart H L A 1953 'Philosophy of Law and Jurisprudence in Britain (1945–1952)' *The American Journal of Comparative Law* 2/3: 355–364 DOI:10.2307/837483.

Hutchinson A C 2010 'The Province of Jurisprudence (Really) Redetermined' in Irving et al 2010: 87–102.

Irving H, Mowbray J and Walton K eds 2010 *Julius Stone: A Study in Influence* Federation Press Annandale.

James F 1994 'Introduction' in Cusack et al 1994: v–xi.

Jennings W I 1938 'A Plea for Utilitarianism' *The Modern Law Review* 2/1: 22–35.

Johns F 2010 'A Gift of Realism: Julius Stone and the International Law Academy in Australia' in Irving et al 2010: 21–38.

Kahn-Freund O 1952 'Inconsistencies and Injustices in the Law of Husband and Wife' *The Modern Law Review* 15/2: 133–154.

Kirby M 2007 'Past, Present & Future' *ALJ @ 80* 16 March Sydney <https://cdn.hcourt.gov.au/assets/publications/speeches/former-justices/kirbyj/kirbyj_16mar07.pdf>.

Kirby M 2012 'The graduating class of Sydney Law School 1962: Talented, lucky, unquestioning' *Australian Bar Review* 36/2: 189–200.

Lacey N 2004 *A Life of H.L.A. Hart: The Nightmare and the Noble Dream* Oxford University Press Oxford and New York.

Lake M 1999 *Getting Equal: The history of Australian feminism* Allen & Unwin St Leonards.

Lawson V 2006 'Fenston, Esmé (Ezzie) (1908–1972)' in V Lawson ed 2006 *Australian Dictionary of Biography* Australian National University Canberra (first published 1996) viewed 18 March 2022 <https://adb.anu.edu.au/biography/fenston-esme-ezzie-10165>.

Le Dœuff M 1991 *Hipparchia's Choice: An Essay Concerning Women, Philosophy, etc.* Trans T Selous Blackwell Oxford (first published 1989).

Maine H S 1912 *Ancient Law* John Murray London (first published 1861).

Mauger J and Hartley J 1985 'Come in Spinner: The Politics of the Toss' *Australian Journal of Cultural Studies* 3/2: 117–125.

Moore N 2012 *The Censor's Library* University of Queensland Press St Lucia.

North M 1990 'The Anatomy of a Best-Seller: The Making of "Come in Spinner"' Master of Arts Thesis (Hons.) University of Woolongong Woolongong.

North M ed 2001 *Yarn Spinners: A Story in Letters, Dymphna Cusack, Florence James, Miles Franklin* University of Queensland Press St Lucia.

Pound R 1948 'Reviewed Work: *The Province and Function of Law* by Julius Stone' *Harvard Law Review* 61/4: 724–737.

Rosanove J 1954 'Australian Divorce Laws' *The Australian Law Journal* 27: 672–677.

Rubenstein K 2016 'Alive in the Telling: Trailblazing Women Lawyers' Lives, Lived with Law' *Law Text Culture* 20: 66–92.

Sawer G 1953 'Husband-and-Wife versus Master-and-Servant: A Collision of Concepts' *The Australian Law Journal* 27: 323–326.

Sheridan S 2012 '"Opposing All the Things They Stand for": Women Writers and the Women's Magazines' in P Kirkpatrick and R Dixon eds 2012 *Republics of Letters: Literary Communities in Australia* Sydney University Press Chippendale: 195–204.

Sheridan S, Baird B, Borrett K and Ryan L 2001 *Who Was That Woman? The Australian Women's Weekly in the Postwar Years* UNSW Press Sydney.

Simic Z 2007 'Butter Not Bombs: A Short History of the Union of Australian Women' *History Australia* 4/1: 07.1–07.15 DOI:10.2104/ha070007.

Star L 1992 *Julius Stone: An Intellectual Life* Oxford University Press in Association with Sydney University Press New York.

Stone J 1950 *The Province and Function of Law: Law as Logic, Justice and Social Control; A Study in Jurisprudence* Maitland Sydney (first published 1946).

Thornton M 1995 'Book Review: Leonie Star "Julius Stone: An Intellectual Life"' *Law in Context: A Socio-Legal Journal* 13: 127–130.

W 1987 'An Anniversary Preface' *The Modern Law Review* 50/6: 673–676.

Woolf V 2001 'Three Guineas' in V Woolf ed 2001 *A Room of One's Own and Three Guineas* Vintage London (first published 1938).

Archival Sources

Papers of Norman MacKenzie, The Women's Library at LSE 7NMA Box FL086- FLO87
1955 'Annual Report' *League of Women Voters of South Australia*: 2 GB106/7/Y/NM 104.

Trove

Barcs E 1947 'It's the law!' *The Daily Telegraph* Sydney 19 April: 19.

Big Law Conference 1951 'Distinguished Guests for Big Law Conference: "Legal Eagles" Will Wear Vivid Plumage for opening session' *The Australian Women's Weekly* Sydney 25 July: 21.

Hambly D 1969 'The Law for the Layman' *The Canberra Times* Canberra 5 July: 12.

'Impressions of Sydney Law Convention' 1951 *Border Watch* Mount Gambier 6 September: 8.

'Jubilee Visits a Stimulus' 1951 *The Advertiser* Adelaide 28 August: 2.

McLeod Z 1951a '27,000 divorced women face lonely existence' *The Australian Women's Weekly* Sydney 10 February: 20–21.

McLeod Z 1951b 'Diverse laws make divorce difficult' *The Australian Women's Weekly* Sydney 3 March: 20–21.

'Party for law visitors' 1951 *The Sydney Morning Herald* Sydney 7 August: 5.

'Their Honors Concurred . . .' 1951 *The Argus* Melbourne 24 August: 5.

'World's Great Legal Men Were There' 1951 *The Argus* Melbourne 9 August: 5.

Essay 3

On Place and Displacement, 1962 (A Jurisographical Exercise Concerning Authors and Their Sources)

Introduction

An aim of this collection of essays is to show the explicit connections that exist between a writer's experience and her writing. To write relationally, and of relations, is not to initiate 'a series of intimate revelations and concessions',[1] but to insist that the inheritance of knowledge is not separate from the experience of its practice. In Essay One, I explained my project in those terms. In Essay Two, I explored debts of technique and genre, and started to show how stories of disciplinary relationship (as much as relations between men's and women's accounts of the experience of law), are never certain, or coherent.[2] In both instances, I have acknowledged the relationship between method and source as a proper subject for jurisprudential and historical enquiry. That said, such accounts are hard to write, especially using law's materials, and often involve the writer trimming the edges off a story to gain a clean line of hindsight. This can obscure sources written outside of or in opposition to public institutions of law (courts and universities),[3] and risks the production of segregated accounts of knowledge and practice. Under-regarded sources and records, which are often written by women but sometimes also written about them, reveal how particular methods gain disciplinary (and interdisciplinary) ascendancy in time and place. This is equally as relevant a concern for jurisprudence, feminism, history (or of course, where these essays are heading), 'law and humanities' as a sub-discipline of its own. I think the activity of reminding this is the case is an obligation of feminist jurisography.

Giving precise form to that obligation is the purpose of this third essay, and I explore more intimately two aspects of relations between method, source, and knowledge to do so. The first is to ask, and historicise, what a method is *for*: who chooses and announces it, what questions it is directed to expose or answer, what it produces. The second is to comment, and reflect on, the situation of the sources available to bring such a story into view. To undertake these tasks, I focus on one book, and the conduct of its production. That book is Norman MacKenzie's *Women in Australia* (1962).

DOI: 10.4324/9780429461132-3

I have wanted to write about *Women in Australia* since I was first introduced to it in the 1990s, primarily because I felt ambivalent about its bequests. On one hand, it is useful and valuable, examining the impediments to Australian women's public participation in the period just before the revolutions of Women's Liberation. On the other, it presents as sincere but misguided, written by a complete outsider to that experience: an English man, whose first and only introduction to Australia coincided with his arrival in 1959 to begin research for the book. It has also intrigued me that *Women in Australia* is well-known as a source book in Australian feminist historiography,[4] but almost unknown in accounts of jurisprudence. This is despite the fact that it contains an appendix on laws affecting women's status in the 1960s (written by the Australian public law scholar Enid Campbell), and many public policy recommendations about access and law reform. Perhaps this absence of interest by a broader audience is an example of philosopher Michèle Le Dœuff's caustic (but nonetheless accurate) observation that books with a title like *Women in Australia* are often found in libraries 'sectioned off under a special heading ("by women, about women, for women") and half their potential readers are deprived of solid reading matter'.[5] It is, in my view, a book of jurisprudence as well as a source book for feminist history writing. It marks the early 1960s as the point when law started to join with other disciplines, and demonstrates how legal problems for a particular class could be methodologically dealt with through collection of data, interview and survey, innovations that are now orthodoxies of socio-legal and empirical research in law faculties all over the world.

These inheritances are equivocal, but are not severable, as I hope to show. To make that story as visible as possible, in what you are about to read, I follow two related sets of sources: one that opens up the official writing of the author, Mr Norman MacKenzie, as a university researcher; and the other that addresses the writing of Australian women (or at least the women with whom he corresponded in the course of his research). Deciding how to represent those sources adequately has taken time. The first iteration of this essay was written in 2013, and I have experimented since then with ways to draw out the ambitions of jurisography and respond to different audiences. My encounter with Mr MacKenzie has appeared as personal notes written while *in situ* in libraries, shared only with a friend; to public talks at universities in Melbourne and in London (noting these were differently conceived and received); to a published essay for a collection in a critical law journal.[6] In each iteration, I have understood better that I was testing my responsibilities for the sources I was reintroducing, and also bringing into view my ambivalence for, and complicity with, institutional knowledge production and custodianship. For a version that belongs to this collection, I have settled on a genre that is part formal essay, part book review, and part travel journal. What I want to come into view, after all, is a tale of translocation: of methods across time, collections, and places; and of researchers (both Mr MacKenzie moving to Australia in the 1960s, and my experience of following him back to London, 50 years later).

University Notes

To present *Women in Australia* as a book of jurisprudence, it is useful to return to Julius Stone, who I introduced in Essay Two,[7] and his scholarly milieu. By the late 1950s, Stone's *The Province and Function of Law* (1946) was a central text on the Sydney University curriculum. The book marked the post-war moment when 'the study of law' started to be seen differently. Law was not removed from life, but was 'a social instrument', that required 'an inquiry into the effects of the interaction of law and human behaviour'.[8] 'We have seen', Stone wrote, 'that there is wide spread modern agreement that any ideal of what "ought to be" in the sphere of law must be based on a prior or concurrent assessment of the concrete situations in which it is sought to realise the idea'.[9] This required, resultantly, a recalibration of the writing and practice of jurisprudence itself, so it could be understood as 'first of all the examination of law in light of other disciplines',[10] (although those other disciplines were to remain in service to law). Stone's innovations, and views, were formed in 'wide spread modern agreement' with his own teachers and colleagues, in England and the United States, where he had trained.[11] The fortunes of the *Modern Law Review* and its contributors demonstrate one lineage of that experience, perhaps best exemplified by jurisprudents based at the London School of Economics (LSE), guided by the spirit of Beatrice and Sidney Webb's *Methods of Social Study* (1932), intent on working across disciplines to produce public work that was socially relevant.[12] The experience of Legal Realists in America forms another. In the 1940s and 1950s, scholars at Yale, Harvard, and Wisconsin had pioneered in very literal terms (as American critical legal scholar David Trubek has argued) that 'it was necessary to leave the library and get "the facts" about what really goes on in areas allegedly affected by legal rules'.[13] In the war and post-war period at least, American Legal Realists' push against purely doctrinal legal scholarship necessitated engagement in activities capable of ascertaining 'whether something [jurisprudents knew] . . . about social life [was] central and representative or . . . merely peripheral and unusual'.[14] Finding 'the right facts' meant, in practice, jurisprudents using social science and its methods as a disciplinary aide, a junior partner whose 'techniques such as surveys, interviews, and multivariate analyses'[15] enabled facts useful to their hypotheses to be collected and generalised. It was through these methods that jurisprudential knowledge would 'evolve through an iterative process',[16] so that Legal Realists could assert a conception of law capable of demonstrating how it 'actually applied and affected people's lives'.[17]

In Australia in the 1950s, it seemed as if these aligned jurisprudential commitments to Stone's nascent practice of 'law in relation' only appeared publicly at the level of proposition. 'Research' (as we might understand it now) was an 'esoteric irrelevancy' for most teachers at Law schools, which were more akin to professional colleges, and staffed by those predominantly at the Bar.[18] There was a pedagogical and theoretical divide, for example, that took material form in Stone's own Faculty, where he held the Chair in the Department of Jurisprudence, sequestered away from the more traditional Department of Law.[19] It was not feasible in the post-war world, however, to pretend that the doctrines and techniques of law, such as status, were separate from social experience (as Erwin Griswold, Dean of Harvard, argued in his address to the Australian Legal Convention 1951, and as I described in Essay Two).[20] Nor was it defensible to pretend that faculty of a modern university, including those with legal expertise, should quarantine themselves from public projects that might have relevance to practical considerations of justice and social participation.[21] But the Australian academic community, although not intellectually isolated, was small; there seemed little opportunity for Stone to form the cross-faculty and federal relationships, and access the funding, necessary to build institutional alliances to gain empirical insights into 'the fact of actual ethical attitudes of real people'.[22] There appeared to be a disjuncture between desire and capability, to put a theory about facts into relationship with fact-finding techniques – let alone build a consensus view on the exact purposes for which those facts might best be gathered, and what precise experiences (or 'ethical attitudes')[23] required testing or response by law (and lawyers), or by their disciplinary allies.

From within the cloistered world of public administration, and captured in their archives, the story reads a little differently. Julius Stone, while he was writing *Province*, had been invited by the Australian Government to participate in the University based Committees on National Morale.[24] Through this committee work he met a different scholarly fraternity, outside of law, but in Australia: professors of anthropology, psychology, politics, and economics, all of whom 'embraced the idea of a science of society', with a 'shared and common purpose and method, marking out a distinctive domain of knowledge' which might be put in place 'to the duty of society as a whole'.[25] Hannah Forsyth, the Australian historian of the modern university, records these men who envisaged a higher duty for universities and themselves as 'god professors' (a term in fact coined in 1963 by historian Geoffrey Serle about his contemporaries).[26] Their common method was, unsurprisingly, a preoccupation with facts,[27] gathered by techniques of observation, analysis, and reasoning. The shared purpose was initially national security, and then after the war, national reconstruction. Engaged in common enterprise, professors who were invited to participate in these committees, in particular Stone, recognised (or hoped to emulate the experiences of colleagues at LSE and elsewhere) that the university had a vital role in the creation of knowledge for practical purposes.[28] By 1952, the Social Science Research Council (SSRC) had been established to undertake that function in post-war Australia.[29] The committee members were neither insular in their world views, nor in their scholarly and life experiences. Many members of the Council had studied or served overseas, were émigrés to Australia, or were collaborators with other men of their intellectual and political inclination at universities outside of Australia.[30] The techniques that in fact inform the drive and institutional purposes behind the SSRC were transnationally developed, but nationally deployed, intended to better understand the specificity of Australian problems and Australian people.[31]

In 1957, the SSRC announced that the status of women would be the topic of its first major funded project,[32] and decided to 'appoint a full-time researcher to conduct the study, possibly from over seas'.[33] Richard Titmuss, who had founded the academic discipline of Social Administration at the LSE and pioneered the British Social Mobility survey in 1954, was visiting Australia when the announcement was made.[34] He recommended a candidate to his friends on the SSRC: Mr Norman MacKenzie.[35] MacKenzie was a polymath, an educator, a modernist, a journalist, a Fabian socialist, a soldier (and possibly a spy). In 1957, he was an assistant editor of *New Statesman*, had recently graduated from the LSE with a degree in politics, and aspired to an academic career. He was later appointed as a foundation professor of sociology at Sussex; with his wife, Jeanne, he wrote about and guarded the reputation of Sidney and Beatrice Webb. MacKenzie had been trained in the modern research practices that interested the committee, and the SSRC appointed him to the job. In 1958, with Jeanne and their two daughters, he moved to Canberra in 1958, to embark on the *Women in Australia* project.[36]

My understanding of the SSRC's promotion of MacKenzie is drawn from my reading of *The Poor Relation* (2010), a history of social sciences in Australia. It is a history written, fittingly, by the late Stuart Macintyre, one of Australia's most eminent (and prolific) historians, with expertise in the 20th century and a scholarly commitment to undertake research that speaks to the ethos of public institutions and explains their origins and purposes. 'The Poor Relation' in the title of Macintyre's book is not a reflection of Australian expertise *vis à vis* London (or even the rest of the Western scholarly world). Rather, it refers to social science as a discipline, and how its innovations were hard to see in the traditional preoccupations of university life. Macintyre's account is based on scrutiny of the records of the SSRC, which reside, fittingly, in the collection of the National Library of Australia in Canberra, a demonstration of the ongoing relationships between the nation state and its national institutions. Macintyre's duties as an historian, however, are not identical to mine, nor should they be. *Women in Australia* appears in his history as one illustration among many of how the bureaucratisation of university knowledge altered the social fabric of Australia. But I have an obligation to notice things and people that Macintyre does not, that lie at the margins, in the footnotes of a story of male scholars of a certain class and mobility, building careers while intellectually building the nation.[37] In Macintyre's account, for example, Mr MacKenzie's appointment is cause for conviviality in the common rooms and university clubs of the LSE, the Australian National University (ANU), and University of Melbourne. But Mr MacKenzie's appointment was also controversial amongst the very constituency that he was appointed to investigate. As Patience Thoms (the first women's news editor of the *Courier Mail* and a self-described feminist)[38] commented, with exasperated emphasis, in 1959:

> 'The absence of women on leading roles in the nation's public and professional life has been frequently the comment of distinguished historians,

economists, and sociologists visiting Australia. The Council's objective is to examine this PHENOMENA in Australia . . . The person chosen to initiate this research is a MAN – a British scholar, Mr Norman MacKenzie'.[39]

My duty is to take my cues from Thoms, rather than the institution of the SSRC, and return the subjects of *Women in Australia* to centre stage.

Library Notes

To understand how women's status was experienced (and not only explained) by the 'Women in Australia' project, I looked outside of national repositories to different kinds of collections, scattered between libraries in Sydney and London. After his two-year visit to Australia, Mr MacKenzie's papers were repatriated with him to London.[40] As a scholar of British post-war life, trained at the LSE, it is appropriate that all of MacKenzie's personal papers found a permanent home at the British Women's Library. The Women's Library, formerly the Fawcett Library, is a repository that includes materials relating to Commonwealth relations (in particular, transnational exchange between feminist organizations on activism and campaigns challenging women's political status in work and marriage). It had been threatened with closure but was occupied (as a feminist collective act of resistance), saved, and then relocated to the LSE Library in central London in 2013.[41]

I went to London in 2013 to view the materials related to Mr MacKenzie's time in Australia. It was an odd experience, as archival work often is, a phenomenon well recorded by those who do it. The cultural and feminist historian Carolyn Steedman, for one example, reflects in her collection *Dust: The Archive and Cultural History* (2002) on what it feels like to visit archives. She writes (somewhat sardonically) about the discomfort and disorientation occasioned by spending hours and days in places of dust, real and metaphysical.[42] What Steedman is exploring, however, is not only a matter of affect, but a philosophical mediation of relationship between source and practitioner, and experience and institution. It is delusional, she suggests, to think that relentless scouring of archival collections will reveal a point of origin or complete recoverability ('a kind of truth'), or that an official repository is removed from the political projects of remembering and forgetting it captures and preserves.[43] The point is that an historian's experience will orient her toward the sources necessary to show her own time as contingent and strange, and her training will offer guidance in acknowledging the nature of her obligations to where those sources are found. This practice is integral to my own experiments of jurisography, although I would also note that it changes to respond to the situation of the writer, and the nature of the project in which they are engaged.

In the case of following Mr MacKenzie, my discomfort was about location. It felt faintly absurd to spend dark November afternoons in London, in the basement of the LSE Library, to discover what London men thought about

Australia and 'Australian women' (a class already limited by association for the men of the SSRC). I recalled fragments of the Introduction to *Women in Australia*, in which Mr MacKenzie summarises Australia of 1962, from the visitor's perspective. He describes 'a notably derivative and dependent society in its culture and institutions',[44] which would have surprised the cultural milieu in Australia at the time who were assertively writing, painting, and thinking in an entirely non-derivative fashion (and also taking it to London, in every sense).[45] He also explained to his readers that Australia is 'a new nation' (which would have rung hollow to Aboriginal leaders like Faith Bandler and Charles Perkins); and 'in a difficult and sometimes harsh environment, still lacking but slowly acquiring the human and material resources to enable its people to fully master it'[46] (which would also have raised eyebrows, I suspect, with WH (Bill) Stanner, HC ('Nugget') Coombs and CD (Charles) Rowley, political allies of Aboriginal peoples, and significant Australian scholars, bureaucrats and public intellectuals, who were, in fact, affiliates of the SSRC).[47] I had conversations with people I knew or met about location and displacement, and my sources. It is axiomatic for most legal scholars and historians that sources capable of showing the experience of the conducts of law and knowledge in Australia reside in, and must be translocatable from, the United Kingdom. But it is not obvious to me (as it seems to be for many others) why that direction and destination is prioritised in such a way that it obscures other experiences. For many Australians, including myself, sources that show inherited experiences of law are not necessarily tied to the UK, but move between Australia and places outside of the direct jurisdiction of the British Empire: to Europe and Asia. Perhaps more importantly (and sometimes more difficult to see) encounters of law that reside in Australian sources (both Indigenous and non-Indigenous) are as inextricably tied to British jurisprudence writing as sources from any other Commonwealth, or former Colonial, jurisdiction. This is an argument my fellow jurisographer Shaun McVeigh has made over time in his work,[48] and reminds that where sources of knowledge about lawful relations are placed (and how they move) is as important for the jurisprudent to take care of as how, by whom, and when those sources were created, collected, or used.

These obligations can often be in competition; my experience of reading Norman MacKenzie's files at the LSE was not severable from what I discovered (and what I discovered was missing). I found, for example, reports from the 1950s, prepared by transnational organisations such as the British Commonwealth League, on the status of Australian people as a legal question. There were research reports detailing the problems occasioned by women's 'dual roles' in public work and family life, across jurisdictions; and articles and reviews of the important book by the Viennese and Swedish sociologists Viola Klein and Alva Myrdal, *Women's Two Roles: Home and Work* (1956), which was the most up-to-date reference on the topic available to Norman MacKenzie when he embarked on his work.[49] There were articles from leading legal scholars, such as RH Graveson, on the questions of status in law.[50] There were reports, prepared by Australian Law Schools, providing a review of existing laws that affected women's status, on a state-by-state and federal basis (that were subsequently used by Enid Campbell in writing her Appendix for MacKenzie's book, a text to which I will return). I found the correspondence between the SSRC and the Law Deans introducing Norman MacKenzie and requesting assistance to produce these reports. They were ultimately prepared by women working in the Law Schools as secretaries and aides, for example at Melbourne University by 'Mrs Rachel Davies, Assistant to [the Dean] Sir Zelman Cowan'.[51] This correspondence exposed the divisions and assumptions of 'law in relation' in the early 1960s: that there were men authorised to explain legal knowledge, and men who could be authorised to explain law's contest and impact, and these remained distinct scholarly enterprises. As ANU Economist, and SSRC member, Heinz Arndt wrote to Sir Zelman Cowan in 1959: 'Mr MacKenzie is also interested to find out something about attempted changes in the law where proposals had substantial backing but failed for one reason or another; but this, I assume, is a question for historians and political scientists rather than lawyers'.[52] It clearly did not occur to Arndt to directly ask women themselves. As I noted in Essay Two, there was plenty of energised and politically adventurous writing by Australian women about the experience of living with law, but in forums and genre unfamiliar to the university. These could have been interpreted as 'information' by the SSRC (but were not).[53] The knowledge the SSRC desired was credentialed research, but in 1958, studies of women's projections for work, or analysis of the politics of the suffrage movement, had not yet been created by university or government personnel (a proof of the very problem the SSRC were seeking to investigate).[54] There was, however, an unauthorised substitute that in the circumstances proved very useful, both to Norman MacKenzie and to me.

The Union of Australian Women (UAW) was an amalgamated group of women's political organisations, many of which had existed since the League of Nations, 'with widely divergent politics, yet similar aspirations to moral respectability, and all lacking significant presence and influence in the academy'.[55] They were commonly invested in agitating for change to women's status in Australia, often doing so through transnational exchange with similar organisations in Britain.[56] The UAW kept meticulously organised files on 'current happenings', and these were 'used extensively by Mr MacKenzie while he was here' (as the UAW President Lucy Woodcock noted, dryly, after the book was finished).[57] In the 1960s, these materials were not yet held by a collecting institution, and were probably viewed for the SSRC project in the UAW headquarters, then in Market Street in Sydney (a task undertaken for Mr MacKenzie by 'Mrs R Grahame . . . of the staff of the Public Library in Sydney').[58] The files nevertheless formed an unofficial archive, a collection that spanned time and addressed the exact topics that were central to the SSRC research hypothesis ('Jury Service, Matrimonial Problems, Social and Welfare Services, Married Women's Property'), and some that were not ('Human Rights, Pensions,

Peace').[59] In the Introduction to *Women in Australia*, Mr MacKenzie lists the help he received from 'members of university faculties, . . . leaders and officials of the political parties, senior public servants, representatives of the business community, officers of trade unions'; and the 'leading personalities in all the professions', most of whom (on the evidence presented by his own book) were men.[60] But he concludes by acknowledging 'a very large number of women's organisations. . . . All of them went out of their way to make valuable information available to me; some permitted access to their files . . . and went to great trouble to provide replies to my questionnaires'.[61]

Mr MacKenzie's requests for assistance to these women's organisations were present in his official collected papers in London. What was absent were their replies to him, their attitudes to his use of their 'information', and their perceptions of his authorisation by the SSRC. Whether some of those materials were excluded by choice, or simply misplaced, interests me greatly (but is the subject of a very kind of different essay). My task here, instead, is to draw attention to the sources' disturbed relationship, as a way to see how disaggregation of knowledge (and miscomprehension between knowledge creators) occurs in different times and places. The UAW files were eventually bequeathed to the State Library of New South Wales, in Sydney; I read them there, at the Mitchell Reading Room, in 2014, a year after my visit to London. The Library is the oldest, and the first truly free, public library in Australia. The Reading Room – located in its own sandstone wing overlooking the Botanical Gardens – is named after David Scott Mitchell, a 19th-century collector of Australian maps, objects, documents, manuscripts, and books, and was designed as an Australian library, devoted solely to Australian content. At the Mitchell, alongside the same files that Mrs R Grahame had accessed in the early 1960s, I also read the letters, Christmas cards, reports, newsletters, and old chocolate box lids (used as notepaper) that told a story of how Mr Norman MacKenzie and some women in Australia began a research relationship, of a kind, and of its time. The correspondence, letters between Mr MacKenzie and the UAW (about the book), and letters between UAW members and other women's groups (about Mr MacKenzie), revealed a sense of these women's irony and forbearance: a relief that after many years of politely trying to gain traction and alert male scholars and politicians to the problems of women's legal status and the effects on their situation, the SSRC had decided to publicly address their agenda, and as such they should cooperate with Mr MacKenzie. Yet there was also a sense of indignation that it was Mr MacKenzie who had been the one chosen to conduct the project, candidly expressed in correspondence between the UAW and a British sister organization, the Six Point Group. The Secretary of the Six Point Group was the Hon. Hazel Hunkins Hallinan (a formidable feminist leader and elder, name dropped by Germaine Greer in the first pages of *The Female Eunuch* when such a book became possible, in 1970).[62] Hunkins Hallinan's view of the intentions and conduct of the SSRC was scathing. 'The scenery of the stage on which we are supposed to have equality is all very lovely to look at', she argued, 'but the acting is bad and so are the back-stage conditions!'[63] As to the selection of MacKenzie as the researcher protagonist, Hunkins Hallinan made her views plain in a letter to the UAW's Lucy Woodcock (a formidable union organiser and educator) on 14 April 1959:

> 'I am a little bit surprised that your Social and Economy Research Council [sic.] has appointed Norman Mackenzie as an investigator into the role of women. I know Mr. Mackenzie slightly in person, and I know very well indeed his work on the *New Statesman*. I have personally never found him in any way interested in women's affairs and he never writes on women's affairs. I feel sure that any job he attempted to do, he would do very well. On the other hand, I would say that this subject is entirely out of his field. Almost any of us in the feminist movement could name half a dozen outstanding women who would do such a job as he has been given with a great deal more knowledge and imagination'.[64]

Even more pointed, perhaps, was an editorial decision made by the editors of the Newsletter of the NSW League of Women Voters (one of the groups who had joined the UAW in 1950). The League had received letters of concern from their members on the topic of Mr MacKenzie's appointment, and reported in their newsletter *Equality* that they had expressed those concerns directly to him, and that he had responded. 'The study', Mr MacKenzie wrote, 'needed someone who was neither a woman nor an Australian for it to be a fair analysis'.[65] The editors published his reply without comment (judging, accurately I think, that it spoke volumes for itself).

Women in Australia

Taking a glimpse of 'the backstage conditions' of the production of *Women in Australia* presents a temptation when reintroducing the final version, published by FW Cheshire in 1962. Hazel Hunkins Hallinan, Lucy Woodcock, and many others who I met through their mail and publications are a recovered chorus for my own ambivalence about Mr MacKenzie's activities. They make very plain that although Norman MacKenzie was content to speak about Australian women empirically, as objects of his survey, Australian women (or at least their registered organisations) were not considered by him as equal collaborators, a slight that they felt keenly. It would be easy, from that perspective, and as an act of historical recovery, to note *Women in Australia*'s casual exclusions (of race and ethnicity), fixed ideas (of class and religion), and self-serving assumptions (of women's intellectual labour and heterosexual domestic arrangements). A writer's relationship to any text, however, is never that straightforward, nor unmediated. As I have noted, part of my task is to reintroduce and review *Women in Australia* as a book of jurisprudence of its time, before joining the official and unofficial sources of its knowledge production back together.

As a book of and about 1962, it is relevant to observe how MacKenzie identified himself as an intellectual heir of JS Mill, and of the Webbs, with attendant commitment to idealised, companionate personal relations between the sexes for the benefit of the public good.[66] '[A] democratic society should develop a system of values and a range of opportunities which enlarge personal freedom for women as well as men',[67] he wrote, and his assessment of Australia's shortcomings (and potential) emanate from that premise. It is also relevant to note that *Women in Australia*, although published as a monograph, in conversation with the world, takes the form of a report to the SSRC in tone and style. It is factual, without flourish, and addressed to university insiders ('we'). The 'women of Australia' are relegated to 'them'. MacKenzie begins with a *sui generis* national overview.[68] He gives a brief historical account of suffrage in Australia, and of the political demands made over time to improve the status of women. He analyses how national policy in the post-war period has altered the lived reality of women, through information collected by survey instruments and available official documentation. He concludes by recommending options for change, predicated on his integrated empirical data. My obligations to *Women in Australia* do not extend to reviewing those policy recommendations (which in many ways are prescient, and had long-term benefits).[69] Instead, they are to notice that in making his report, MacKenzie formalised Stone's view of 'law in relation' to other disciplines, as both as a matter of method ('social and economic policies may affect the status of women on the basis of insufficient knowledge'),[70] and by giving a jurisprudential account of his own. To do so, he relies on the materials collected by the Law Deans and collated by Enid Campbell in an Appendix to the published book. She is not named as a co-author. Campbell's Appendix is the only direct contribution by a legal scholar to *Women in Australia* and, for that reason, deserves reintroduction on its own terms.

In 1960, Dr Enid Campbell became the first woman appointed to an academic position in a Law School in Australia, marking the start of a significant career in public law scholarship. At the time there were only 318 legally qualified women in Australia (a fact MacKenzie reports).[71] When she was invited to participate in the SSRC project, Campbell had just commenced her lectureship at Sydney University in the Department of Law (not in Julius Stone's distinct, and arguably more intellectually adventurous, Department of Jurisprudence).[72] Campbell's Appendix, 'The Legal Status of Women in Australia', is in the style of much mid-century legal writing, a doctrinal review, with little commentary. Her text begins, however, with an instructive epigraph, borrowed from Austrian-American US Supreme Court Justice Felix Frankfurter:

> 'The law must have regard for woman in her manifold relations as an individual, as a wage-earner, as a wife, as a mother, as a citizen. Only those who are ignorant of the nature of law, and of its enforcement, or indifferent to the exacting aspects of women's life, can have the naivete, or

> the recklessness, to sum up a woman's legal position in a meaningless, and mischievous phrase about "equal rights"'.[73]

Campbell organises her work around strict status categories (wife, mother, professional, office holder) to report on how each has been ascribed legal capacity by common law, and how each has been modernised by the 'progressive attitudes' of representative democracy, through 'supreme legislative authority'.[74] She attaches her discussion of progress to different practice areas for easy reference: public law (nationality, citizenship, work and education, 'public function', tax) and private law (matrimonial causes, succession, contract, and tort). Campbell does include, however, a short introduction, briefly offering her own views of the SSRC project. She does not attend to any of the methodological concerns that underpin either the Legal Realist or Social Scientist visions of transformative empirical research that shape MacKenzie's main text. She makes plain that what she reports is intended by her solely as a legal text, not a feminist critique, nor a social science experiment. Campbell endorses, for example, the fact that legislatures have modernized status but 'protected rights' by maintaining separate, sexed personae for women under law. She does not speculate on whether the nature of that protection is in fact warranted or welcome. There is no suggestion, for example, that women's differentiated experiences might provide an alternate point of entry to how status operates, and influences, the inhabitation of those sexed roles in everyday life. This jurisprudential view is not surprising for 1962, but it is still important to note. Campbell is clear that men and women have distinct legal personality, based on their biological and social difference, and that the role of law (and the lawyer) if asked to research any difficulties in those arrangements is to 'observe and reform', not to 'amend nature'.[75] For that reason, she cautions avoidance of:

> '[t]he phrase 'equality of rights' (so often invoked by extreme feminists as a convenient label for past and intend achievements in law reform) as it . . . obscures the inescapable fact that . . . former legal disabilities have been removed, [and] the law has moved and is still moving toward more ample protection of women as wives, mothers, and employees'.[76]

MacKenzie, in his own conclusions, presents a similar argument. The injuries occasioned to women by discriminatory laws of status, for example, are '[o]bstacles progressively eliminated in living memory'.[77] But because he is a sociologist rather than a lawyer, MacKenzie concedes that this positive progression ('the difficulties that remain are vestigial and doomed to disappear')[78] does not necessarily eliminate barriers to women's public participation, it merely changes their quality and character. This resonates, to a degree, with Simone de Beauvoir's observation that formal equality is never enough for a woman to accomplish herself.[79] In her attention to the situation of woman in Paris, in 1949, Beauvoir asserted woman's own experience and agency to transform the conduct of relations with institutions with which she is complicit (such as marriage), as well as the intimate experience of reciprocity with men, in everyday life. MacKenzie is similarly interested in identifying and addressing the conditions of society and culture relevant to Australia in 1962, which may prevent women from taking up the promises of equal participation and contribution. (There is a 'gap between their potential and achievement', he concludes.)[80] In contrast with Beauvoir's text, however, where woman is presented as an agent of her own life, for MacKenzie, woman remains part of a class, distinguishable from other women only by her educational attainments, and demarcated from men because of her maternal and marital obligations. What matters to MacKenzie is not the process of transformation and freedom, but the result. By accepting status-based capacities as predicated on relations between men and women that are natural, or inevitable, it was not possible to ask (as Beauvoir did) how women might first realise themselves as human beings. 'The problem', he writes, 'is no longer how to overcome the obstacles that law and custom presented to emancipation, but how to cope with its implications'.[81] The major implication is that 'they [sic.] have access to education and the professions, but the[re] are limits set by circumstances of life'.[82] In MacKenzie's summation, unencumbered entry into higher education is such 'an emancipation' for women, and can be engineered through social policy as a way to advance the prospects of the national economy; but he is clear that those policies should not alter women's 'enduring goal of success as wives and mothers'.[83]

MacKenzie's contribution in *Women in Australia* was to argue on the basis of empirical evidence that women's diverse public and private personae were dual rather than divided, and 'may be consecutive rather than alternative'.[84] This was significant for the time. But what he failed to see, or hear, after his visit to Australia was that for many women their roles inside and outside 'the home' were already experienced simultaneously, and for others were contested altogether. The 'objective researcher' persona he chose for himself did not ameliorate those concerns. Writer Thelma Forshaw, for example, reviewed *Women in Australia* for the left literary paper *Nation* in 1962, and laconically described MacKenzie as 'landing a cuckoo's egg in our nest: a common practice of visiting sociologists'.[85] For other readers, senior members of the women's organisations MacKenzie had approached for help, the book was disconcertingly inaccurate (and against the evidence of their own files). As Lucy Woodcock wrote later, '[w]e feel [his] statement that [Australian] women were given the vote without any struggle is not true when one considers how every little step towards equality is fought even today'.[86] For some younger women, trying to assert their own methods and find forums for their own intellectual experiences, the book was perplexing. Dr Jean Battersby, for example, wrote in exasperation to her friend, Alan Stout, Professor of Moral Philosophy at the University of Sydney (and a member of the SSRC): 'Am I mistaken or did you have something to do with the body which sponsored Norman MacKenzie in Australia?'[87] Battersby held a doctorate in French literature (partly completed at the Sorbonne), and was a public broadcaster, scholar, and later founding Executive Officer of the Arts Council of Australia. In the early 1960s, she had multiple and varied roles of her own (as diplomatic wife and mother, as teacher at Canberra University College, and as a panellist on *Women's World*, an ABC program dedicated to exactly the issues that exercised the SSRC, but debated by women from a range of viewpoints).[88] She had read both Betty Friedan's *The Feminine Mystique* (1963) (which clearly did offer an educated woman's argument about her exclusion from full public participation, and had deep resonance internationally with many women who had similarly experienced the injurious effects to self that such waste enabled)[89]; and Norman MacKenzie's *Women in Australia*. For Battersby, one book exposed the limits of the other: 'I felt very up in the air at the end of MacKenzie', she write to Stout in 1963, 'as though he hadn't even *asked* the really significant questions'.[90] Her response (which seems understandable, as well as logical) was to undertake a university-based research project of her own, collaborating with senior male colleagues across disciplines, in which personal experience could be recast as public politics and social debate. Battersby sought funding from the SSRC for her project. She was unsuccessful.[91]

Coda

What should be brought into focus from those reviews and responses is how *Women in Australia* was a shot across the bow, of what it meant to some Australian women, by 1962, to be relegated to the status of the object of research, rather than the subject practitioner of knowledge generated about their own experience, and their own conditions of living. In telling these stories in the way that I have, however, I want to be very clear. There is no pivot to be discovered, in either the sources of libraries or universities, that reveals the moment when knowledges, authorised and experienced differently by men or women, become visible to each other. There is also no teleological catalogue of books that divulge how that occurred. I have instead made an example of *Women of Australia* to show how sources for knowledge, and representation of methods, are contested, varied, and imbricated.

From that perspective, it is important to underscore, by way of conclusion, why Mr MacKenzie is a central subject of my own account. The fact remains that in 1957 it was Norman MacKenzie that Australian male jurists (and scholars) invited to consider the status of women's lives in Australia. He then performed in his own writing and research the reinvestment of woman as objects of legal imagination, and despite his book's success, and historiographical significance, in the process of his practice he denied Australian women their subjecthood. MacKenzie gestures toward Beauvoir's project in his epigraph to *Women in Australia* in 1962. He quotes:

> 'Women have never constituted a closed and independent society; they form an integral part of the group, which is governed by males and in

> which they have a subordinate place. Hence the paradox of their situation: they belong at one and the same time to the male world and to a sphere in which that world is challenged'.[92]

MacKenzie does not consider in his text, however, what such a project might mean as a matter of collaboration, or change in his own disciplinary practice. It is necessary to show that this, his own paradox, is odd, and has implications. Drawing juristic and social science together, but denying the experiences of some subjects of law in the process, has had calculable, and observable, consequences. Mr MacKenzie's book, when read with the letters and reports of how women experienced the book's production, destabilises the ordinary assumptions that law's overt gesture to the social and political was uncomplicatedly progressive or could only be written in book-length form (by those given access to do so), or in journals known and acceptable to academic culture.

Women in Australia, as a book of 1962, recalibrated intimate relations between man and woman as a question of a particular kind of social fact that enabled different kinds of legal response. But in doing so, it also missed a reimagining of how to understand the conduct of relations, including scholarly relations, from the perspective of those who experienced them. Understanding why that matters is a responsibility of my own project. In writing about *Women in Australia* for *Feminist Jurisography*, I have tried to show how feminist disruptions to the scholarly production and orientation of jurisprudence hide in plain sight, and in the process name women as originators of methodologies of our own. In Australia (as elsewhere) this practice of naming is an act of political disturbance to what a discipline thinks it knows, and how it conducts itself. It is part of a feminist tradition that I inherit; and how woman becomes the one who knows and writes (within institutions, as well as outside) I will bring into view, in the essays to follow.

Notes

1 Morris 1988: xi.
2 Please refer to Essay One and Essay Two, *Feminist Jurisography*.
3 The stories of origin and tradition of critical jurisprudences are not immune from being pruned and cultivated in this way. See Douzinas 2014 as an example.
4 For the historiographical significance of MacKenzie's book, see Curthoys 1998: 40.
5 Le Dœuff 2003: 16.
6 A version of Mr MacKenzie's adventures appeared in Genovese 2016.
7 See Essay Two, *Feminist Jurisography*: 39–41.
8 Stone 1950: 387.
9 Stone 1950: 386.
10 Stone 1950: 386.
11 Stone 1950: 386; and see Essay Two, *Feminist Jurisography*: 39.
12 W 1987; Webb & Webb 1932.
13 Trubek 1984: 584.
14 Trubek 1984: 580.

15 Trubek 1984: 584.
16 Trubek 1984: 580.
17 Trubek 1984: 583.
18 Griswold 1952.
19 Star 1992: 109–110.
20 Griswold 1951; and see Essay Two, *Feminist Jurisography*: 43–45.
21 Their comparison, for one example, was with Faculty of the London School of Economics from the 1930s onwards. For a discussion, and comparison with Australia relevant to the discussion in this essay, see Macintyre 2010: 144.
22 Stone 1950: 386.
23 Stone 1950: 386.
24 Macintyre 2010: 35.
25 Macintyre 2010: 31; Star 1992: 56–80.
26 Forsyth 2014: 80.
27 There is a longer story to tell here about the function of facts in modern knowledge production, as argued by Poovey 1998.
28 Macintyre 2010: 33–39.
29 See Macintyre 2010: 107.
30 Macintyre 2010: 61.
31 See Macintyre 2010: 143–174 for description of early influential SSRC-funded projects, including Charles Rowley's research, later developed as *The Destruction of Aboriginal Society* (1970).
32 Macintyre 2010: 144.
33 Macintyre 2010: 143–144.
34 Macintyre 2010: 144. Macintyre notes that Mick Borrie, ANU demographer and economic historian, who had also trained at the LSE, instigated the project in 1957. Borrie had a close personal and professional relationship with Titmuss. Another member of the SSRC, the German, LSE-trained, ANU economist Heinz Arndt, knew the candidate too; they had met in London, after the war, and he also endorsed the appointment.
35 Macintyre 2010: 144.
36 Purcell 2013; MacKenzie 1978; MacKenzie & MacKenzie 1982–1985.
37 Macintyre 2010: 144 does note – without commentary – that the SSRC (which had no women members) were 'anxious' to secure 'female representation' on the project's advisory committee, and later appointed University of Melbourne historian Kathleen Fitzpatrick, and political scientist Ruth Atkins, although both resigned.
38 Butterworth 2019.
39 Thoms P 1959.
40 Smith College, Massachusetts, also holds a collection of Mr and Mrs MacKenzie's papers: *Norman Ian and Jeanne MacKenzie Papers 1935–1964*, Smith College, database.
41 Reclaim It 2015; Liddington 2013; Murphy 2022.
42 Steedman 2002: 17–37.
43 Steedman 2002: 3–6.
44 Mackenzie 1962: xii, quoting La Nauze 1959: 10. Jeanne Mackenzie (1961) wrote her own book echoing similar themes. The book details her own experiences and observations of 'The South' between 1958–1960. I have written about Jeanne MacKenzie and Norman MacKenzie's books in Genovese 2016.
45 The material on this subject is vast. See for an example of a contemporaneous source: Blackman et al 2006; Serle 2014.
46 MacKenzie 1962: xiii. It is important to note that race, and Aboriginal experience, do not feature in the 'Women in Australia' research, or in the final book, in any form. For the influence of Aboriginal leaders through this period there is a large amount of scholarship, exemplified by Maynard 2007.

47 For the involvement of Rowley and Stanner in the life of the SSRC, and the foundation of the Institute of Aboriginal and Torres Strait Islander Studies, see Macintyre 2010: 155–164.
48 McVeigh 2016.
49 Myrdal & Klein 1956.
50 Graveson 1941.
51 'Correspondence, Prof. Zelman Cowan to Prof. Heinz Arndt' 1959.
52 'Correspondence, Prof. Heinz Arndt to Prof. Zelman Cowan' 1959.
53 MacKenzie did try to engage the *Australian Women's Weekly* as a 'research agent' to run surveys through the magazine, but was unsuccessful: 'Correspondence, Esme Fenton to N MacKenzie' 1960.
54 MacKenzie 1962: 377 in fact recommends the creation of these reporting requirements within the bureaucracy, and also recommends the front runner of the Office for the Status of Women.
55 Curthoys 2000.
56 The UAW closed its Melbourne office in 2020, but continues to campaign through petitions, letters and submissions: Morrison 2013. See also Simic 2007.
57 'Correspondence, Mrs L G Woodcock to Prof. S Encel' 1967. They are corresponding about proposed revised edition of MacKenzie's 1962 book. Lucy Woodcock was a former teacher, equal pay campaigner, and officer holder at the NSW Teachers' Association. See Mitchell 2006.
58 MacKenzie 1962: xvi.
59 *Union of Australian Women Papers, Mitchell Library, State Library of New South Wales, MLMSS 2160.*
60 MacKenzie 1962: 197–222.
61 MacKenzie 1962: xv.
62 For a consideration of Hallinan, and her contributions to twentieth century feminist practice, including other affiliations to Australia beyond MacKenzie's text, see Spender 1983: 11–44; Greer 1971: 11.
63 'Correspondence, Mrs Hazel Hunkins Hallinan to Mrs L G Woodcock' 1959.
64 'Correspondence, Mrs Hazel Hunkins Hallinan to Mrs L G Woodcock' 1959. Note, however, that Madge Dawson, a tutor in Adult Education at Sydney University, undertook surveys of women graduates and made her findings available to MacKenzie. Enid Campbell, the first woman appointed to Sydney Law School, wrote the appendix on Women's Legal Status in the completed book. Dawson's contributions are hidden as acknowledgments, in the preface. Campbell's are presented as an appendix, in her own name. Neither, however, have their name on the cover as co-authors.
65 'LET US RESPOND TO THE CHALLENGE' *Equality: The Newsletter of NSW League of Women Voters* 1959.
66 For example, JS Mill is given the last word in the manuscript: MacKenzie 1962: 345.
67 MacKenzie 1962: 338.
68 MacKenzie 1962: 324.
69 MacKenzie 1962: 338–340.
70 MacKenzie 1962: 338.
71 MacKenzie 1962: 205.
72 Lee 2010; Campbell 1995.
73 Campbell 1962: 360, quoting Schienfeld 1947: 303. Scheinfeld is quoting a statement made by Frankfurter before the US Senate Judiciary Committee, on 8 February 1938.
74 Campbell 1962: 359.
75 Campbell 1962: 360, quoting Schienfeld 1947: 303. Scheinfeld is quoting a statement made by Frankfurter before the US Senate Judiciary Committee, on 8 February 1938.
76 Campbell 1962: 360.

77 MacKenzie 1962: 324.
78 MacKenzie 1962: 324.
79 Beauvoir 2011: 152. She reminds her readers this ambiguity carries particular weight and warning in 1949, one year after the UN Declaration of Human Rights: Beauvoir 2011: 15. This point is discussed in Essay Two, *Feminist Jurisography*: 29–32.
80 MacKenzie 1962: 344.
81 MacKenzie 1962: 324.
82 MacKenzie 1962: 325.
83 MacKenzie 1962: 325.
84 MacKenzie 1962: 325.
85 Forshaw 1962.
86 'Correspondence, Mrs LG Woodcock to I McCorkandale' 1967. They are corresponding about proposed revised edition of MacKenzie's 1962 book.
87 Macintyre 2010: 146.
88 Lawson 2009; Berg 1972.
89 Friedan 2013. For reception of Friedan in Australia, see Curthoys 1998: 40; in the US, see Coontz 2011.
90 Macintyre 2010: 146.
91 Macintyre 2010: 147.
92 MacKenzie 1962: ix, quoting Beauvoir 1953. MacKenzie specifies his source but not the page.

References

Beauvoir S de 1953 *The Second Sex* Trans and Ed H M Parshley Jonathan Cape London (first published 1949).

Beauvoir S de 2011 *The Second Sex* Trans C Borde and S Malovany-Chevallier Vintage New York (first published 1949).

Berg H de 1972 *Jean Battersby Interviewed by Hazel de Berg in the Hazel de Berg collection* [sound recording] National Library of Australia Canberra.

Blackman C, Boyd A, Boyd D, Brack J, Dickerson B, Perceval J, Pugh C and Smith B 2006 'The Antipodean manifesto (1959)' in A Stephen, A McNamara and P Goad eds 2006 *Modernism & Australia: Documents on Art, Design and Architecture 1917–1967* The Miegunyah Press Melbourne: 694–697.

Butterworth L 2019 *Thoms, Patience Rosemary (1915–2006)* The Australian Women's Register The University of Melbourne and The National Foundation for Australian Women Melbourne and Canberra viewed 28 April 2022 <www.womenaustralia.info/biogs/PR00216b.htm>.

Campbell E 1962 'The Legal Status of Women in Australia' in MacKenzie 1962: 359–421.

Campbell R 1995 *Enid Campbell Interviewed by Ruth Campbell in the Law in Australian society oral history project* [sound recording] National Library of Australia Canberra.

Coontz S 2011 *A Strange Stirring: The Feminine Mystique and American Women at the Dawn of the 1960s* Basic Books New York.

Curthoys A 1998 'Cosmopolitan Radicals' in B Caine, M Gatens, E Grahame, J Larbalestier, S Watson and E Webby eds 1998 *Australian Feminism: A Companion* Oxford University Press Melbourne: 39–48.

Curthoys A 2000 'Adventures of Feminism: Simone de Beauvoir's Autobiographies, Women's Liberation, and Self-Fashioning' *Feminist Review* 64/1: 3–18 DOI:10.1080/014177800338927.

Douzinas C 2014 'A short history of the British Critical Legal Conference or, the Responsibility of the Critic' *Law and Critique: Journal of Critical Legal Studies* 25/2: 187–198 DOI:10.1007/s10978-014-9133-9.

Forsyth H 2014 *A History of the Modern Australian University* NewSouth Publishing Sydney.

Friedan B 2013 *The Feminine Mystique* W W Norton & Company New York (first published 1963).

Genovese A 2016 'About Libraries: A Jurisographer's Notes on Lives Lived With Law (in London and Sydney)' *Law Text Culture* 20/1: 33–65 DOI:10.1080/13200968.2013.10854482.

Graveson R H 1941 'The Movement from Status to Contract' *The Modern Law Review* 4/4: 261–272 DOI:10.1111/j.1468-2230.1940.tb00778.x.

Greer G 1971 *The Female Eunuch* Paladin London.

Griswold E N 1951 'Divorce Jurisdiction and Recognition of Divorce Decrees: A Comparative Study' *The Australian Law Journal* 25: 248–266 DOI:10.2307.1336891.

Griswold E N 1952 'Observations on Legal Education in Australia' *Journal of Legal Education* 5/2: 139–154.

La Nauze J A 1959 'The Study of Australian History, 1929–1959' *Historical Studies: Australia and New Zealand* 9/33: 1–11 DOI:10.1080/10314615908595147.

Lawson V 2009 'Arts patron who fought bureaucracy' *The Sydney Morning Herald* Sydney viewed 10 January 2022 <www.smh.com.au/national/arts-patron-who-fought-bureaucracy-20090303-8nca.html?page=-1>.

Le Dœuff M 2003 *The Sex of Knowing* Trans K Hamer and L Code Routledge London and New York.

Lee H P 2010 'A Tribute to Professor Enid Campbell' *Australian Law Librarian* 18/3: 182–183.

Liddington J 2013 'Fawcett Saga: Remembering the Women's Library Across Four Decades' *History Workshop Journal* 76/1: 266–280 DOI:10.1093/hwj/dbt026.

Macintyre S 2010 *The Poor Relation: A History of Social Sciences in Australia* Melbourne University Press Melbourne.

MacKenzie J 1961 *Australian paradox* F W Cheshire Melbourne Canberra and Sydney.

MacKenzie N 1962 *Women in Australia* F W Cheshire Melbourne Canberra and Sydney.

MacKenzie N ed 1978 *The Letters of Sidney and Beatrice Webb* Cambridge University Press Cambridge.

MacKenzie N and MacKenzie J eds 1982–1985 *The Diary of Beatrice Webb* Virago London.

Maynard J 2007 *Fight for Liberty and Freedom: The origins of Australian Aboriginal activism* Aboriginal Studies Press Canberra.

McVeigh S 2016 'Jurisprudent of London: Arts of Association' *Law Text Culture* 20/1: 189–215 DOI:10.2139/ssrn.3169144.

Mitchell B 2006 'Woodcock, Lucy Godiva (1889–1968)' *Australian Dictionary of Biography* Canberra viewed 8 March 2022 <https://adb.anu.edu.au/biography/woodcock-lucy-godiva-9172>.

Morris M 1988 'Foreword' in A Curthoys ed 1988 *For and Against Feminism: A Personal Journey into Feminist Theory and History* Allen & Unwin Sydney: viii–xii.

Morrison C 2013 'History and Background' *Union of Australian Women Melbourne* viewed 31 March 2022 <http://uaw.org.au/about_us.html>.

Murphy G 2022 'The Women's Library' *London School of Economics and Political Science* London viewed 7 April 2022 <www.lse.ac.uk/library/collection-highlights/the-womens-library>.

Myrdal A and Klein V 1956 *Women's Two Roles: Home and Work* Routledge & Kegan Paul London.

Poovey M 1998 *A History of the Modern Fact: Problems of Knowledge in the Sciences of Wealth and Society* University of Chicago Press Chicago.

Purcell H 2013 'Norman MacKenzie obituary' *The Guardian* London viewed 13 December 2021 <www.theguardian.com/education/2013/jun/24/norman-mackenzie>.

Reclaim It 2015 'Voices from The Women's Library occupation' *Feminist Review* 109/1: 156–168 DOI:10.1057/fr.2014.51.

Rowley C D 1970 *The Destruction of Aboriginal Society* Australian National University Press Canberra.

Schienfeld A 1947 *Women and Men* Chatto & Windus London.

Serle G 2014 *From Deserts the Prophets Come: The creative spirit in Australia 1788–1972* Monash University Publishing Clayton (first published 1973).

Simic Z 2007 'Butter Not Bombs: A Short History of the Union of Australian Women' *History Australia* 4/1: 07.1–07.15 DOI:10.2104/ha070007.

Spender D 1983 *There's Always Been a Women's Movement This Century* Pandora Press London and Boston.

Star L 1992 *Julius Stone: An Intellectual Life* Oxford University Press in Association with Sydney University Press New York.

Steedman C 2002 *Dust: The Archive and Cultural History* Rutgers University Press New Brunswick.

Stone J 1950 *The Province and Function of Law: Law as Logic, Justice and Social Control; A Study in Jurisprudence* Maitland Sydney (first published 1946).

Trubek D M 1984 'Where the Action Is: Critical Legal Studies and Empiricism' *Stanford Law Review* 36/1–2: 575–622 DOI:10.2307/1228692.

W 1987 'An Anniversary Preface' *The Modern Law Review* 50/6: 673–676.

Webb S and Webb B 1932 *Methods of Social Study* Longmans, Green and Co. London New York and Toronto.

Archival Sources

Baillieu Library Special Collections, University of Melbourne

Forshaw T 1962 'Condition Female' *Nation* November 17: 21–22.

Norman Ian and Jeanne MacKenzie Papers, 1935–1964, Smith College, database.

Papers of Norman MacKenzie, The Women's Library at LSE 7NMA Box FL086-FLO87

1959 'Correspondence, Prof. Heinz Arndt, Social Science Research Council, The Australian National University to Prof. Zelman Cowan, Dean of the Faculty of Law, University of Melbourne' September GB106/7/NME/2.

1959 'Correspondence, Prof. Zelman Cowan, Dean of the Faculty of Law, University of Melbourne to Prof. Heinz Arndt, Social Science Research Council, The Australian National University' September GB106/7/NME/2.

1960 'Correspondence, Esme Fenton, Editor, *The Australian Woman's Weekly* to N MacKenzie' 25 February GB106/7/NMA/5 Historical.

Thoms P 1959 'This Is a MAN'S [sic] Country . . . Our Women Are so Complacent, but WHY?' *Courier Mail* 29 September GB106/7/NMA/5 Historical.

Union of Australian Women Papers, Mitchell Library, State Library of New South Wales, MLMSS 2160

1959 'Correspondence, Mrs Hazel Hunkins Hallinan, Six Point Group to Mrs L G Woodcock, Union of Australian Women' 14 April Y 793 Folder 'Status of Women'.

1959 'Let Us Respond to the Challenge' *Equality: The Newsletter of NSW League of Women Voters* News Sheet No 47 Fawcett reels MLM2312 [microfilm of materials held at Fawcett Library City of London Polytechnic].

1967 'Correspondence, Mrs L G Woodcock, Union of Australian Women to I McCorkandale, National Women's Christian Temperance Union' 27 November Add on 427 4(6) Folder 'Correspondence 1963–1970'.

1967 'Correspondence, Mrs L G Woodcock, Union of Australian Women to Prof. S Encel, University of New South Wales' 9 October Add on 427 4(6) Folder 'Correspondence 1963–70'.

Essay 4

On Books and Institutions, circa 1970 (A Jurisographical Examination of Relational Practices)

Feminist Jurisographical Exercises

Feminist Jurisography is a book of six writing exercises, in which I work alongside traditions of feminism and jurisprudence that I have inherited. My writing experiments prioritise how an argument is carried through method, with redescription as its punctuation. Redescribing the methods of those who transformed my disciplines, but which may be not in direct sight today, can be understood as an activity of reimagining their practical relevance for contemporary projects of disciplinary relations. Naming jurisography as my own practice is a necessary part of that activity, as it organises how I address my own situation, and shows what feminist and jurisprudential writing offer to any project worried about the conditions of living, and quality of relationships, in law and life. In one view, each exercise speaks for itself. I have refused the convention of an academic monographic that prioritises a single thesis in which the author remains silent, while their hypothesis of cause and consequence, problem and perspective, emerges chapter by chapter as a *fait accompli*. I have, instead, embraced the essay and note, forms which draw guidance from women writing experientially and dialectally, and (until very recently) at institutional peripheries, which I explained in Essay One.[1] The feminist books and guides I am following centre ambivalence, and what it means to think and write with more than one point of view, to be very clear that lives lived on (and off) the page are connected rather than reducible, and capable of change as a result. It is one of my intellectual duties to demonstrate how these relational techniques are rigorous contributions to disciplinary knowledge, which answer back to the normativity and formalism of much academic writing. Another is to show how feminist innovations have influenced transformative practices within disciplines, and to draw feminist assertions of knowledge into open (rather than clandestine) conversation with jurisprudence writing worried about the quality of law in social life. From that standpoint, I have been following a loose chronology of the conditions in which accounts of feminism and jurisprudence are written and come into relationship. The exercises can therefore also be read together, as a story of how personal relations between men and women have

DOI: 10.4324/9780429461132-4

been addressed since 1949. I have given material (and allegorical) shape to that narrative by bringing into view both official and unofficial jurisprudence writing, by credentialed male authors in the university, and by women writing out of office (or at least in offices not recognised, or misapprehended, by those with authority to publicly care for the conducts of law).

Until now, I have kept these registers of technical form and self-formation slightly at arm's length from each other. The reason is that the scholarly persona of the feminist, whose conduct of intellectual life disturbs the certainties of what it means to authorise knowledge, did not declare herself in writing until the 1970s. I cannot easily join my essays together without a consideration of how writing that came from the Women's Liberation Movement transformed the status of 'woman' from object of study to subject author. My concern in this fourth essay is to give an account of that transformation, through a jurisographical examination of books created and shared by Women's Liberationists. These books can be understood now as an international reading list of early feminist theory, and include *Sexual Politics* (Millett 1970), *The Dialectic of Sex* (Firestone 1970), *The Female Eunuch* (Greer 1970), and *Woman's Estate* (Mitchell 1971).[2] At the time, all were popular best sellers and on the shelves of radical repositories all over the world. I have chosen one of these guides to examine in detail: *Woman's Estate*. This is because, for my purposes, *Woman's Estate* can also be read as a book of unofficial jurisprudence, at a time when 'feminist theorising about the law' (as Canadian feminist legal scholar Kathleen Lahey noted, looking back in 1985) was 'an uncatalogued item, a yet-to-be recognised enterprise'.[3] The persona 'feminist' needed to be imagined before it was possible to be a feminist at law, and I want to consider how that persona was formed.[4] Mitchell, a scholar of Marxist theory and active in British New Left politics, used her training to recast relations of class and interests, and challenge the everyday experience of women's status and condition (a duality that I have been following in *Feminist Jurisography*, and which is integral for feminist jurisprudence to come).

The cultivation of intellectual personae through writing is not, obviously, confined to feminists. In Essays Two and Three, I staged a dialogue between men's and women's writing to show distinct addresses to the lived experience of law. I introduced books by men holding juristic office first, to make an historical point.[5] But in this essay, my consideration of Feminist Books comes first, to leave no doubt about who created 'interdisciplinary' writing. My consideration of Law Books comes at the end, where I will revisit the work of the exemplary jurisprudent who has been guiding my story, Julius Stone. I will share my notes on an expansive lecture Stone delivered at the University of Texas in late 1967: 'Trends in Jurisprudence in the Second Half Century'.[6] The lecture offers insight into how Stone reflected upon his body of work, and its influence, over a 20-year period. The lecture also enables me to consider the nature of his views on the methodologies that enabled law and society to become known to each other, at universities and outside, in a heady and uncertain time.

Before I begin, I want to make a note about the presentation of my jurisographic exercise in this essay. Re-joining 'the times, the means, the spaces'[7] to show how books read and books written create relations with others is not novel. I have taken guidance in how to represent methods from many sources. One that is important to me is the work by the Italian theorists of sexual difference, The Milan Women's Bookstore Collective, who wrote collectively and anonymously about their experiences in Milan in the 1970s and 1980s. The Bookstore in Milan (modifying to their circumstances an idea they borrowed from *Libraire des femmes*, opened by the Psychanalyse et Politique group in Paris in 1968, and soon proliferating all over Italy)[8] stated that their ambition was to generate 'a way of doing'. They named a practice of relationship grounded in the material, 'to have daily meetings, build a center, have adequate spaces where the separation between the private and the political can be surmounted'.[9] Their 'new' political terms were to *create* 'female social spaces in order to transform the given reality', and to *transform* 'both the women involved in the project and society'. For the Collective, the point was to understand how these actions were 'not two distinct aims but two sides of the same process'.[10] The Milan Women's Bookstore was therefore 'intended as a space in which "-the new-will be gathered and communicated so that it may become collective wealth."'[11]

These are ideas that circulate (as I shall explore in relation to an Australian experience).[12] From that perspective, I am borrowing the term 'bookstore' in this essay symbolically, to organise and place my own ideas about books, writing, and relationships. A space claimed, rented, owned, or inhabited is not only about bricks and mortar, as the South African-British writer Deborah Levy reminds with force and precision in her most recent instalment of living memoir, *Real Estate* (2021). It is also about creative invention as a political intervention; a status based on the ownership of your own traditions and ideas, and the production of your own work, a sharp rebuke to the presumptions in law and life of men as landlords viewing 'every female writer as a sitting tenant on his land'.[13]

Guides for Living

To locate my own bookstores and bookshelves, I need to return to Beauvoir and *The Second Sex*. As I discussed in Essay One, and noted by many before me, *The Second Sex* was never a manifesto.[14] But it was a guide for imagining a different kind of life. Beauvoir's intentions were very plain on this point, both in the original book, and in the interviews, essays, memoirs, and journalism that she continued to publish for the rest of her life. She wrote to comprehend and 'to translate . . . a situation that is showing itself to be historical precisely in that it is in the process of changing'.[15] Although not offering anything as programmatic as a plan for universal action, or rules of morality to be followed slavishly and adhered to without deviation, what Beauvoir did do in *The Second Sex* was address the question of woman's experience of relations both intimately and eruditely, and talk to her reader in the first person. This attitude changed everything.

The Second Sex was a best seller from the time of its first edition.[16] Although no book is a static artefact, the extent to which *The Second Sex* has provided 'reference points for understanding'[17] and been continually renewed over the past 70 years is remarkable. It has energised generations of readers (myself included), but for readers in 1960s and early 1970s – when there was little else in the library – *The Second Sex* was a fulcrum for a new experience of freedom for women. It showed how interrogation of one's own circumstance could open a different politics of radical action, and provided a model of how to assert oneself in writing, and with knowledge and with men, in a way that shifted focus from woman's emancipation to her liberation of the self as human being. Identification with Beauvoir was sometimes contemporaneously cited. Canadian radical feminist theorist Shulamith Firestone, for example, dedicated her *Dialectic of Sex* (1970) to Simone de Beauvoir 'who endured'.[18] The brilliant essay 'The Master's Tools will Never Dismantle the Master's House', written by Black, queer, feminist scholar Audre Lorde in 1979 for a conference dedicated to *The Second Sex*, rebukes white, heterosexual feminist participants for attempting to ossify and claim Beauvoir rather than understand what she opened up to everyone.[19] More commonly, Beauvoir has been openly discussed by feminist authors of the 1970s when reintroducing their own writing, to capture and explain the ethos and dynamism of a time of personal and collective self-invention. Juliet Mitchell, for her part, described *The Second Sex* in an interview in 2006 as a 'brilliant depiction of an analysis of the oppression of women' that inspired her, and offered something outside of the limitations of Marxist theory and the British New Left's forestalling on woman's condition and class interests.[20] The American literary and feminist theorist Kate Millett did not openly acknowledge Beauvoir in her own ground-breaking blockbuster *Sexual Politics* in 1970, but wrote later: 'I owe a great debt to *The Second Sex*. I could not have written *Sexual Politics* without it'.[21]

In *Hipparchia's Choice*, French philosopher Michèle Le Dœuff (who I have been reading alongside in these essays) reflects on her experience as a young student and activist of being introduced to Beauvoir in text and in person in late 1960s Paris. 'Reading *The Second Sex*', Le Dœuff recalled, 'taught us to objectify the question ["what is wrong with me?"], to look at the social world with a critical eye, instead of looking within ourselves for some hidden cause of existential incapacity. It taught us simply to situate some of our difficulties and thus free ourselves from their internalization'.[22] Importantly, Le Dœuff also emphasises that 'between 1949 and 1971' Beauvoir herself did not 'put down her pen and wait until the . . . Movement began'.[23] She wrote constantly, and paid attention to her own changing situation in Paris, listening 'first to writers . . . then to the collective thoughts of groups from the Movement'.[24] Beauvoir 'caught hold of emerging ideas', Le Dœuff recalls; circa 1970, her work had evolved (in particular around questions of labour, reproductive rights, sexuality, and anti-colonialism) through meeting 'young feminists' with whom she was 'entirely in sympathy' because of their desire 'to change the world that has been made by men'.[25] Le Dœuff's point is that '[f]eminist books are generally a prospective memory of a movement which constantly needs to be taken up again'.[26] These forms of exchange, of entrustment through text and experience and over time, do not detract from, but rather supplement and demonstrate, how *The Second Sex* 'galvanised women's movements everywhere'.[27]

The Australian experience of reading Beauvoir is well documented. The late film critic and essayist Sylvia Lawson, in her acerbic collection *How Simone de Beauvoir Died in Australia* (2002),[28] wrote about what it felt like to encounter Beauvoir for the first time in Sydney. Lawson was already an established writer by the late 1950s, but the act of reading a book – in public, by a known French intellectual, *who also happened to be a woman* – was to 'leave oneself open to rebuke for precocity and pretension'.[29] To set oneself apart was, however, exactly the point, and the source of its enjoyment. 'To be caught reading [*The Second Sex*] in a coffee shop – or better still in Sydney, Lorenzini's wine bar', Lawson wrote, 'was decidedly chic, like smoking Gauloises, or serving vermouth with salami and black olives'.[30] In her own essay on discovering Beauvoir in the mid-1960s, 'Adventures in Feminism' (2000),[31] historian Ann Curthoys recalls a preference for reading Beauvoir's novels, but above all her autobiographies. Curthoys writes about how as a student she was enthralled by depictions of Beauvoir's conduct of relationships and daily life: how Beauvoir and her lovers lived apart, yet how Beauvoir met Sartre each day to talk about lives and 'unwritten books', walking the streets of Paris, stopping to take a bowl of borscht for lunch, and a cup of chocolate at La Cupole for supper.[32] These details of wine and food and community are not incidental. They are given, deliberately, by both Curthoys and Lawson, to convey a sense of what became possible, for their own future work, through reading, and relationship. In style, attitude and genre, both essays demonstrate how Beauvoir's books were training manuals in crafting a different kind of public writing persona as a woman ('If we were intellectuals we read Simone de Beauvoir', as the poet and writer Kate Jennings recalled 40 years later).[33] But they also demonstrate that what they learned was a certain ethos of life, sharp and focussed but alive to pleasure, that made it easier to navigate their own situation, that was also 'showing itself to be historical precisely in that it is in the process of changing'.[34]

Bookstores

Beauvoir, of course, did not achieve 'Women's Liberation' singlehandedly in 1970 merely because she had written *The Second Sex* in 1949. She did not, for example, envisage a collective women's movement as a means of redressing oppression.[35] But as the American literary critic Judith Thurman has argued, 'revolution cannot begin until the diffuse, private indignation of individuals coalesces into a common cause'.[36] As noted, Beauvoir is name dropped and acknowledged as germinal to that common cause in the 1970s, as she offered a way to perceive how the personal was not only political, but that such a politics might be definable as 'an international movement . . . not in organisation, but in . . . identification and shared ideas'.[37] To assume that happened only in your own home missed the point. To move the personal to the political involved an exchange of ideas in real time, and that required somewhere to meet.

Before 1970, to say you were going to a 'women's group' suggested one of two things. The first was membership of an auxiliary to a political organisation ostensibly concerned with universal questions but in fact predicated on male experience, organised for the benefit of men (for example, the experience of many women in The New Left).[38] The other was to organise a concerted rebuttal to institutional exclusion based on sex, advocated courageously and separately by the excluded (as the UAW did, in my examples in Essay Three).[39] Around 1970, these designations expanded and changed. A women's group became a transformative active project of finding together the words, and the means, to expose and then overturn the expected order of things from a point of view that did not originate from men at all. The Australian feminist scholar Dale Spender importantly reminded in 1983 that *There's Always Been a Women's Movement This Century*.[40] But the problem in 1970 was that the questions asked by women as collective groups in earlier decades of the 20th century, and the ways of asking them, stood in contrast to the self-characterisation of their own burgeoning community as a sisterhood with 'dangerous ideas'.[41] This is a point that the Australian feminist historian (and my first feminist teacher) Susan Magarey made as early as 1986, in her apt and instructive article 'I Never Wanted to be an Administrator of Anything'.[42] There was not, then, a ready-made template for unorthodox institutional and social life. 'In such a situation', Curthoys recalled in 2000, 'the world of books became paramount. . . . Reading was a way of thinking about alternatives'.[43] Beauvoir's work (already read, already guiding the individual) helped transform the act of reading from a 'one-to-one dialogue'[44] to a 'collective and profoundly sociable enterprise'.[45] Beauvoir 'taught us how to live', as Curthoys puts it, and showed that it was possible 'to forge an alternative to the narrow options then facing women, and to live according to a different conception of femininity, intellectuality, independence, sexuality and friendship'.[46]

The spaces created by women for women's groups were as a consequence integral to forging these alternatives. Women's resource centres, houses, bookstores, and libraries were specific to the politics of their location. What their collectives shared, however, was a desire to tear up the rules of membership of orthodox institutional space – the Chamber, the House, the Library, the Faculty, the Committee room – by creating membership protocols of their own. These women's collectives also shared a mode of conduct, an awakened obligation to reanimate the power of words that filled those spaces (what was spoken, what was read, what was written) to express the reformulation of relationships adequate to the times, and their own desires and discoveries.[47]

The women's space I want to visit to explore those ideas is Women's Liberation House, at 67 Glebe Point Road, in inner city Sydney.[48] This is for a personal reason. One of the young scholars who gathered there, circa 1970, was Ann Curthoys. By the 1990s, she was my PhD supervisor, when I moved to Glebe, to study. It was from Ann that I learned how cultivate a certain attitude to life and writing. So it was appropriate to the exercise of this essay about books, institutions, and the inventions of feminist relational practices to return to 'radical Glebe' (as Ann has described the experience of being there at the time),[49] and to Women's Liberation House, where *The Second Sex* sat symbolically on the first shelf.

Bookshelves

67 Glebe Point Road, when I first moved to Sydney in 1993, was a second-hand shop (if I recall correctly). More recently, it was a café. In 1970, it was a rented share house, but one with an open-door policy, an ephemera of pamphlets and books, a Roneo machine, and a Letraset.[50] In accounts by feminist custodians, Women's Liberation House at 67 Glebe Point Road appears as both a shared historical location, and a repeated referent of how ideas, and people, were brought into relationship with each other. Women's Liberation House defined itself outside of the expected protocols of membership, by word of mouth, and by association. 'You didn't actually "join"', Curthoys recalled in 1988, 'you just went along'.[51] 'Going along' was not limited to 20-something Anglo-Australian university students, although they undoubtedly provided the intellectual and political energy, and the actual keys to the house.[52] 'There [were] women across class, across race barriers, across ethnic origins . . . across ages – and that was one of the things that was really exciting', the labour activist Laurie Bebbington noted in an interview in the 1990s. 'There [were] Koori women . . . women who were still at secondary school . . . And there were women who were fifty or sixty . . . no matter where you came from there were relevant issues about why you were where you were'.[53]

In their recollections of this time, feminist custodians offer descriptions of Women's Liberation House making it possible to walk through the front door with them, and to enter into a world. The front room was the meeting room, the 'point of solidarity' for consciousness-raising activities.[54] (A shorthand today, consciousness raising was defined by Juliet Mitchell in 1971, for those seeking to try it, as speaking with other women in local groups to 'generalise phenomenon' and engender solidarity through difference, in order to 'change the pain that must be protested' and understand it '*is* the politics – the turning of many individual experiences into a collective struggle').[55] In the second room, downstairs, there were things to read.[56] 'We gorged . . . on underground rags', Kate Jennings recalls, many of which were coming from America, but also Britain and Europe courtesy of personal connections,[57] and were then copied on the Letraset to meet demand.[58] These 'rags' titles were intentionally provocative but tongue-in-cheek: *Off the Pedestal, Off Our Backs, Up From Under, No More Fun and Games*.[59] The journals soon shared shelf space with a new genre of popular books, produced by and for members of women's liberation groups in New York and London, and which were a sensation when they appeared in the first years of the 1970s. 'As a poet', Jennings recalled, 'I gravitated to . . . Robin Morgan, Ti-Grace Atkinson, and Valerie Solanas [author of the SCUM Manifesto]. Unafraid to be emotional, luminous with rage. Hard line, hard-core. Manifestos and poems that jumped off the page. I loved it'.[60] Others, like Curthoys and Magarey, training to be historians, and emerging from the New Left, it was Millett's *Sexual Politics* primarily, and also Mitchell's *Woman's Estate*, that 'were integral' to the 'development of our ideas'.[61] These books gave clues to their readers about how to speak about the category woman as experienced in the immediate political moment, using some expected scholarly techniques, but a reversal of authorial voice, a disturbance of the idea that disciplines were contained and bound by their methods and traditions, and a keen recognition that the writing was for a general audience (with no kudos attached to scholarly obfuscation and certainly no evidence of performance anxiety).

By 1972, the second room upstairs at 67 Glebe Point Road had expanded to become a writing room and an editorial suite. At first, Curthoys recalled, '[we] were . . . energetically soaking up ideas [from overseas] borrowing, reprinting, reworking, quoting at length, discussing, explaining'.[62] But in rapid succession, and with a sense of what feminist artist, writer, and broadcaster Virginia Fraser would later call a 'mad confidence',[63] Australian women's liberationists 'initiat[ed] then develop[ed] our own style'.[64] They published Australia's first women's liberation newspaper, *Mejane*, in 1971; by the end of 1972, they had started a journal, *Refractory Girl*, that 'represented the more academic side of women's liberation with longer more scholarly articles'.[65] By 1973, Sydney Women's Liberationists had armed themselves to begin an institutional disciplinary argument with the university, and its forms of knowledge and traditions. This argument was staged as the Philosophy Strike at University of Sydney, an event well cared for by many Australian feminists ever since (not only in oral histories and memoirs, but in academic writing and public art).[66] By 1975, Australian feminist scholarship arrived at traditional publishing houses, with a remarkable launch of six now-classic books in a single year (including Anne Summers' *Damned Whores and God's Police*): a whole bookshelf of original feminist writing directed to our own specific history and located politics.[67]

I have a temptation to retell the stories of these achievements (they are great stories). But in paying attention to the bookshelf at Women's Liberation House, I simply want to show that women's liberationists created a new persona for themselves: the feminist intellectual. Her books were written outside of universities, by authors who were students undertaking intellectual apprenticeships, but who also were in daily conversation with women with all kinds of experiences and problems different to their own. Her books also demonstrated that writing on 'the woman question' was no longer 'to justify a particular state of things by reference to some nature or necessity'.[68] Collectively, feminist intellectuals showed there was 'no destiny' for 'woman', singular, as a 'writing and reading subject'.[69] The lesson of the book – *The Second Sex*, circa 1970, and those it inspired – was that it deprived the categorisation of woman of 'any subjective guarantee'.[70]

Juliet (Feminist Books, circa 1970)

To examine to these accomplishments, I will take just one book off the shelf: Juliet Mitchell's *Woman's Estate*. My copy of *Woman's Estate* is 182 pages long, a Penguin paperback bought second-hand. It retains its original sticker recommending a retail price of $2.25, and fits in a large pocket, or a small handbag. *Woman's Estate* is a good read, as it moves with pace and energy, perhaps reflecting what Mitchell described, 30 years later, as its 'long gestation' but 'shot-gun birth' (she wrote it in just six weeks).[71] The book is organised in in two parts with short sections, for easy reading on the bus, or at a collective meeting. Like *The Second Sex*, *Woman's Estate* traverses texts and disciplines as a point of necessity, as the only way to comprehensively analyse woman's status as secondary. Part One is an overview of Mitchell's own present situation, but cast as a collective survey of the reasons and purposes of the arrival of the Women's Liberation Movement. In order to adequately write about contemporary politics and theory in motion, Mitchell presents a hybrid genre: part sociological survey and political science thesis, part 'how to' book of 'principles of organisation'[72] and a primer of 'concepts'.[73] The book was therefore tailor-made for readers seeking guidance in how to engage with practices (like consciousness raising), and ideas now named for public dissemination (sexism, patriarchy, feminism). In Part Two, Mitchell presents a theoretical analysis that depends on her training as Marxist intellectual, but uses the theory she has mastered as a set of methods for her own redeployment.[74] As Mitchell has reflected on the writing of *Woman's Estate*, and its precursor essay from the *New Statesman* 'The Longest Revolution' (1966), '[f]or us, in the 1960s, Marxism was not out there as "Marxism". One was also self-critical . . . [and] understood where we had to expand it intellectually'.[75] In Mitchell's case, she did not 'stick within the terms' that 'giant theorists' (Marx, but also Freud) had set.[76] Instead, following techniques learned from *The Second Sex*, and identifying Beauvoir as a theorist to work with alongside the male 'giants',[77] she reintroduced thought in order to respond to the 'concrete situation'[78] that she experienced ('after all you are in a different historical epoch') and observed ('and in a different social context').[79] Mitchell acknowledged that Marx, and importantly Engels, had not ignored 'the woman' question (or woman's spheres of influence and forms of labour).[80] However, Mitchell also observed that those who came after them 'inherited a tradition of thought which simply pointed to the a priori equation of socialism with feminine liberation without showing concretely how it would transform woman's condition'.[81] 'The size of absence of women in socialist theory and practice is immense', she argued, and where 'analysis has been offered clearly it has been inadequate, for the resulting practice has seriously failed to match it'.[82]

What Mitchell argued in response seems so obvious today that it is easy to forget its radical force. First, she stated that women were an oppressed class, with definable interests able to be organised and promulgated by giving voice to women's experience as a 'class consciousness'.[83] Second, she took Beauvoir's transformative declaration in 1949 ('I write it', which deviated existentialist philosophy from male assumption to feminist inversion, and claimed woman as a subject self),[84] to argue for 'a specific theory of women's oppression' that deviated from Marxist orthodoxy.[85] '[T]hough we cannot, in Women's Liberation, in any sense rely on previously developed analyses', Mitchell argued, 'we may be able to use them, to modify and extend'.[86]

Mitchell's ambition was to 'reject . . . the idea that woman's condition can be deduced derivatively from the economy (Engels) or equated symbolically with society (Marx)'.[87] By acknowledging that 'women are exploited at work, *and* relegated to the home', Mitchell began to examine how 'the two positions compound' oppression: 'subservience in production is obscured by [women's] assumed dominance in their own world – the family'.[88] The family, in Mitchell's emergent feminist theory, was then neither natural nor identifiable only as ideology. In 'ask[ing] the feminist questions, . . . to try to come up with some Marxist answers', 'the family' instead could be understood as superstructure, in which the diverse aspects of women's situation within it produced a 'complex unity' – production, reproduction, sexuality, and the socialisation of children.[89] These required separation and disentanglement in order to understand how each was maintained and could be changed. In this way, Mitchell fragmented the category 'woman' as it had been used in existing thought, to topple the pre-eminence of the subordinated status of women preordained in culture and written into law. Sounding remarkably like Beauvoir in 1949, she argued: 'There is nothing inevitable about the form or role of the family, any more than there is about the character or role of women',[90] and insisted that how personae of wife, lover, and mother operated was something able to be theorised, and redefined, by woman herself. '[E]xamining the concrete role and nature of today's family from within',[91] in terms of both its psychology and its economy, was an intellectual activity necessary for woman to exercise agency and define her freedom. Significantly, such a project was not understood to be a burden for women alone (something often forgotten). 'How can one sex be free without the other?', Mitchell argues, again following closely Beauvoir's arguments about reciprocal relations in *The Second Sex*.[92] For women's relationship to children to be totally voluntary and self-determined, rather than expected or legally required, for one example, meant acknowledging alliance with (rather than reliance on, or sublimation to) men. 'Both sexes are oppressed by sex role stereotypes . . . don't you think men would like to be more at home with their children. . .?',[93] Mitchell wrote, radically arguing that the inevitably of 'the family', as a realm which depended on certain status for man and woman (he as property owner, father, household head; she as property, mother, housekeeper) be 'decomposed into a new pattern' as acts of mutual obligation and radical reorganisation.[94]

Mitchell's emergent 'feminist theory of oppression' was in these ways less interested in institutional equality (or marriage law reform) as a primary aim, but saw it as something that would come when woman (and by extension, man) liberated themselves as 'whole people'.[95] That said, the fact that 'the agents and institutions of power' were 'men (and/or male dominated society)',[96] who could proscribe a 'natural destiny' based on sex, was an 'ideological concept' that had to be fought.[97] The duty of the feminist intellectual, with that insight, Mitchell argued, was to present ways in which '[t]theoretical analysis *and* revolutionary action . . . restructure and destroy the inevitability' of 'woman's place'.[98]

Woman's Estate as a feminist book did not directly address legal doctrine as part of its project of destruction and reconstruction, but Mitchell's contribution to unofficial jurisprudence writing lives in the book's title and carries something forward. An 'estate' of course operates at common law as inherited rights, interests, and entitlement, from which woman has been historically excluded on the grounds of legal status. By virtue of her argument, Mitchell reminds that an 'estate' is also a state of being, or condition of life, and open for transformation though redefinition and action. In these ways, I think, *Woman's Estate*[99] not only attaches the subject woman to a class with interests of their own, who can collectively disturb social and economic functions of a body politic, and reorient its expected sites of contest. It also says something about Mitchell's own state of being: that she refused to relinquish her experience as either scholar, or women's liberationist; and by joining them together in the style, content and argument of her writing, provided guidance to others to do the same.

Julius (Law Books, c.1970)

In my Introduction to this essay, I was frank about the limits and arrangement of my attention to official law books of this era. I note, however, that in the late 1960s and early 1970s, law scholars were engaged in all kinds of activities that announced that the scholarly persona 'jurisprudent' was open for renewal.[100] An alternative non-doctrinal tradition[101] (empirical and building upon the Realist enterprise that I have been watching in Essays Two and Three)[102] had become established enough that new kinds of writing about law could be institutionally categorised. A review essay in the *Stanford Law Review* in 1973, by the American legal scholar Richard Abel, provides a useful example. In his essay, Abel delineated the differences between 'law books' (the work of legally trained insiders, that formed an integral part of the professional legal enterprise), and 'books about law' (a genre that presented 'a mode of reflection', and drew on 'the humanities and social sciences' with objectives 'outside of the legal system', and a commitment to understand and 'illuminate legal phenomena').[103] His categorisation was not a straightforward repurposing of 'law on the books' and 'law in action', but a considered exercise of analysing what the new genre of 'books about law' might contribute to jurisprudence, and how such 'interdisciplinary studies' might be 'judged'.[104] Arguably, a book like *Woman's Estate* met Abel's positive criteria of a 'book about law'. It illuminated perspectives (by women) on 'legal phenomena' that might have been useful to legal scholars at a time when the Western world was moving rapidly toward no fault divorce, and a transformation from 'personal relations' to what we understand now as 'family law'.[105] Feminist books and law books circa 1970 remained, however, at arm's length from each other. Some of the reasons they did not meet are obvious, such as the fact that the writers of each deliberately cultivated a specific audience who remained, for the time being, in different spaces, with access to entirely different bookshelves and reading materials. But there are other reasons that are obscured, but important to draw into view.

To explain what I mean, I will give one example: a lecture delivered by my exemplary jurisprudent, Julius Stone, at the University of Texas in 1967. Stone had been invited by his friend, the pre-eminent 20th-century American Law Librarian and Tarlton Professor of Law, Roy Merksy, to revisit ideas first introduced in *The Province and Function of Law* (first published in 1946),[106] and that had become world renowned in the intervening twenty year period. By the late 1960s, Stone's 'sociological jurisprudence', or law in relation, had been adapted and updated by him in new texts for teaching: *Social Dimensions of Law and Justice* (1966b), in *Law and the Social Sciences in the Second Half Century* (1966a).[107] The influence of Stone, and his writing, for the generation of law students of the late 1960s and early 1970s (most of whom were men, and many of whom became leading professors and judges, law reform commissioners and counsel in Australian, and elsewhere) has been well documented.[108] The lecture, 'Trends in Jurisprudence in the Second Half Century', offers something additional to that study of influence, a self-reflection, specific to the times.

Stone's central themes in his work were 'the sociological nature of law, the indeterminacy of the law in judicial interpretation, and the principled exercise of discretion in interpreting law'.[109] What I have been drawing out in my accounts is not the influence of his thought on the discipline, or what influence that has had on the law *per se*, but the methodological inheritance of his commitment to law being bought 'into relation'. Stone's sociological jurisprudence made it permissible to ask 'what law is' in relation to society, and then to also argue that a relation between social/human sciences and jurisprudence was permissible in order for society to be knowable to law.[110] Stone argued consistently in his many publications, books, speeches, broadcasts, and lectures from 1946 that jurisprudents had a duty to observe how other disciplines offered evidence about 'the actual ethical attitudes of real people',[111] drawn from 'a mass of data' (or facts) that 'displayed law behaviour in society'.[112] The preferred techniques by which this data was produced were empirically based anthropology, or political science; as others have noted, this was accompanied by a scepticism towards Marxist thought and influence.[113] Stone's work also made clear that in the exchange of law in relation, the task of jurisprudent was to retain control over which (and whose) 'existing conditions'[114] could in fact be recognised and dealt with by, and in, law.

In his 1967 address, Stone re-emphasises a theme in his earlier writing: that jurisprudents have responsibilities to understand how law's subjects experience social change, and how their own discipline therefore also changes. He noted, carefully:

> 'What men have already learned cannot be "open" in the full sense. Each generation needs constantly to renew it, review it, and even revise it for its own situation. It cannot be entitled simply to forget what has gone before . . . [we] require knowledge of the particular community, in its particular time and place, among whose members we are to make a just distribution'.[115]

In language which would not be amiss in a report written by Beauvoir, reminiscent of both of their experience and obligations of writing into a post-war world, he reminds his audience to 'consider . . . the frailties of thought thrust upon us by our situation in time and place even when we struggle hardest to overcome them'.[116] This carries with it, however, 'vital corollaries' for the legally trained.[117] One is about inheritance: 'the need to carry with us in our own brief journey what earlier generations had learned in and for their situations; not to forget lightly what they struggled to reach, even when we may have moved beyond'.[118] The other is about contingency of social situation, and renewal: 'the need to recognize [what is] provisional . . . [to have an] "openness" towards the future, provided we see that this can be an openness only towards what we still have to learn'.[119]

With those cautions and duties in mind, the key technical point Stone makes in his 1967 speech is that 'law in relation' as a set of research practices was now accepted, after twenty years debate, within the law academy itself. 'It is no longer necessary to browbeat lawyers into admitting to their concern for the ethical and sociological imports of law', he stated, 'or to propagandize for inter-disciplinary teamwork or the integration of all contributions to our knowledge of human society whatever the disciplinary boundaries from which they came'.[120] The relationship between political science, sociology and jurisprudence, and the measured and rational ways that law had made use of the data provided by those disciplines,[121] ensured that 'law in relation' had become an 'important intellectual instrument by which modern societies', (and by 1967 this was not limited by Stone to Western traditions),[122] could understand (and perhaps improve) 'the turbulent responses of law and its agents to economic, social and ideological change'.[123]

Despite Stone's advocacy of jurisprudential attention to changing social circumstances, there were ideas and techniques that he also resisted. Stone is clear, for example, that interdisciplinary work should be done by teams (as we saw in Essay Three), in which the legal scholar's overview is dominant. (The idea that an interdisciplinary work could be entirely produced by one person, driven by the nature of her technical questions and abilities, was not conceivable). Stone also remains uneasy about social and human sciences if they emphasise 'interests'.[124] There is a qualitative difference between the currency of ideas shaping methods when Stone first published in 1946 (how to give an account of self in terms of action and agency), and those that gave an urgency to university life for the students in 1967 (how collective organisation aggregated lived experience into political interests, capable of disturbing institutions as representations of the *status quo*). Stone, however, consistently argued that 'interests' cannot properly benefit law's objective social need. 'Interests', for Stone, are aligned with Marxist practices, which are thinly disguised in Stone's speech as something to avoid because they are partisan and disturb good 'objective' social science practice. Stone argues that 'it remains basic that this concern of [social science in relation with] jurisprudence seek detailed empirical understanding and solution of ad hoc practical problems . . . concern with the larger more visionary enterprises ought never to obscure this truth'.[125] If jurisprudence were to open itself, unguarded, to such partisan enterprises, jurists would 'have to raise, almost immediately, important doubts as to the whole notion of men's "interests" as an organizing category for marshaling empirical data, or for theorizing about justice'.[126]

This belies a tension; Stone's grappling with this tension reminds that jurisprudence writing (as he himself noted) is never temporally untethered, and that this particular time was turbulent. 'In the study of law and society as a contemporary phenomenon we remain still undoubtedly dominated by the attempt to understand law as a manifestation of the pressure of men's changing de facto interests in a given time and place',[127] Stone contends. '[Despite] the value of the notion of interests', which Stone conceded were 'the center of grave philosophical and sociological questions [about contemporary society]', questions about the value of those interests for law remained solely for the jurisprudent to determine. As Stone, argued, this was due to 'the difficulty of limiting . . . reference to phenomenon objectively observable' by methods acceptable to orthodox jurisprudence. 'Some of these difficulties are perhaps easily avoidable', Stone eventually concluded for his gathered audience of Law Faculty and students, '[and] we need not refer to them'.[128]

Relational Practices

By writing this jurisographical account of 'the times, the means, the spaces',[129] there are two practices I hope I have drawn back into view.

The first is how 'law in relation' was (and is) a methodological practice of experience, in content and form. What counts for jurisprudential writing concerned with 'law in relation' is open to destabilisation at different times, and by scholars with diverse obligations of audience, different technical inheritances, and new political urgencies. As examples of Law Books and Feminist Books, *c.*1970, Stone and Mitchell's texts can each be understood as a presentation of intellectual experience. The writing of Julius and Juliet do not, however, co-exist in any straightforward way. I have brought them together because I carry more than one scholarly inheritance, and to deliberately show that they were institutionally misaligned, and not in easy temporal communion. From that vantage point, obscured characteristics of a putative relationship between feminism and jurisprudence can be seen.

Stone's 1967 reflection, for example, reminds that jurisprudence writing moves with time and is capable of embracing a changing society. That capacity, and its recognition in writing, enables important things to happen in Australian jurisprudence and law reform, well into the 1980s, although the focus of the legally responsible actor and knower in making change remains fixed on the institutions and practices of law, from the inside. The outside, the life beyond the gates of the university, is understood as essential to understand, but remains subordinate, and addressed when spoken to or written about by jurisprudents, jurists, and lawyers. The techniques of the other discipline by which a changing world can be known, who its subjects might be, and how their experiences and interests might be tested, remains, for jurisprudence, strangely fixed.[130] This is despite the fact that by the late 1960s, the jurisprudential techniques Stone advocated had started to occupy the same space as new disciplinary assertions, by writers like Mitchell, that were intent on transforming the ways social experience could be known.

It would be a critical fantasy to suggest feminists were the only writers taking on an intellectual project of looking at something slantways, to critique or refract, in the early 1970s, and it would be a feminist fantasy to suggest that women's liberation could occur without a direct intervention to juridical practices. But feminist writing circa 1970 did pay attention to something precise that was distinct and new for jurisprudence. Scholars writing as feminists started asking law questions (or questions about living with law) for themselves, without the imprimatur of the legal hierarchy, and in doing so displaced 'law in relation' and its version of interdisciplinary scholarship. It was feminists who learned to interrogate the premises of their own disciplinary practices and engage in the robust suspicion of methods that had relegated their personal and collective interests into categories outside their experience of life. And it was feminists who saw the necessity of approaching interdisciplinary engagements as about more than a matter of empirical verification, but as projects of deconstruction, and reintroduction, disturbing idealised forms as they wrote. The challenge to 'empirical objective' method, the idea of an unmediated singular subject who can be studied and known, and seen and read only in authorised ways, was destabilised by writers like Mitchell and many others. Their techniques – such as asking feminist questions to reach Marxist answers – forced into view *who* the subject and author of institutional and disciplinary observation might be, rather than relying on how objects of study ('woman', 'family') could be uniformly measured. It was this practice that feminists then took with them to law school, into legal practice, into law reform, and, most importantly for my project, into the legal academy. By asking feminist questions to reach different disciplinary answers, feminists circa 1970 liberated the idea that knowledge was privileged and contained. They demonstrated that it was possible to break the intellectual fourth wall between personae and personal experience, and as a consequence, refuse expectations of grand theory but nevertheless operationalise traditions of thought through writing. It is these activities of feminist scholarly life that I think transform law and humanities scholarship in ways that we do not see so easily now.

The second practice is how writing that was able to be described as 'feminist' from the early 1970s did not seek internal agreement but did propose a different formulation of knowledge relations.

I started this essay with an acknowledgment of the work of Italian feminist writers, to make a point about the integral role of spaces to the creation and transformation of those relations. The experience of what happened at the Bookstore in Milan is not of course transposable to Women's Liberation House in Sydney or Women's Library in London, for just some examples. But the encapsulation of what happens when you and your friends stock the shelves of those spaces I think remains instructive, and aids my own exercise of naming and explaining feminist jurisography. The activity of women's liberationists was not simply to read a shelf of women's work that carried shared meaning because it was already known and admired. It was to 'search for language of gendered mediation'[131] in those books – books like *The Second Sex*, in the Australian example – because of the work the author did to reassess and rethink 'the horizon' of imbalanced knowledge, where the 'measures of value are male'.[132] Examining the writing of those who wrote before you, those who understood and exposed disparity and imbalance as a problem, and a lived experience, became an activity in and of itself: a creation of a different symbolic ordering. 'As long as the imbalance registered was one of women compared to man the horizon was neutral', the Milan Collective wrote in 1979. 'A neutral justice ordered women not to compare themselves to one another, promising to bring them to equality with men, with that result that female experience stayed imprisoned in itself, without social translation'.[133] Instead, the starting point and practices of reading then writing, they argued, and as experiences at 67 Glebe Point Road showed, could be relations of trust with each other, in and over time.

My point is that the books written by those who learned from these shelves circa 1970 transformed the aspiration of a neutral, and naturalised, knowledge production and transmission. The texts of feminist intellectuals were, and remain, acts of social translation in which female experience was liberated with rigour, attitude, and style. Their material and symbolic conducts with knowledge authorised a different starting point for all kinds of writing and new institutional relationships. It is this legacy that I will explore further – as an act of acknowledgment, and of literal genealogy of my own experience – in my next instalment of *Feminist Jurisography*.

Notes

1 See Essay One, *Feminist Jurisography*.
2 Millett 1970; Firestone 1970; Greer 1970; Mitchell 1977.
3 Lahey 1985: 519.
4 There are many early exemplars and contemporaries of Lahey, in this point. For two, see Thornton 1986; O'Donovan 1985.
5 See Essay Two and Essay Three, *Feminist Jurisography* for discussion.
6 Stone 1967.
7 This formulation is borrowed from the original Italian, in a 1976 leaflet called 'Il tempo, i mezzi e i luoghi', recorded by The Milan Women's Bookstore Collective 1990: 83.
8 The Milan Women's Bookstore Collective 1990: 91.
9 The Milan Women's Bookstore Collective 1990: 84.
10 The Milan Women's Bookstore Collective 1990: 84.
11 The Milan Women's Bookstore Collective 1990: 91. They are quoting a leaflet from 1974 in the section entitled 'The Milan Bookstore and the Parma Library': 90–96.
12 For another account of the Milan Women's Bookstore Collective and their practices, see Martinis Roe 2018. I return to these texts and ideas in Essay Six, *Feminist Jurisography*.
13 Levy 2021: 258.
14 Le Dœuff 1991: 57. See discussion of this point in Essay One, *Feminist Jurisography* at Note 35.
15 Beauvoir 2011: 750.
16 Moi 2010.
17 Le Dœuff 1991: 57.
18 Curthoys 2000: 17.
19 Lorde 2018.
20 Çakmak, Mitchell & Somay 2006: 17.
21 Curthoys 2000: 17.
22 Le Dœuff 1991: 57.
23 Le Dœuff 1991: 132.
24 Le Dœuff 1991: 132.
25 Le Dœuff 1991: 132.
26 Le Dœuff 1991: 16.
27 Le Dœuff 1991: 57.
28 Lawson 2002: 179.
29 Lawson 2002: 179.
30 Lawson 2002: 179.
31 Curthoys 2000.
32 Curthoys 2000: 6.
33 Jennings 2010: 3.
34 Beauvoir 2011: 750.
35 Mitchell 1977: 82.
36 Thurman 2011: xv.
37 Mitchell 1977: 11.
38 Jennings 2010: 7–9.

39 See discussion of this point in Essay Three, *Feminist Jurisography*: 57–61.
40 Spender 1983.
41 Magarey 2014a.
42 Magarey 1986. See also Magarey 2014b.
43 Curthoys 2000: 11.
44 Le Dœuff 1991: 57.
45 Curthoys 2013a: 58.
46 Curthoys 2000: 13.
47 Alongside earlier references in this essay to experiences in France and Italy, see for examples from the UK and US: Delap 2016; Spain 2016.
48 For a discussion of these spaces in Australia more broadly, see Magarey 2014a: 57–72.
49 Curthoys 2013b.
50 Curthoys 2013b.
51 Curthoys 1988: 2. See also Magarey 2014b: 380.
52 Curthoys 2013b; Magarey 2014a: 25–42.
53 Quoted in Magarey 2014b: 380–381. See also Magarey 2014a: 25–42.
54 Curthoys 2013b.
55 Mitchell 1977: 58 (my emphasis).
56 Curthoys 2013b.
57 Curthoys 2013b.
58 Magarey 2014a: 25–42.
59 Curthoys 2013b.
60 Jennings 2010: 3.
61 Curthoys 2013b; Magarey 2014a: 25–42.
62 Curthoys 2013b.
63 Fraser 2010.
64 Curthoys 2013b.
65 Curthoys 2013b. See also Magarey 2014b; Luker 2019.
66 See for example: Bashford 1998; Martinis Roe 2017.
67 Dixson 1976; Summers 1975; Ryan & Conlon 1975; Kingston 1975. Susan Eade (Magarey), Peter Spearritt and Ann Curthoys also guest edited a special issue of *Labour History*, 'Women at Work': Curthoys, Eade & Spearritt 1975. For historiographical analysis of these texts, and those that slightly preceded, see Curthoys 1996.
68 Le Dœuff 1991: 112.
69 Le Dœuff 1991: 112.
70 Le Dœuff 1991: 112.
71 The 'long gestation' includes the publication of Mitchell's essay 'Women: The Longest Revolution' in *The New Left Review* in 1966, which was incorporated into *Woman's Estate* in 1971: Shin 2015.
72 Mitchell 1977: 56–61.
73 Mitchell 1977: 62.
74 Singh 2011; Çakmak, Mitchell & Somay 2006.
75 Singh 2011: 2.
76 Singh 2011: 2.
77 Çakmak, Mitchell & Somay 2006; Mitchell 1977: 81–82, 101.
78 Mitchell 1977: 14.
79 Singh 2011: 2.
80 Mitchell 1977: 80.
81 Mitchell 1977: 81.
82 Mitchell 1977: 75
83 Mitchell 1977: 75.
84 For an explanation of this argument in *The Second Sex*, see Essay One, *Feminist Jurisography*: 10–12.

85 Mitchell 1977: 75. This argument is sustained throughout Chapter Four: Mitchell 1977: 75–96.
86 Mitchell 1977: 75.
87 Mitchell 1977: 100.
88 Mitchell 1977: 99 (my emphasis).
89 Mitchell 1977: 99–100.
90 Mitchell 1977: 100.
91 Mitchell 1977: 159.
92 Mitchell 1977: 56.
93 Mitchell 1977: 56.
94 Mitchell 1977: 107.
95 Mitchell 1977: 14.
96 Mitchell 1977: 14.
97 Mitchell 1977: 100.
98 Mitchell 1977: 100 (my emphasis).
99 'Woman's Estate' is also taken from a poem by the English Romantic poet William Blake, quoted on the title page of Mitchell's book, and can be argued to carry double meaning. For Blake's ambiguous attitude toward women in his own work, see Fox 1977.
100 This story has been recorded elsewhere, notably by participants: see Tomlins 2013. See also Genovese & McVeigh 2015 and discussion in Essay Five, *Feminist Jurisography*: 107–111.
101 As described by Trubek 1984.
102 See discussion in Essay Two, *Feminist Jurisography*: 39–41 and Essay Three, *Feminist Jurisography*: 54–57.
103 Abel 1973: 175–176.
104 Abel 1973: 176.
105 For discussion of that transition see Halley 2011. Interestingly, the subject of Abel's review was Rheinstein 1972.
106 Stone 1967: i. See discussion in Essay Two, *Feminist Jurisography*: 39–41.
107 Stone 1966a, 1966b.
108 For a discussion on this point, see Essay Two, *Feminist Jurisography*: 39. One important example referred to is by Irving, Mowbray & Walton 2010.
109 Irving, Mowbray & Walton 2010: 1.
110 See Essay Two, *Feminist Jurisography*: 40–41 for a full discussion on this point.
111 Stone 1950: 386.
112 Stone 1950: 387.
113 Baxi 2010: 78.
114 Stone 1950: 409.
115 Stone 1967: 48.
116 Stone 1967: 47.
117 Stone 1967: 47.
118 Stone 1967: 47.
119 Stone 1967: 48.
120 Stone 1967: 18 (Stone's emphasis).
121 Stone 1967: 17.
122 Stone 1967: 18.
123 Stone 1967: 17.
124 Stone 1967: 29.
125 Stone 1967: 30.
126 Stone 1967: 31–32.
127 Stone 1967: 31–32 (Stone's emphases).
128 Stone 1967: 33–34.

129 From 'Il tempo, i mezzi e i luoghi', recorded by The Milan Women's Bookstore Collective 1990: 83.
130 Genovese & McVeigh 2015.
131 The Milan Women's Bookstore Collective 1990: 113.
132 The Milan Women's Bookstore Collective 1990: 112.
133 The Milan Women's Bookstore Collective 1990: 115.

References

Abel R L 1973 'Review: Law Books and Books About Law' *Stanford Law Review* 26/1: 175–228 DOI:10.2307/1227916.

Bashford A 1998 'The Return of the Repressed: Feminism in the Quad' *Australian Feminist Studies* 13/27: 47–53 DOI:10.1080/08164649.1998.9994886.

Baxi U 2010 'Revisiting Social Dimensions of Law and Justice in a Post-Human Era' in Irving et al 2010: 69–86.

Beauvoir S de 2011 *The Second Sex* Trans C Borde and S Malovany-Chevallier Vintage New York (first published 1949).

Çakmak E E, Mitchell J and Somay B 2006 'There is never a psychopathology without the social context: An interview with Juliet Mitchell' *Cogito* 44–45.

Curthoys A 1988 *For and Against Feminism: A Personal Journey into Feminist Theory and History* Allen & Unwin Sydney.

Curthoys A 1996 'Visions, nightmares, dreams: Women's history, 1975' *Australian Historical Studies* 27/106: 1–13 DOI:10.1080/10314619608595993.

Curthoys A 2000 'Adventures of Feminism: Simone de Beauvoir's Autobiographies, Women's Liberation, and Self-Fashioning' *Feminist Review* 64/1: 3–18 DOI:10.1080/014177800338927.

Curthoys A 2013a 'A feminist voice' in A Clark and P Ashton eds 2013 *Australian History Now* NewSouth Publishing Sydney: 56–72.

Curthoys A 2013b 'Radical Glebe' *Glebe Society's Glebe Voices Series* 22 February Sydney <https://glebesociety.org.au/socialhistory/radical-glebe-a-personal-view-by-ann-curthoys/>.

Curthoys A, Eade S and Spearritt P eds 1975 *Women at Work* Australian Society for the Study of Labour History Canberra.

Delap L 2016 'Feminist Bookshops, Reading Cultures and the Women's Liberation Movement in Great Britain, c. 1974–2000' *History Workshop Journal* 81/1: 171–196 DOI:10.1093/hwj/dbw002.

Dixson M 1976 *The Real Matilda: Woman and Identity in Australia 1788 to 1975* Penguin Books Melbourne.

Firestone S 1970 *The Dialectic of Sex: The Case for Feminist Revolution* Morrow New York.

Fox S 1977 'The Female as Metaphor in William Blake's Poetry' *Critical Inquiry* 3/3: 507–519 DOI:10.1086/447903.

Fraser V 2010 'Mad Confidence: A Book About Australian Women' in N King ed 2010 *Up Close: Carol Jerrems with Larry Clark, Nan Goldin and William Yang* Heide Museum of Modern Art and Schwartz City Melbourne: 94–101.

Genovese A and McVeigh S 2015 'Nineteen eighty three: A jurisographic report on *Commonwealth v Tasmania*' *Griffith Law Review* 24/1: 68–88 DOI:10.1080/10383441.2015.1022891.

Greer G 1970 *The Female Eunuch* MacGibbon & Kee London.

Halley J 2011 'What Is Family Law?: A Genealogy Part II' *Yale Journal of Law & the Humanities* 23/2: 189–294.

Irving H, Mowbray J and Walton K eds 2010 *Julius Stone: A Study in Influence* Federation Press Annandale.

Jennings K 2010 *Trouble: Evolution of a Radical, Selected Writings 1970–2010* Black Inc. Melbourne.

Kingston B 1975 *My Wife, My Daughter and Poor Mary Ann* Thomas Nelson Melbourne.

Lahey K A 1985 '. . . Until Women Themselves Have Told All That They Have to Tell . . .' *Osgoode Hall Law Journal* 23/3: 519–541.

Lawson S 2002 *How Simone de Beauvoir died in Australia* UNSW Press Sydney.

Le Dœuff M 1991 *Hipparchia's Choice: An Essay Concerning Women, Philosophy, etc.* Trans T Selous Oxford Blackwell (first published 1989).

Levy D 2021 *Real Estate* Hamish Hamilton London.

Lorde A 2018 *The Master's Tools Will Never Dismantle the Master's House* Penguin London (first published 1984).

Luker T 2019 'Women into print: Feminist presses in Australia' in M Arrow and A Woollacott eds 2019 *Everyday Revolutions: Remaking Gender, Sexuality and Culture in 1970s Australia* ANU Press Canberra: 121–138 DOI:10.22459/ER.2019.07.

Magarey S 1986 'I Never Wanted to Be an Administrator of Anything' *Women's Studies International Forum* 9/2: 195–202.

Magarey S 2014a *Dangerous Ideas: Women's Liberation – Women's Studies – Around the World* University of Adelaide Press Adelaide.

Magarey S 2014b 'Women's Liberation Was a Movement, Not an Organisation' *Australian Feminist Studies* 29/82: 378–390 DOI:10.1080/08164649.2014.976898.

Martinis Roe A 2017 'It Was About opening the Very notion That There Was a Particular perspective' *The National: New Australian Art* Sydney viewed 21 April 2022 <www.the-national.com.au/artists/alex-martinis-roe/it-was-about-opening-the-very-notion-that-there-was-a-particular-perspective/>.

Martinis Roe A 2018 'A story from Circolo Della Rosa: The Milan Women's Bookstore Co-Operative and their practice of collective difference' in A Martinis Roe ed 2018 *To Become Two: Propositions for Feminist Collective Practice* Archive Books Berlin: 47–74.

The Milan Women's Bookstore Collective 1990 *Sexual Difference: A Theory of Social-Symbolic Practice* Trans P Cicogna and T de Lauretis Indiana University Press Bloomington (first published 1987).

Millett K 1970 *Sexual Politics* Doubleday & Company New York.

Mitchell J 1966 'Women: The Longest Revolution' *New Left Review* I/40: 11–37.

Mitchell J 1977 *Woman's Estate* Penguin Books Harmondsworth (first published 1971).

Moi T 2010 'The Adulteress Wife' *London Review of Books* 32/3 DOI:10.1093/oso/9780190608811.003.0006.

O'Donovan K 1985 *Sexual Divisions in Law* Weidenfeld & Nicolson London.

Rheinstein M 1972 *Marriage Stability, Divorce, and the Law* University of Chicago Press Chicago.

Ryan E and Conlon A 1975 *Gentle Invaders: Australian Women at Work 1788–1974* Thomas Nelson Melbourne.

Shin S 2015 *Juliet Mitchell: Looking back at Woman's Estate* Verso Books London viewed 14 April 2022 <www.versobooks.com/blogs/1836-juliet-mitchell-looking-back-at-woman-s-estate>.

Singh S 2011 'Emancipation in the heart of darkness: An interview with Juliet Mitchell' *The Platypus Review* 38: 1–6 <http://platypus1917.org/2011/08/05/emancipation-in-the-heart-of-darkness-an-interview-with-juliet-mitchell/>.

Spain D 2016 'Feminist Bookstores: Building Identity' in D Spain ed 2016 *Constructive Feminism: Women's Spaces and Women's Rights in the American City* Cornell University Press Ithaca: 84–110.

Spender D 1983 *There's Always Been a Women's Movement This Century* Pandora Press London and Boston.

Stone J 1950 *The Province and Function of Law: Law as Logic, Justice and Social Control; A Study in Jurisprudence* Maitland Sydney (first published 1946).

Stone J 1966a *Law and the Social Sciences in the Second Half Century* University of Minnesota Press Minneapolis.

Stone J 1966b *Social Dimensions of Law and Justice* Maitland Publications Sydney.

Stone J 1967 'Trends in Jurisprudence in the Second Half Century' in B D Hathaway compiler 1980 *Julius Stone: A Bio-Bibliography Including "Trends in Jurisprudence in the Second Half Century," an Unpublished Speech Presented 24 March 1967 at the University of Texas School of Law* Tarlton Law Library Austin: 17–51.

Summers A 1975 *Damned Whores and God's Police: The Colonization of Women in Australia* Penguin Books Melbourne.

Thornton M 1986 'Feminist Jurisprudence: Illusion or Reality?' *Australian Journal of Law and Society* 3: 5–29 <http://classic.austlii.edu.au/au/journals/AUJlLawSoc/1986/7.pdf>.

Thurman J 2011 'Introduction' in Beauvoir 2011: ix–xvi.

Tomlins C 2013 'Law "And", Law "In", Law "As": The Definition, Rejection and Recuperation of the Socio-Legal Enterprise' *Law in Context: A Socio-legal Journal* 29/2: 137–163.

Trubek D M 1984 'Where the Action Is: Critical Legal Studies and Empiricism' *Stanford Law Review* 36/1–2: 575–622 DOI:10.2307/1228692.

Essay 5

On Personae, 1988 (A Jurisographical Study of Theoretical Relations)

1988

This fifth instalment of *Feminist Jurisography* begins in the 1980s, and moves between Sydney, Paris, and London, to the present day. It is an account of a perennial problem that I have been following in this collection of essays: how knowledge has been transmitted, conducted, and written about to reflect male experience. This essay also extends my study of a feminist response to that problem: how a certain attitude to writing prioritises difference, and suggests by design a different way to conduct relations of knowledge. In essays Two and Three, I watched how forms of writing in the 1950s and 1960s – by women novelists, philosophers, essayists, and activists – interrupted the expectations of who was authorised to become a subject holder of knowledge. In Essay Four, I wrote about how that writing gave substance and succour to the self-formation of the 'feminist intellectual' in the early 1970s.[1] My concern in this fifth essay is to show how through the 1980s those inhabiting this new persona of 'feminist intellectual' brought 'feminist theory' into public view, as a cosmopolitan humanities tradition in its own right. It is also to make some observations about what feminist intellectuals, who inhabited a postmodern sensibility, had to say about relations of knowledge as a consequence.

Before I start the story, however, I want to be clear about my intentions, and my own practice and experience of 'the postmodern'.[2]

Beginning a chapter in the 1980s strongly suggests a way my narrative ought to run, that would be a logical point of extension in *Feminist Jurisography* with its loose chronology. I could reflect on the stories of arrival of feminists to law school faculties in the 1980s,[3] and contribute by historicising the relations between local feminist politics and domestic law that conditioned the production and transmission of their work. Alternatively, I could follow the intellectual and political inheritance of law in relation to social sciences, discussed in Essay Three, to watch how it developed into feminist socio-legal studies.[4] Instead, my concern is with 'the post' because it emerges from a tradition of humanities, rather than social sciences, which has its own feminist routes in Australia. In offering you 'a 1980s chapter' that takes this particular turn, I do

DOI: 10.4324/9780429461132-5

not intend to elevate postmodern contributions to the exclusion of others (not everyone was having a *postal* experience in the 1980s, as I have written about elsewhere).[5] Nor do I want to suggest 'the post' is past, or only epochal. Rather, I want to take the opportunity to remind how it is not. From that viewpoint, returning to 'the 1980s' is not to tie down a mode of scholarship as a formative first step in projects of contemporary political formation ('then and now') for either critical feminist or critical legal theory, to shoehorn or smooth out disputes, rivalries, or preoccupations into discreet themes or phases.[6] Those projects of capture and review can be written in multiple traditions (including the theoretical, socio-legal, historical or the biographical), and are important. Their writers may also ask how the methods they deploy are useful to tell a story. But they do not often place into view how and why methods are, in fact, the story. That is my practice, and the project of jurisography. My task is to locate and report on what techniques 'the post' offered to feminists *and* jurisprudents in the 1980s, because it was the first time both had institutional status, and, in some circles, a shared ethos in the production (and disruption) of academic writing through a new set of humanities writing practices. These different scholarly personae may not have recognised each other's distinctiveness or shared aesthetic sensibilities at the time (or necessarily since).[7] But in telling a story about their techniques and attitudes, and the nature of their rapport, I can say something about a jurisographer's relationship to her own sources, her situation, her experience, and her collaborators. This allows me, in other words, to give a partial account of how I enter the story myself.

For those that haven't been reading *Feminist Jurisography* in any particular order, or for those joining me for the first time now, I introduced the persona of jurisographer, and activity of writing jurisography in Essay One.[8] I explained in that earlier essay how and why jurisography, as an invented practice, belongs to the conduct of life scholarly tradition. A brief digression on how that tradition was presented in the 1980s is relevant here, to make the subject matter of this fifth essay clearer.

As part of his *History of Sexuality* project, the French postmodern philosopher and historian Michel Foucault wrote explicitly about conducts of scholarly life, and a scholar's self-awareness of the responsibility they took for their 'arts of existence'.[9] As Foucault wrote in *The Use of Pleasure* (1984), a scholar must 'problematise' what they do in the conditions 'of the world in which they live'.[10] This writerly project involved a task of making 'life into an *oeuvre* that carries certain aesthetic values and meets certain stylistic criteria'.[11] Foucault argued that these kinds of activities required an engagement with 'practical' texts, which offer opinions and advice, 'designed to be read, learned, reflected upon, and tested out', adding that such texts 'serve as functional devices that would enable individuals to question their own conduct, to watch over and give shape to it, and to shape themselves as ethical subjects'.[12] It is important at this juncture to remind that in Essay One I examined closely Simone de Beauvoir's original iteration of these 'arts of existence'. Her book *The Second Sex*

(1949) radically altered the trajectory of the tradition of scholarly conduct, by directly demonstrating how these arts were relational, that the persona of the scholar and her experience of writing were not distinct from each other. Her work therefore not only predates *The Use of Pleasure* (1984), but can be read as a 'practical text' for those that followed. What interests me as a question for the 1980s is what such an inheritance inferred, if you happened to be a feminist who had already learned something of Beauvoir's 'stylistic criteria' before you encountered Foucault, his *The Use of Pleasure*, and the critical oeuvre that he and other fellow travellers inspired.

The subject of my study is *The Pirate's Fiancée: Feminism, reading, postmodernism* (1988a). *The Pirate's Fiancée* is a collection of essays written over a ten-year period by Meaghan Morris, the Australian feminist, critic, and interlocutor/translator of Foucault (among others). As a feminist intellectual and as a postmodern critic, Morris' work enables close examination of how those personae were not always distinct by the late 1980s. Her work also makes visible what a feminist intellectual had to say about how knowledge remained sexed, but why a relationship between feminist knowledge and other disciplinary know-how might not play out to an inevitable or predictable conclusion by 1988.

'Study' as a genre has a precise meaning in this context. In certain traditions, as the Italian writer and literary theorist Italo Calvino explained in 1980, to write 'a study' does not always mean presenting a focused case for extrapolation, or providing a third-person literary analysis. A study can be, instead, a public activity of rhetorical engagement with another's writing, and 'phenomenological' (in the sense I described examined in Essay One).[13] A study of this kind involves exemplification, through close reading of a chosen text, of experience of political and intellectual provocations, relationships, and disputes in time and place.[14] A study, in these traditions, is a genre that does double duty, and operates as a training exercise, in the language I have been using in this book.[15] How I represent and organise my own work for you, in other words, is not separate from the act of reading, and re-presenting, the work of those I follow.[16]

Choosing *The Pirate's Fiancée* for my study is therefore important for *Feminist Jurisography*, as it gives me a direct line of sight to an ethos of intellectual life that I directly inherit as an Australian feminist scholar. Morris writes with a precise focus on the formation of feminist personae, in a way that orients and connects with my own work.[17] My choice is personal, as I read *The Pirate's Fiancée* for the first time in the mid-1990s, when it guided me through writing my first article. I also met Morris herself, as she was then a scholar at my University, and she generously discussed her text, and some of the circumstances of its production, to help me undertake my own.[18] I hope to show in what follows some of the debates and tensions of intellectual life, circa 1988, and why naming a practice for yourself (such as jurisography) is, in its own way, an acknowledgment of the continuing relevance of *The Pirate's Fiancée* as a 'practical text' concerned with 'analysing a particular discourse in its self-determination'.[19]

Feral Publishers

Meaghan Morris came of age intellectually and politically in Sydney, in the early 1970s. She was a student of French and English at Sydney University; but, as was the case for many of her contemporaries, the curriculum and training offered inside the University at that time was not entirely accommodating of her experience, nor inspirational as regards her political interests.[20] Morris became involved in the Sydney milieu of 'self-taught intellectuals'.[21] She also, importantly, became a feminist. Through her involvement in bohemian intellectual culture idiosyncratic to inner city Sydney, where the personnel of Women's Liberation, The Sydney Push, academics, and film critics could meet together socially (if not always agreeing politically), Morris encountered imported French, but also English and American, critical texts.[22] Throughout the 1970s, books and pamphlets by Juliet Mitchell, Jacques Lacan, Louis Althusser, and early translations of Michel Foucault (notably *Discipline and Punish* (1977))[23] were debated in reading groups, largely outside the university, by men and women engaged in the politics of the antipsychiatry, prison reform, and gay and women's liberation movements. Through her involvement in these groups, Meaghan Morris met Paul Foss.[24] Together, they contributed translations of French texts to *Gay Liberation Press*, a small independent journal that had started in 1973. By 1976 it had changed its name to *Working Papers in Sex, Science and Culture*. Later it was simply called *WP*. The *WP* collective included philosophers, art and film critics, and feminists.[25] The first two issues dealt 'primarily with psychoanalysis and Marxism', focussing on local debates about the 'political utility' of psychoanalysis to disturb the ownership of knowledge's practices. Juliet Mitchell's book *Psychoanalysis and Feminism* (1974) was a key text.[26] In 1976, Morris travelled to University of Paris 8, Vincennes (a 'major centre of psychoanalytic theory')[27] on a French Government scholarship. She took Mitchell's book with her, and 'somewhat paradoxically' gave seminars on *Psychoanalysis and Feminism* 'to a French audience who had had little previous contact with non-French applications of psychoanalysis'.[28] She attended lectures by Deleuze, Lacan, Foucault, and Barthes.[29] She became involved in the feminist scene and disturbances surrounding the Psychanalyse et Politique (Psych et Po) group in Paris, and encountered the work of Michèle Le Dœuff and Luce Irigaray.[30]

In 1978, Morris returned to Sydney. She began work as a film critic for major Australian broadsheets, and continued to work with her friends in the *WP* collective.[31] Around that time, the collective decided to employ a different 'editorial strategy'.[32] On a minimal budget, they created an imprint, Feral Publications. The ambition of Feral Publications was to place Continental theory and political events (French, but also Italian)[33] into dialogue with radical politics of opposition in Sydney.[34] The collective set out to produce 'monographs, translations and collected essays', released 'on an irregular basis', to explore 'the analysis of the functioning of languages and discourses . . . in inventing political strategies . . . and modes of resistance to the action of power through and upon sexuality'.[35] The first production of Feral Publications was *Language, Sexuality and Subversion* (1978), edited by Meaghan Morris with her friend Paul Foss. The second was *Michel Foucault: Power, Truth, Strategy* (1979), edited by Morris with the philosopher Paul Patton (who had also spent time as student in Paris, in the period after 1968).[36] *Language, Sexuality & Subversion* (1978) included translations of essays by Jean Baudrillard, Gilles Deleuze, and Felix Guattari, and significantly, Luce Irigaray's 'That Sex Which Is Not One' (1977).[37] *Power, Truth, Strategy* (1979) imported and translated some of Foucault's later essays and interviews, including 'Truth and Power'.[38] Interposed with these European texts were photographic, theoretical, and experimental essays by Australian scholars and intellectuals.

What I want to emphasise are the forms of collaboration and writing inherent to the Feral Publishers in the publication of these guides. Morris worked with others in her milieu (men and women) as a commitment of intellectual life. This extended from the practical production of dossiers with Paul Foss or Paul Patton in the late 1970s to the opening up of public conversations through those texts (conversations that were often deliberately challenging) to 'foster radical thought' into the 1980s.[39] These styles of collaboration, upfront and open as a strategy (Morris, Foss, and Patton were not 'editors' in the way we might usually understand it), were also acts of reimagination, in the sense I have been working with and described in Essay One.[40] Morris and the members of the Feral Publications collective were interlocutors with their chosen authors and their readers in terms of textual selection, translation, arrangement, and the commission of new Australian work explicitly presented as on equal terms. The form of their work took a rhetorical stance that tested how 'writing is the transformational act',[41] and showed how that that was not done alone.

The influence of Feral Publications travels in many directions.[42] To give a personal example, my friend the jurisprudent Peter Rush took *Language, Sexuality and Subversion* (1978) with him from Sydney to Cambridge in 1984, when he began both his postgraduate studies and his involvement with UK critical legal studies.[43] A significant destination, in Australia, was to the new cultural studies, and feminist (later gender) studies programs at Universities. Morris' contributions and experience are rightly often located at the juncture between these new disciplines. In Australia, first participants in these programs – and their direct descendants – have recorded disciplinary biographies of both cultural studies and feminist studies. The organising conceit of these accounts is that both possessed a commitment to 'radical theoretical writing',[44] and a distinctive intellectual hybridity in their relations with cosmopolitan thought, and with each other.[45] Some scholars (feminists) have argued that who made the first move also requires acknowledgment.[46] They have traced how critical studies was indelibly influenced by local feminism, because it was feminist practitioners who had already 'managed to reframe French theory', for local markets, but also to 'export those French-Australian ideas to an Anglo-American audience'.[47] This was not isolated to the feminist intellectuals who resided between the intersection of feminist theory and cultural studies. Morris shared a sensibility and skills with many of her feminist friends in Australia. Together, they had recognised the usefulness and charge of a whole range of cosmopolitan thinking for original articulations of how to join thought and action, in multiple disciplines, and brought 'feminist theory' into public view as an intellectual tradition in its own right.[48] I have been following that story in my fourth essay in this collection too.[49] For the purposes of this fifth essay, what is important to underscore is simply that Foucault did not arrive in Sydney by himself, or graft[50] onto the Australian fabric of humanities unaided by feminist intellectuals.[51] One consequence was that, by the 1980s, it was possible for feminists to discuss relations of knowledge (between women and men, and between feminists and orthodox disciplinary roles) as not only conducted in the experiential or empirical realms, but also figuratively, and as relations of theory.

Feminist Intellectuals

Theoretical relations, and how to write about them, is exactly what I wish to study in *The Pirate's Fiancée*. I want to make three observations about Morris' exemplification of the persona and situation of the feminist intellectual, circa 1988, before showing how they were instantiated in her writing.

My first observation is about what kind of institutional office Morris and her collaborators (both feminists and critics) inhabited. They were not 'of the university' in the sense we might understand theoretical workers now. In 1988, Morris noted she wrote '*for*' if not 'from' an academic context, for a 'mixed' public 'to be encountered at events organised on the thematic or political, rather than purely professional, principles'.[52] This was a description of Foucault's 'specific intellectual', a persona which Morris acknowledged 'has been particularly useful both in allowing institutional struggles to occupy a field of "everyday life" rather than being relegated to an "ivory tower" divorced from a "real world"'.[53]

In her introduction to the *The Pirate's Fiancée*, Morris wrote:

> 'One of the most important consequences of the notion of the "specific intellectual" is . . . to begin to accept . . . that this movement can run the other way: academic theorization can and should transform its practices by learning from the experiences, the concepts, and the methodologies developed by people in broader social and political movements'.[54]

Morris was, however, cautious about how scholars learned 'the vernacular'.[55] By 1988, it was certainly true that noticing there was a 'real world' beyond the university gate was not a political activity limited to feminists. But it was also true that joining everyday experience to practises of knowledge was, by then, a public duty acknowledged as *specific* to intellectuals who also happened to be feminists. Although '[f]eminism has both profited from, and helped to produce, this kind of reconceptualization of academic politics',[56] Morris argued, it was nevertheless 'the relationship between feminist theory and the various women's movements [that have] operated historically in this two-way sense'.[57]

My second observation is about the conduct of feminist knowledge. By 1988, the fact that the door of the university was ajar to a cohort of feminist intellectuals for the first time brought a new obligation to care for 'feminist knowledge' itself. There were two foci in work that undertook that care (supported by publishers savvy enough to supply a new market when they saw one).[58] Both shaped *The Pirate's Fiancée*. One was outward facing: in relation to feminists working in the law, for an example, the task was explaining to (a mostly male) Academy exactly how knowledge was sexed, as well as how feminist knowledge was a recognisable entity.[59] This writing was both pedagogical and vigilant, but either way an act of assertion that required technical precision.[60] The other focus runs underneath and is inward facing, toward how a feminist writer should negotiate that relationship between social experience and the institutionalisation of her thought, circa 1988.

There is of course a central proposition that links these foci together, that had a drive and charge of its own by 1988. This proposition, radically staged by Beauvoir in *The Second Sex* in 1949, and directly addressed by many Australian feminist intellectuals in 1988,[61] was that 'knowledges of *human* social, personal and linguistic relations, while they may be about men *and* women, represent the perspectives and interests of only one sex [. . .]'.[62] When woman began writing herself into public view and into authority, she challenged those perspectives and interests. That activity of writing did not, however, give her a free pass to political complacency, or self-satisfied certainty that her ways of doing were above reproach, or set in stone. She had to reimagine these things for herself, as an act of her own agency. Beauvoir demonstrated how that kind of 'operative philosophy' (as the French philosopher Michèle Le Dœuff described in her own iteration, 1979)[63] required the writer to constantly watch how the targets of her questions changed because of her own situation, and to respond and adapt her projects to their times accordingly.[64] The Australian feminist philosopher (and member of the Feral Press Collective) Elizabeth (EA) Grosz described the projects of 1988 as taking up this tradition with renewed force, and self-consciousness, because it was '[o]nly in the late 1980s' that 'feminists acquired a perspective from which to assess traditional knowledges from the point of view of their capacity to accommodate women's particularity'.[65] Those methods of assessment could not, she and others argued, replicate either patriarchal know-how, or the liberation ethos that preceded, and enabled, their own. The technical work for feminist intellectuals was to problematise 'the unsettling *and* subversive place of feminism *within* knowledge' and to be wary of how feminist knowledge, once it started to reside literally in the offices of law or state or academies, should guard against 'effacing its own masculine . . . orientations'.[66] To put that another way, as historian Ann Curthoys did in her 2000 reflection on this inevitable development, 'feminism was the site of the reinvention of the category "woman" in the 1970s, and then of its deconstruction in the 1980s and 1990s'.[67] By the late 1980s, that deconstruction took all sorts of forms, and not only in and for Australia.[68] The American scholar Judith Butler has described these diverse projects (including their own groundbreaking queer/feminist text *Gender Trouble* (1990))[69] as the result of feminist intellectuals 'bringing critical attention to bear on [feminisms'] premises in an effort to become more clear about what [they] mean . . . and to negotiate conflicting interpretations'[70] of sexuality, gender, race, ethnicity, class, and role. Feminist texts that worried about these problems were also attached to place, 'never fully distinct'[71] from a specific engagement in everyday life (as Butler, a scholar of Beauvoir, has made clear).[72]

This leads to my last observation, about the situated obligations of feminist intellectuals. In Australia, the agency and privilege attached to inventing and inhabiting institutional personae in the 1980s was more often than not the experience of non-Indigenous scholars, but it came with distinctive duties to know that their place belonged to someone else. Morris, alongside some of her contemporaries, worried aloud about how to address those responsibilities in her work.[73] The German-Australian feminist scholar of multiculturalism and diaspora, Sneja Gunew, for example, argued in the introduction to one of the many publications that came out around 1988 (*Feminist Knowledge: Critique and Construct*)[74] that the contributors were 'conscious that the absence of accounts from Aboriginal women signifies glaringly our own lack'.[75] It is without question that the training in how to recalibrate intellectual duties in a place like Australia was given tirelessly by Aboriginal knowledge holders[76] (a point made forcefully and correctly by the Goenpul Quandamooka feminist and scholar Aileen Moreton-Robinson, later, in her 2000 text *Talkin' up to the white woman*).[77] But it is notable the extent, even by 1988, that re-forming difficult relations between knowledges were practices integral and familiar to non-Indigenous Australian feminists, able to be drawn from within their own repertoires, if they cared to look (as Moreton-Robinson has also noted).[78] Significantly, 1988 was the Bicentenary of British Imperial Invasion of Gadigal country on which Sydney was built. It was marked by Indigenous Australians in acts of sovereign assertion, and demand for Makarrata, or treaty, with the Australian State. It was marked by the State in a series of wilfully deaf, and lurid, replications of the original violence. These endorsed 'celebrations' of 'settlement' (and an uncompromisingly unsophisticated idea of what 'Australia' was) were openly debated and critiqued.[79] Some (but certainly not all) feminist texts were aware of the need to think hard about 'tactics for undermining any versions of complacent postcolonialism'.[80]

Let me be clear: I am not making this observation to tick a box, or suggest that feminist intellectuals had the answers, in 1988, or today. Formation of lawful relations in Australia, between Indigenous and non-Indigenous knowledge, and between Indigenous and non-Indigenous feminists, is unfinished and continual work, and the duties for its address require constant attention. But I am underscoring a point about the ways in which Western feminist traditions of practice, predicated on the relational, operated in Australia in 1988. These texts of the 1980s do not respond directly to questions asked of the 2020s. But they do give guidance (if like me, you are seeking what in your own traditions of knowledge might be sufficient to the task of meeting well). This guidance is both technical and ethical: about how to develop capability for clear sighted acknowledgment of one's situation, to understand protocols for engagement between knowledges, and to take seriously the responsibilities that accrue with recently acquired authority. That training is useful now as it was then. *The Pirate's Fiancée*, in my study, is of course a working example of such a feminist guidebook; and I turn now to examine exactly how Morris produced, and spoke in, the text.

Pirates' Fiancées

The Pirate's Fiancée: Feminism, reading, postmodernism was published by Verso in 1988 as part of its 'Questions for Feminism' series.[81] The series introduced itself as aiming 'to address, in a lively way and on an international basis, the wide range of political and theoretical questions facing feminism'.[82] *The Pirate's Fiancée* provided the opportunity to collect together Morris' work over the previous decade, recognising the significance of its contribution to that international project. It included essays written for the Feral Publications, her film criticism for newspapers, and pedagogical exercises from her part-time teaching roles. In any capacity, the task of writing across diverse outlets, and to deadline, in her day jobs, had often been 'arduous'.[83] But it also had its personal pleasures, because of what these essays represented as exercises for her: '[t]he activity of thinking and writing about theories that might inform my practice'.[84] Most of the essays, Morris noted in her Introduction, were written for 'fun'. 'Fun' is not innocuous. Rather, it is a description for her motivations, as well as used to sting the ponderous presentations of theoretical workers who mistook arts of lightness, humour, and play for lack of intellectual rigour and hard work. 'Fun', Morris wrote, 'of course, can incorporate any number of reasons for writing something – enthusiasm, amusement, admiration, a sense of a challenge to learn, but also concern, irritation, anxiety, or bemusement, a desire to confront something bothersome'.[85] (I can relate).

Each of the essays chosen for *The Pirate's Fiancée* skewed from some or all of these motivations. The texts that stage her practices included: Mary Daly's radical separatist *Gyn/ecolgy*; the film *Crocodile Dundee*; shopping centres; the philosophy of Michèle Le Dœuff, Jean-François Lyotard, Michel Foucault, and Luce Irigaray; the photographs of Lynn Silverman, the criticism of Susan Sontag, the feminine writing of Hélène Cixous, and always Australia, and how its complex intellectual and cultural experiences could be understood, represented, and challenged. For students of academic feminism (the discipline in which people like me, who started university coincidentally in 1988, could in fact be trained) the essays showed something else too. That was the working out, on the page, of how to speak as and for yourself. 'Most of these essays in this volume', as

Morris explained, 'were written as an effort to produce a speaking-position in a particular political, critical and publishing context'.[86] That self-fashioning of a rhetorical voice involved two key tasks. One was to describe the debates, intent and operation of contemporary 'critical speaking' that 'tends to deny *all* critics a place from which to speak or the possibility of something to say'.[87] The other was to respond directly 'to work which is explicitly concerned with the positioning of women, and with thinking about subjectivity, modes of address, and reference, in particular historical contexts'.[88] Morris' chief achievement in *The Pirate's Fiancée* is showing how feminist knowledge operates, unapologetically, in both tasks. As she argued,

> 'In none of these essays . . . is the production of a speaking-position understood as a matter of inventing a 'personal voice' for '<u>me</u>' . . . On the contrary, I think that producing a 'position' is a problem of rhetoric, of developing enunciative strategies (or ways of 'play acting'). . . precisely in relation to the . . . conventions that make speaking difficult or impossible for <u>women</u>'.[89]

In that vein, *The Pirate's Fiancée* is a book of strategy to locate a feminist speaking position for the author, and a relationship advice guide to other feminists seeking that 'elusive *reference-point*'[90] in their own work. Importantly, for jurisographers-to-be, that advice had a lot to do with writing. In *The Pirate's Fiancée*, a feminist speaking position is 'a recognizable genre in criticism'.[91] Through her own writing Morris invents strategies to speak *within* texts of contemporary theory and knowledge, but also *about* them, as a response to a moving target.

In redescribing these strategies, it helps to remember that Morris is a reader, translator, and interlocutor of the work of Michèle Le Dœuff, who has been making guest appearances throughout all of my own essays. Morris argued that Le Dœuff had written 'one of the few feminist commentaries on *The Second Sex* to try to come to grips with that work as a productive political text, rather than an emanation from its author'.[92] Le Deouff's 'operative reasoning' is the subject of an essay of its own in *The Pirate's Fiancée* (first published in 1981/1982), and I think sits in dialogue with Morris's own activities, or at least the ones that speak most clearly to me. Like Beauvoir, Morris writes, '[Le Dœuff draws] attention to the importance of asking how philosophical [or other] discourses can *work* in particular contexts, rather than debating their (imagined) intrinsic *worth*'.[93] This activity of 'the specific intellectual' requires resisting the 'fixing' of a position, particularly a feminist one, such as ' "it's phallogocentric" '.[94] That kind of rigidity 'repeats the structure of . . . philosophical (and psychoanalytical) propositions'[95] that are in fact the subject of challenge. That should be of concern to any scholar, she argues (this is not a book able to relegated to 'the women's section'); but particularly for women inhabiting all kinds of new intellectual personae who are interested in changing relations of discourse and knowledge through figuring out 'how to work as a feminist in philosophy, and how to utilize philosophy as a feminist'.[96] What these personae need to watch closely, the dialogue between Morris and Le Dœuff shows, are the terms of the give and take, the 'political (and rhetorical) flexibility' that enables 'feminist interventions in different institutional and discursive contexts'[97] to 'modify' the starting point by which either feminism (or the other party in the relationship) speaks. Their combined advice for feminists entering into productive theoretical relations with their disciplines by the 1980s (be it philosophy, postmodern theory, or for this reader, jurisprudence) 'disengages from the debate which assumes that some stable relationship' is in fact desirable between feminist and other knowledges in the first place; or, that it needs to be 'fixed as contestation *or* cooperation, [or] refusal'.[98]

Noticing how that activity was conducted as a writing aesthetic is important to my study. Women writing about relations to knowledge (and knowledge as sexed) is not new. As I have discussed elsewhere, before the 1970s and 1980s, such writing did not assume orthodox scholastic forms or deploy expected analytical styles.[99] Techniques of reintroduction, parody, allegory, doubling, and personification became important to women inventing personae to do their work, long before the linguistic turn.[100] But the 'textual strategies'[101] that became available *because* scholars like Meaghan Morris joined their traditions to postmodern theory extended a feminist repertoire to figuration, 'quotation, revision, mimicry . . . discourse *piracy*'.[102] By 1988, Morris could place the elusive contentions and pulls of the 'real world' (the *de jure* relations of men and women as matters of status and of intimacy), and the relationship problems that kept recurring in scholarly texts between feminist and other knowledges, onto an imaginary plane, to see them all the clearer. This did not infer writing a fictive or metaphorical account of sexed relations between men or women. The 'feminist imaginary' (as the Australian philosopher Moira Gatens explains in *Imaginary Bodies*, essays she wrote between 1983 and 1994, which I greatly admire) refers instead to a set of technical propositions. These are the 'images and symbols . . . through which we make sense of social bodies' to 'determine, in part, their value, their status, and what will be deemed their appropriate treatment'.[103]

Morris' recurring figure – the Pirate's Fiancée – made her first appearance in an essay for Feral Publications' *Michel Foucault: Power, Truth, Strategy* (1979). Morris' epigraph to that essay was 'Feminists and Philosophers, or maybe tonight it'll happen',[104] and the essay begins with a direct intervention, that feels as if the reader has been pulled aside at a party to get some advice before they get carried away. 'I would like to make a few slanted suggestions about the possible value of Foucault's work to feminists who might be reading it',[105] Morris confides. She explores the benefits of Foucault's work (a refusal of a unitary experience, concern with embodiment, disturbance of knowledge's power over its subjects). But she is adamant too that those qualities, or ways of doing, are not lacking in many forms of feminist disciplinary engagement already. On paper, 'Foucault and Feminism' seem a good match, able to conduct a dalliance that is neither clandestine, nor submissive. But Morris also sounds a word of caution, with her tongue in cheek. It is not that feminists should be sceptical of any promises to becoming committed to 'post-modern theory' as proffered by Foucault (or Derrida and Lacan) just 'because [it] is all too cocky for words'.[106] Foucault is a 'profoundly androcentric writer', Morris writes, and 'any feminists drawn in to sending Love Letters to Foucault would be in no danger of reciprocation [as his] work is not the work of a ladies' man'.[107] What matters, instead, Morris advises feminist readers, is that you go into this kind of knowledge relationship with your eyes open, and that you set the terms for an unconventional engagement yourself, for the benefit of all parties.

Fiancées and wives make all kinds of clichéd and discomfiting appearances in philosophical discourse. Some feminist scholars have chosen to rewrite these roles rather than 'confine [them] to the museum of dead terms'.[108] Toward the end of her book *The Sex of Knowing* (2003), Michèle Le Dœuff, for example, addresses how woman has been cast (and cast-off)[109] as Cynical spouse (Hypatia), eroticised muse (Heloise), rejected fiancée, and, of course, as longsuffering cosmopolitan lover (the whole scholarly obsession with the embodiment of what was going on in the relationship of Beauvoir and Sartre, rather than reading what Beauvoir actually did to transform relations of knowledge in her work). Le Dœuff shares an anecdote about why these figures are not only bothersome but representative of the whole problem that requires feminists' 'constant vigilance'. She tells us that after *Hipparchia's Choice* (1991), her second book, was published:

> '[the philosopher] Gilles Deleuze wrote to tell me he hoped I would at some point write about the figure of the fiancée in Kierkegaard's writing. I confess I saw no urgent reason to comment upon this personage, a young girl courted by a Pygmalion who, by abandoning, subtly completes the process of endowing her with a mind'.[110]

Le Dœuff questions what is assumed in this (intriguing) exchange, that 'when a woman undertakes an intellectual emancipation that is not a separation, society judges her initiative more severely that it does the devious strategy of Kierkegaard's [male] fiancé, who seduces only to abandon'.[111] From that perspective, the rejected figure of (female) fiancée is indeed of great interest to Le Dœuff in order to respond from within the imaginary realm, to Deleuze's assumptions:

> 'And what next? . . . The figure of the rejected fiancée suggests that we are dependent on the other sex for freedom we may obtain, and that freedom comes from separation from them . . . [but that] denies a woman's capacity to take the initiative for establishing even the ever-so-slight distance that emancipation implies'.[112]

Taking that 'initiative', Le Dœuff suggests, requires a scholar to recast relations of knowledge in their work as conducts of amity and tolerance, to inhabit different kinds of personae and play with different kinds of figuration, as 'every freedom gained by the other opens a space . . . for a dialogue that has at last become necessary'.[113]

Morris' figure of the fiancée certainly rises to the challenge. *The Pirate's Fiancée* is the name of a film made in 1969 by the French-Argentinian writer director Nelly Kaplan, shown at the 1970 Women's Film festival in Sydney. 'It made a profound impression on many women in the audience', Morris recalls, 'and I have never forgotten it'.[114] The plot was a fable. Kaplan's fiancée has no betrothed in sight. She lives alone, on the edge of a village, 'with her goat, and her bit of high tech: a tape recorder' and 'she makes her rent' from men, and from cleaning. The villagers 'spurn her and fear her because of her sharp, insolent tongue'. But in the confines of her house, she secretly records the confidences men share with her. She saves their money, and 'has saved their words'. One day she leaves, and as she 'sets off down the road' the villagers listen to 'not the voice of a curious girl, but [their] own most intimate secrets and confessions, playing loudly, in public, for all to hear'.[115]

Morris reads the film against other pirate's fiancée fables to show exactly what Kaplan turns around, and makes available to others. In Bertold Brecht's *The Threepenny Opera*, the song 'Pirate Jenny' is 'a cleaning woman's dream of being recognised as a pirate queen, possessing a secret knowledge that will give her the power to humiliate and destroy'. The song, Morris notes, was embraced 'enthusiastically in the uncompromising ambience of the early women's movement . . . as an allegory of vengeance and liberation'. What Morris reminds, however, is that Pirate Jenny's song was only ever 'an embedded fiction of a fantasy', sung by the character on the eve of her marriage to the protagonist, MacHeath. In Kaplan's version, 'a fable of political action' becomes 'a political act of transforming fables'.[116] Morris' own practices of criticism and reading (of the film and the song) do something else again, to reorder relations figuratively (between feminists and Foucault, and other male theorists), on her own terms:

> 'the fiancée doesn't dream of waiting for her hero to arrive on stage in a moment of revolutionary rapture. She makes do herself by acting critically upon her everyday conditions of existence – to transform her position within them . . . It is [the] everyday conduct [of male protagonists] that is now framed as "play-acting" – and after the performance there can't be any more of it in quite the same old way.'[117]

Postmodern Jurisprudents

I realise some readers of this study must be waiting to get 'to the law bit'. So, to examine how feminist intellectuals (and pirate's fiancées) showed ways to set terms of engagement with jurisprudence in postmodern times, I need to introduce some legal writing.

By the early 1980s, some jurisprudents working at the edges of the university started to take up the office of critic in order to inhabit in new ways the 'law in relation' question (that I have been following in these essays).[118] The generation that preceded them, the post-war legal scholars of the 1950s and 1960s, had pioneered systematised empirical and Social Science techniques to open jurisprudence to the complexities of lived experiences of law. But as discussed in earlier essays, these methods perpetuated the place of 'law' as a dominant partner in consciously modern cross-disciplinary projects, which carried consequences (mostly careless rather than intentional), such as a failure to see and hear the specificity of law's subjects.[119] Legal Critics, on the other hand, saw themselves, and their relationship to legal knowledge in the 1980s, very differently. The critics wrote about jurisprudential practices in dialogue with postmodernist thought, and challenged the very idea of a totalising experience or representation of human life and knowledge, including 'law' itself. This differently conceived relationship to theoretical knowledge and expertise outside of law's domain was accompanied by political conviction, and with aesthetic swagger. A critical legal scholar could start, for example, to interrogate law as literature and literature as law. They could argue that the texts of jurisprudence were not limited to what was produced by and for the legal enterprise, and to make claims about why that might have significant repercussions for the representation of justice.[120]

My chosen example of these innovations in genre, style, and attitude is *Postmodern Jurisprudence: The Law of Text in the Texts of Law* (1991), by Costas Douzinas, Ronnie Warrington, and Shaun McVeigh.[121] Douzinas, Warrington, and McVeigh were key provocateurs in the critical legal studies movement in the UK from the 1980s, and the text (although not often mentioned now) was part of the arrival of the 'law and humanities' movement.[122] *Postmodern Jurisprudence* showed what happened to jurisprudence writing in England, in the time just after Lyotard's *The Postmodern Condition: A Report on Knowledge* (1979) was translated, and became accessible to an Anglophone, British intellectual world.[123] Part satire and part critical and textual analysis, the book is intended to be 'an exploration of the ethics and politics of reading the law in an age of uncertainty'.[124] Just as Lyotard asks what work the orthodox account of Enlightenment truth and justice does for the postmodern project, Douzinas et al do not set out to 'trash' orthodox jurisprudence as other scholars with whom they engage, such as the US critical legal studies scholar Stanley Fish, might have suggested at this same time.[125] Instead, they are very clear that jurisprudence as a scholarly practice already has certain duties, that preconfigure the arrival of 'the post'. Orthodox jurisprudence, they remind us, 'sets itself the task of determining what is proper to law. . . . Its method is to apply legal procedures to the law itself'.[126] This includes 'giving evidence of its truth' in order to 'narrate its story',[127] and 'construct[ing] theories that portray the law as a coherent body of rules and principles, or of intentions and expressions of a sovereign will'.[128] This is because the 'predominant strategy' of jurisprudence 'is to try and weave the legal texts into a single, seamless veil in which authorised and symmetrical patterns are endlessly produced, circulated and repeated'.[129] The task or duty of the jurisprudent taking up the post is to 'distrust all attempts to create large-scale, totalising theories in order to explain social phenomena'.[130]

This involves particular practices to 'destabilise the very conception' that there is a coherent certainty in what stories or narrative events can be heard and told by Law. This means a postmodern practice of jurisprudence:

> 'tells small scale and provisional open stories about our lives and the world. A sensitivity to different forms of speaking and writing; an attention to the repressed and opposed dialects and idioms that are always within but apparently excluded from complex texts; an intention to disrupt apparently closed systems and memoires of meaning'.[131]

Taking up the post for Douzinas et al is then a matter of 'tactics' that can be as useful to the reading (and writing) of texts of jurisprudence as they can to those of philosophy. These tactics include, importantly (as the subtitle might give away), thinking carefully about the text of law in relation, or dialogic encounter, with the law of text; and that part of that encounter is to bring to the notice of the readership the fine-grained work that Lyotard, and Derrida in particular, offers to scholars of law, as well as to legal subjects. The project is not to reinscribe totality of another kind – of a critical legal studies yet to come, as a rival orthodoxy. Instead, the book as a whole shows what the jurisprudent can do with 'the post' as a series of techniques, attitudes, styles, and genres – as a practice to be applied – in order to question traditions of telling and experiencing law (as judgment, as doctrine, or as a relation of social or political justice).

I bought my copy of *Postmodern Jurisprudence* in 1994, in a book store in Fremantle, on summer holidays. I was 24, and had recently started my PhD thesis in Sydney. My copy is riddled with marginalia, Post-It notes, and regrettable pink highlighting. I sought in my PhD project to explain what happened when feminist activism and experience met legal doctrine, and was writing about criminal cases in Sydney, and the Sydney Women's Liberation Movement. But what motivated me was figuring out how to be *interdisciplinary:* how to think with narrative theory to write 'a feminist legal history' of a very particular kind. I was intensely interested in 'the postmodern'. We postgraduate Humanities students at the University of Technology, Sydney thought of 'the post' as a set of tools to 'apply' to our projects. This perhaps was not a surprise, as our supervisors and other mentors at the Faculty at the time included Ann Curthoys, and, as I have already disclosed, Meaghan Morris herself. Deciding not to undertake this project in a law school was a particular choice.[132] My ambition was to use whatever techniques were available to destabilise 'law' and 'history' as totalising projects that had excluded feminist knowledge. I also felt opportunities to address the relations between my disciplines ('the slippage' as I wrote in the margins of my copy of *Postmodern Jurisprudence*) were not of scholarly interest to most academics in Australian law schools in the very early 1990s (or so I felt, or knew, at the time). So finding this book was exciting. It offered a conversation about practices of jurisprudence that made sense to my own concerns and experiences (although of course I knew that these experiences were probably – in every sense – a world away from those of the book's authors).

Returning to *Postmodern Jurisprudence* for this study, two interrelated things struck me. The first was how much I had defaced the book, but also that my marginalia was in fact a diary of an assertion of my own practices in the mid-1990s. These are not particularly illuminating, but a sign of youthful enthusiasm and a slingshot approach to reading. (For example, page 28: 'useful: . . . how this intersects with feminist theory', or, 'My stuff: two levels of the unrepresented: one which identifies the other: woman becomes the category'). The second thing that seemed very clear now, and it wasn't then, was that I was making these connections, doing my *work*, because the book itself is almost silent as regards its own engagements and conversation with feminist experiences of writing and thinking 'the post' (for jurisprudence, or anywhere else) that were available. Although Douzinas et al were clear that 'the post' did not replace 'one set of certainties with another'[133] and that this could be used to reanimate the tasks of jurisprudence, the question of how jurisprudence created binaries based on sex, and how certainties of (male) voice and authorship were deployed or critiqued in creating binaries, was not addressed.

Interestingly, for Douzinas et al, feminist practise of politics and thinking (alongside marginalised Others) could be acknowledged, in one sense. As they wrote:

> 'Feminist critiques of education were the first to argue that the logic of the law reproduces a narrow, partial, patriarchal and patrial view of the world. Feminism questions the "reason" of the law'.[134]

These practices, however, remained separate but parallel to the work of postal jurisprudence. As the authors explained:

> 'This interrogation of the reasons of reasons, whether from a feminist, ethnic, or postmodernist perspective, is part of a common enterprise to enable the voice of the other, the "unpresentable" not so much to speak (protests have been made) as to be acted upon'.[135]

Despite the concessions and faint praise, the job for a postmodern jurisprudent was understood as robustly distinct to that of a feminist-at-law undertaking her version of critique. For the postmodern jurisprudents of *Postmodern Jurisprudence*, only one figurative relation was in play. As they wrote, father to son, and as *men of action*, '[o]ur readings of the law of our fathers are designed to legitimate the Oedipal overthrowing that these critiques commence'.[136]

My point, for this study, is that guides such as *The Pirate's Fiancée* had taught me ways to read books like *Postmodern Jurisprudence*. Instead of feeling outside or critical of Douzinas' project, and I suppose I could have, I was, as my notes at the time reminded, far more interested in what he and his colleagues made available: a particular form and style of doing jurisprudence that was clearly in theoretical relationship with feminist thought of the times (whether *Postmodern Jurisprudence* acknowledged that or not). The work of Morris, and other feminist intellectuals, had shown with wit, aesthetic skill, and intellectual rigour the characteristics of agency and complicity within feminist theory circa 1988, that enabled the formation of all kinds of relationships and collaborations, and through language as action. These guides showed how to observe the differences between scholarly relations lived in the everyday (between men and women, and also between feminists) which were often based on alliance, and the theoretical sublimation of feminist intellectual innovation, that allowed feminist expertise in relating sites and experience of knowledge to be mispresented, carelessly used, or ignored. Without proper and mature acknowledgment, Morris argued, and let readers like me see and understand, critical theory was reduced to a 'peculiar feat of reconstituting an overwhelming male pantheon of proper names to function as ritual objects of academic exegesis and commentary'.[137] To refuse to own up to a relationship with feminist knowledge by 1988 (if you happened to be a fellow traveller, a conspiratorial 'specific intellectual') was to perpetuate a 'singularly ponderous phallo-centred conversation' that 'wondered where the women were',[138] and to stall the projects that informed the points of view, and meeting points, for feminists and crits alike.

I read *Postmodern Jurisprudence* differently now, of course, because I collaborate and am friends with one of its authors, Shaun McVeigh. That does not mean I am unfazed by the muted gesture to feminism in *Postmodern Jurisprudence* just because he has told me entertaining things about its production (such as much of it was written on the Tube in London, on the Northern Line between Kennington and Hendon). On the contrary, the authors' half-hearted concession to a feminist intellectual self-assertion ('protests have been made') seems both more risible and more vexatious every time I read it. But that book also provides a through line, an experience of a text of law, to show what I have been writing about all along: how jurisprudence writing (and the writing of jurisprudence), its reception and reimagination, is a matter of duty, relationship, and circumstance. Shaun trained himself to consider what the tasks of the jurisprudent might be by writing *Postmodern Jurisprudence* in 1991 in London, and since then in Australia. I trained myself to consider what the tasks of the feminist historian of jurisprudence might be when I read it, and wrote my own work in Sydney, with the guide of texts like *The Pirate's Fiancée*. It is because of those experiences that we can consider the practices of jurisography in the ways we collaborate on today.

Within the confines of my study, then, neither *The Pirate's Fiancée* nor *Postmodern Jurisprudence* are academic remainders: objects of the 1980s, fit now only for critique or curiosity. But joining them together has been to show something additional: how the arts of relational thinking are integral to feminist thought, and became obvious outside it at a certain time. It is also to make clear that taking care of those arts *within* jurisprudence writing accrues as a direct, and current responsibility, if you happen to be trained as both feminist and as jurisprudent (as I am).

Jurisographers

There are many other things to say about the experience of 'the post', circa 1988.[139] In law world, for example, a scholar could write a revisionary record of the intellectual experience of Australian legal scholars' relationship with the humanities. Or they could map the channels of reception between 'feminism' and 'jurisprudence' (or postmodernism) across institutional and geographical channels, and temporal and political ones too. Or they could write a critique of why contemporary 'law and humanities' scholarship, as open to political and historical rejection of colonisation as it is, fetes its critical progenitors in a way that remains depressingly gendered and jurisdictionally predictable. But this study of 1988 is approximate by design. I have not written it to claim that one rival account of the theoretical relations I have discussed is definitive. Nor have I written it to claim 'a "personal voice" for "*me*"'.[140] Instead, as I explained at the start, I wrote it to speak from the self-invented persona (or office, if your inheritance permits) of jurisographer, and to demonstrate the naming of their practice.[141]

Jurisography – as a collaboration with Shaun McVeigh and Peter Rush – has been a way for us to publicly name, as a political act, how we care for writing that worries about conducts and relations of law. In the traditions to which jurisography belongs, as I hope to have shown, acts of reading and writing are not passive nor incidental, but draw directly from the traditions and situation of the writer. The style of reading and writing texts that became available in the 1980s, for obvious reasons, apprise the reasons for inventing a name for a practice in the first place, as well as exemplify how it might be conducted.[142] This essay, then, like the others you have been reading in this book, has been a technical writing exercise, concerned with finding ways to inhabit (and recommend) that persona: the jurisographer.

In undertaking those exercises in my other essays, I reported on all kinds of writing (from Julius Stone to Juliet Mitchell) and was open about the moves I made in working with and between feminist and jurisprudential texts, all of which I inherit. In this essay, the tone, you may have noted, is different, because this time my exercise was conducted within feminist thought itself. I chose to present a study, so as to consider my 'cultural participation . . . in the information conveyed'.[143] The writers I am writing about are known to me. So, I have (to a degree) let the texts speak for themselves. This was intentional. There is a literary and literal genealogy to note, as in my other essays. But debts of acknowledgment, this time round, are also personal and immediate, and for that reason I have stood slightly to one side. By way of conclusion, however, I want to show my hand and say something direct about the form and intent of this fifth exercise.

Cleary, the hermeneutic and aesthetic projects of the 1980s – the displacement of the problems of knowledge as experienced onto a theoretical plane – are not simply (or only) attributable to institution, or the structure of language.

They are also oppositions of genre and role. When writing about writing (as jurisography does), I am not just 'talking about texts'. What matters most to me in my study is to be explicit about what the acts of writing, and the ethos and comportment of feminist writers like Morris in the 1980s, offers to me (or anyone else) writing now. These writers, in speaking eloquently from the page, not only set the tone for the rigorous work necessary to establish a dialogue about theoretical relations (the speech act of writing); more importantly, they displayed an attitude in that writing, created a public disposition for feminist writers regardless of discipline that demanded, and demands, serious attention. There is a feminist maturity about writers like Morris, and Grosz, Curthoys, Gatens, Butler, and many other scholars who arrived in public at this time, and whose work I acknowledge as integral to the formation of this essay. They created a vocabulary and a cadence – a fearless speech – that is cool and unfazed, yet harnesses and redirects impatient indignation as regards what other kinds of writers and writing might want from them, or expect of their work. They don't write to be accepted by (or acceptable to) male thought, or men. They don't write to divide or conquer; flatter or flirt; cajole or berate. They are not performing the tired versions of exceptionalism that have historically prevailed when women speak from their experience (and their talent) when they write. They do not hide themselves behind their work, nor do they become complacent in that work. They do not pretend to be satisfied with the compromised conditions in which the exercise and display of their knowledge is produced. They are not tranquil about acts of intellectual piracy or vandalism occasioned against the originality of their traditions and the courage of their convictions. The comportment and ethos of this persona who announced herself in the 1980s – woman writing her intellectual authority in full view – is for these reasons a guide of relevance and significance for those who follow. In the context of my own work, I can inhabit and reimagine this persona, adapted to my own tasks and questions, when speaking in public through my own writing. I can voice as well as show my own version and experiences of the recurring problems of knowledge as sexed (be it the fields of theoretical relations, or within jurisprudence and its methodological rivalries), and take what I have earned and learned into my collaborations. So from that perspective, I hope that my own exercise in writing this study has demonstrated exactly what the invention of a practice, and the conduct of a jurisographer, owes to the feminist intellectual, circa 1988, and her work; as well as commend her example when determining a language and style for your own craft and projects.

Notes

1 See Essay Two, Essay Three and Essay Four, *Feminist Jurisography*.

2 There is a vast amount of commentary and analysis of 'the postmodern turn'. For one overview example relevant to the discussion in this essay, see McVeigh 2013.

3 For examples from Australia, see Davies 2002; Genovese 2015; and Essay Six, *Feminist Jurisography*: 130–135.

4 See, for example, Auchmuty & van Marle 2012. See discussion of this point in Essay Three, *Feminist Jurisography*: 51–57.
5 Genovese & McVeigh 2015.
6 I am not alone in making this observation. It is a point made persuasively over many years. For four excellent examples, see Brown 1991; Bottomley 2004; Conaghan 2009; van Marle 2012.
7 See, for example of this form of misrecognition, Douzinas 2014: 188–189.
8 See Essay One, *Feminist Jurisography*.
9 Foucault 1992: 11.
10 Foucault 1992: 10.
11 Foucault 1992: 11.
12 Foucault 1992: 12–13.
13 Calvino 1997: 305. Collection first published in Italy, 1980, Einaudi. See Essay One, *Feminist Jurisography*.
14 Calvino 1997: 305.
15 See Essay One and Essay Six, *Feminist Jurisography*.
16 I elaborate on this point in Essay Six, *Feminist Jurisography*: 126–130.
17 I do not mean to suggest there was no other work concerned with postmodernism by feminist scholars in law, 1988–1992. The purpose of my text selection relates to its relationship to my location and experience, as discussed. For a non-exhaustive sample of other influential texts, most from the US, that were also important to me at this time: Ashe 1988; Cornell 1990; Fineman & Thomadsen 1992; Frug 1992; and in Australia, Rothfield 1990.
18 Genovese 1996.
19 Morris 1988b: 73.
20 See Essay Four, *Feminist Jurisography*; Lewis 2004: 51.
21 Lewis 2004: 51. See also: Frow & Morris 1993; Curthoys & Docker 2017.
22 I reiterate here I am telling, intentionally, a located story about Sydney, and acknowledge there were disputes and rivalries between an emergent set of practices and different cities in Australia. See King 2008.
23 Lewis 2004: 53; Morris 1984; Foucault 1995.
24 Foss, later the 'long term editor of the [Australian critical] journal *Art and Text*', was in the mid-1970s a student of the history and philosophy of science at UNSW: Lewis 2004: 53.
25 For example: Paul Foss, Meaghan Morris, George Alexander, Terence Bell, Elizabeth Grosz, and Graeme Tubbenhauer. See Foss & Morris 1978: 1.
26 Lewis 2004: 54, quoting Muecke 1991: 61; Mitchell 1974.
27 Lewis 2004: 54. See also Martinis Roe 2018.
28 Lewis 2004: 54.
29 Lewis 2004: 54.
30 Martinis Roe 2018: 104–105.
31 Morris 1988a: 7.
32 Foss & Morris 1978: 11.
33 For example, between essays by Jean Baudrillard and Meaghan Morris was work by Umberto Eco 1978.
34 Lewis 2004: 53; Foss & Morris 1978: 8.
35 Foss & Morris 1978: 11.
36 Morris & Patton 1979.
37 Irigaray 1978.
38 Patton and Morris 'made a significant contribution to the importation of French Theory to Australia by introducing audiences to these later essays': Lewis 2004: 54.
39 Alexander 1978; Morris 1984.
40 See Essay One, *Feminist Jurisography*: 16–18..

41 Alexander 1978: 43.
42 See for examples King 2008; Martinis Roe 2018; Felski & Sofia 1996.
43 Personal communication, June 2019, quoted with permission. Rush also noted that he had encountered critical legal studies prior to 1984, at the University of New South Wales.
44 Morris 1984: 58.
45 Morris 1984; Frow & Morris 1993; Felski & Sofia 1996; Lewis 2004; Curthoys & Docker 2017.
46 Felski & Sofia 1996; Lewis 2004.
47 Lewis 2004: 55.
48 Morris 1984; Genovese 2014; Battersby 2000; Lewis 2004; Martinis Roe 2018.
49 See Essay Four, *Feminist Jurisography*.
50 'Grafting' is a key term used by feminists to describe these relationships and activities, for example Sheridan 1988.
51 As the critical studies scholar Tania Lewis has argued (and I agree), for feminist writers in Australia, this was 'an exemplary moment of transnational intellectual exchange'. Lewis 2004: 55; Felski & Sofia 1996: 385–386; Frow & Morris 1993: xxvii. See also Gunew 1990. Gunew (1990: 1) notes: 'We have long been frustrated by the map of international feminisms which traces a line between Britain, America and France but rarely includes other groups. As Australian feminists we are excellently placed to be a clearing house for those mainstream feminisms and have towards them a degree of eclecticism which allows us to adapt what we need and to be more generally critical toward the rest'.
52 Morris 1988a: 8.
53 Morris 1988a: 8. Morris is quoting and responding to Bennett 1987.
54 Morris 1988a: 10.
55 Morris 1988a: 8.
56 Morris 1988a: 8.
57 Morris 1988a: 10.
58 A non-exhaustive survey of scholarly books by Australian feminists or by feminists located in Australia, published in the single year 1988, serves an example that seems remarkable now: Morris 1988; Curthoys 1988; Sheridan 1988; Caine, Grosz & de Lepervanche 1988; Pateman & Gross 1988; Pateman 1988.
59 For the earliest example of outward-facing critique in Australian scholarly feminist jurisprudence, see Thornton 1986.
60 The point made repeatedly across texts is that feminist knowledge was unlike patriarchal knowledge, and needed to be genealogically and politically asserted as such: 'the constant across the range of its expressions' was that feminist knowledge was 'limited, politically implicated, and representative of some, not all interests': Grosz 1988a: 57.
61 See, for example, Gatens 1988.
62 Grosz 1988a: 55; 57. Grosz's emphasis.
63 Le Dœuff 1980. Morris address this relationship directly: see Morris 1988b: 71–102.
64 See Essay Four, *Feminist Jurisography*: 76–77.
65 Grosz 1988b: 92.
66 Grosz 1988a: 57, my emphasis.
67 Curthoys 2000: 3.
68 In the context of this study, it is perhaps enough to note as representative for those in the know, or those following their own routes through this story, the diverse work of Hélène Cixous, Luce Irigaray, Julia Kristeva, and Michèle Le Dœuff in France; Luisa Muraro, Adriana Cavarero, and The Milan Women's Bookstore Collective in Italy; the m/f collective in the UK; Rosi Braidotti, Meaghan Morris, EA Grosz, and Moira Gatens and others in and from Australia; and in the US, Donna Haraway, Drucilla Cornell, Kimberlé Crenshaw, Audre Lorde, and Judith Butler.

69 Butler 2007.
70 Butler 2004b: 175.
71 Butler 2004b: 175.
72 Butler 2007: 11–17; Butler 2004a: 232–250.
73 For two examples circa 1988: Morris 1988d: 241–269; Curthoys 1988.
74 Gunew 1990: 1.
75 Gunew 1990: 1. This self-criticism extended to those like herself who worked to understand multiculturalism and its own diasporic experiences of difference, and absence.
76 For a notable early example: O'Shane 1976; and into the 1990s, see Huggins 1993; Behrendt 1993.
77 Moreton-Robinson 2000.
78 Moreton-Robinson 2013.
79 Morris 1988d: 241–269; Bellear 1988; Langton 1988; Cook & Goodall 2013.
80 Gunew 1990: 1; Curthoys 1993.
81 This series was edited from the UK by a group of feminist intellectuals (Michèle Barrett, Annette Kuhn, Anne Phillips, and Ann Rosalind Jones), each of whom interrogated in different ways the value of feminist thought for Marxist and psychoanalytic theory, and vice versa.
82 Morris 1988a: frontispiece.
83 Morris 1988a: 6.
84 Morris 1988a: 7.
85 Morris 1988a: 7.
86 Morris 1988a: 6.
87 Morris 1988a: 6.
88 Morris 1988a: 6.
89 Morris 1988a: 7 (Morris' emphases).
90 Morris 1988a: 6, Morris' emphais.
91 Morris 1988a: 7.
92 Morris 1988a: 100.
93 Morris 1988b: 100 (Morris' emphasis).
94 Morris 1988b: 101.
95 Morris 1988b: 101.
96 Morris 1988b: 101.
97 Morris 1988b: 101.
98 Morris 1988b: 100.
99 For example, Gatens 2007. This point is also as discussed in Essay One, *Feminist Jurisography*: 14–16.
100 See discussion of these terms and ideas in Essay One, *Feminist Jurisography*.
101 Morris 1988a: 5.
102 Morris 1988a: 4 (Morris' emphasis).
103 Gatens 1996: viii. The sexed personifications of subjects and forms of reasoning is a point made by Beauvoir in *The Second Sex* also. See discussion on this point, Essay One, *Feminist Jurisography*: 12 and Essay Two, *Feminist Jurisography*: 30–31.
104 Morris 1979: 148. This epigraph was not replicated in version of the essay reproduced in Morris 1988c.
105 Morris 1988c: 51.
106 Morris 1988c: 59.
107 Morris 1988c: 55.
108 Morris 1988c: 4.
109 Le Dœuff 2003: 1–3.

110 Le Dœuff 2003: 217.
111 Le Dœuff 2003: 219.
112 Le Dœuff 2003: 217.
113 Le Dœuff 2003: 220.
114 Morris 1988a: 1.
115 Morris 1988a: 1.
116 Morris 1988a: 2.
117 Morris 1988a: 2.
118 See for examples of reflective pieces Douzinas 2014; Goodrich 2017.
119 See Essay Two and Essay Three, *Feminist Jurisography*.
120 For a contemporaneous example from the British tradition, see Douzinas, McVeigh & Warrington 1992; Hunt 1986. And from the US tradition, Tushnet 1986; Unger 1983; Trubek 1984. Also see Note 17, earlier.
121 Douzinas, Warrington & McVeigh 1991.
122 Douzinas 2014.
123 Lyotard 1984.
124 Douzinas, Warrington & McVeigh 1991: ix.
125 Douzinas, Warrington & McVeigh 1991: 138–139. The authors are responding in particular to Fish 1987.
126 Douzinas, Warrington & McVeigh 1991: 25.
127 Douzinas, Warrington & McVeigh 1991: 25.
128 Douzinas, Warrington & McVeigh 1991: ix.
129 Douzinas, Warrington & McVeigh 1991: ix–x.
130 Douzinas, Warrington & McVeigh 1991: x.
131 Douzinas, Warrington & McVeigh 1991: x.
132 I elaborate on this point in Essay Six, *Feminist Jurisography*: 131–132.
133 Douzinas, Warrington & McVeigh 1991: xiii.
134 Douzinas, Warrington & McVeigh 1991: xiii.
135 Douzinas, Warrington & McVeigh 1991: xiii.
136 Douzinas, Warrington & McVeigh 1991: xiii.
137 Morris 1988a: 12.
138 Morris 1988a: 12.
139 As Margaret Davies, for one, has done: Davies 2002.
140 Morris 1988a: 7.
141 For a discussion about the differences between the use of 'office' and 'persona', see Essay One, *Feminist Jurisography*: 5–6.
142 See Essay One and Essay Six, *Feminist Jurisography*.
143 Calvino 1997: 305.

References

Alexander G 1978 'Introduction: On Editorial Strategies' in Foss et al 1978: 15–43.

Ashe M 1988 'Mind's Opportunity: Birthing a Poststructuralist Feminist Jurisprudence' *Syracuse Law Review* 38/4: 1129–1174.

Auchmuty R and van Marle K 2012 'Special Issue: Carol Smart's *Feminism and the Power of Law*' *Feminist Legal Studies* 20/2: 65–69 DOI:10.1007/s10691-012-9203-z.

Battersby C 2000 'Learning to Think Intercontinentally: Finding Australian Routes' *Hypatia* 15/2: 1–17 DOI:10.2979/HYP.2000.15.2.1.

Beauvoir S de 2011 *The Second Sex* Trans C Borde and S Malovany-Chevallier Vintage New York (first published 1949).

Behrendt L 1993 'Aboriginal Women and the White Lies of the Feminist Movement: Implications for Aboriginal Women in Rights Discourse' *Australian Feminist Law Journal* 1/1: 27–44 DOI:10.1080/13200968.1993.11077108.

Bellear L 1988 'Koorie History and the Bicentenary' *Lilith* 5: 68–70.

Bennett D 1987 'Wrapping up postmodernism: the subject of consumption versus the subject of cognition' *Textual Practice* 1/3: 243–261 DOI:10.1080/09502368708582016.

Bottomley A 2004 'Shock to Thought: An Encounter (of a Third Kind) with Legal Feminism' *Feminist Legal Studies* 12/1: 29–65 DOI:10.1023/B:FEST.0000026078.52409.A6.

Brown B 1991 'Litigating feminisms' *Economy and Society* 20/4: 423–444 DOI:10.1080/03085149100000023.

Butler J 2004a 'Can the "Other" of Philosophy Speak?' in J Butler ed 2004 *Undoing Gender* Routledge New York: 232–250.

Butler J 2004b 'The End of Sexual Difference?' in J Butler ed 2004 *Undoing Gender* Routledge New York: 174–203.

Butler J 2007 *Gender Trouble: Feminism and the Subversion of Identity* Routledge New York (first published 1990).

Caine B, Grosz E A and de Lepervanche M 1988 *Crossing Boundaries: Feminisms and the critique of knowledges* Allen & Unwin Sydney.

Calvino I 1997 'In Memory of Roland Barthes' in I Calvino ed P Creagh trans 1997 *The Literature Machine: Essays* Vintage London (first published 1980): 300–306.

Conaghan J 2009 'The Making of a Field or the Building of a Wall? Feminist Legal Studies and Law, Gender and Sexuality' *Feminist Legal Studies* 17/3: 303–307 DOI:10.1007/s10691-009-9136-3.

Cook K and Goodall H 2013 'Bicentennial' in K Cook and H Goodall eds 2013 *Making Change Happen: Black and White Activists talk to Kevin Cook About Aboriginal, Union and Liberation Politics* ANU Press Canberra: 335–366.

Cornell D 1990 'The Doubly-Prized World: Myth, Allegory and the Feminine' *Cornell Law Review* 75/3: 644–699.

Curthoys A 1988 'Post-colonialism, ethnic identity and gender' in A Curthoys 1988 *For and Against Feminism: A Personal Journey into Feminist Theory and History* Allen & Unwin Sydney: 145–149.

Curthoys A 1993 'Feminism, Citizenship and National Identity' *Feminist Review* 44/1: 19–38 DOI:10.1057/fr.1993.18.

Curthoys A 2000 'Adventures of Feminism: Simone de Beauvoir's Autobiographies, Women's Liberation, and Self-Fashioning' *Feminist Review* 64/1: 3–18 DOI:10.1080/014177800338927.

Curthoys A and Docker J 2017 'Stuart Hall and Cultural Studies, Circa 1983' *Cultural Studies Review* 23/2: 162–173 DOI:10.5130/csr.v23i2.5824.

Davies M 2002 'Ethics and Methodology in Legal Theory: A (Personal) Research Anti-Manifesto' *Law Text Culture* 6/1: 7–26.

Douzinas C 2014 'A Short History of the British Critical Legal Conference or, the Responsibility of the Critic' *Law and Critique* 25/2: 187–198 DOI: 10.1007/s10978-014-9133-9.

Douzinas C, McVeigh S and Warrington R 1992 'The Alta(e)rs of Law: The Judgement of Legal Aesthetics' *Theory, Culture & Society* 9/4: 93–117 DOI:10.1177/026327692009004005.

Douzinas C, Warrington R and McVeigh S 1991 *Postmodern Jurisprudence: The Law of Text in the Texts of Law* Routledge London and New York.

Eco U 1978 'Silence is L(e)aden' in Foss et al 1978: 77–81.

Felski R and Sofia Z 1996 'Introduction' *Cultural Studies* 10/3: 383–392 DOI:10.4324/9780203990780.

Fineman M A and Thomadsen N S eds 1992 *At the Boundaries of Law: Feminism and Legal Theory* Routledge New York.

Fish S 1987 'Dennis Martinez and the Uses of Theory' *Yale Law Journal* 96/8: 1773–1800.

Foss P and Morris M eds 1978 *Language, Sexuality & Subversion* Feral Publications Sydney.

Foucault M 1992 *The Use of Pleasure: The History of Sexuality: Volume 2* Trans R Hurley Penguin Books London (first published 1984).

Foucault M 1995 *Discipline and Punish: The Birth of the Prison* Trans A Sheridan Vintage Books New York (first published 1977).

Frow J and Morris M 1993 'Introduction' in J Frow and M Morris eds 1993 *Australian Cultural Studies: A Reader* Allen & Unwin Sydney: vii–xxxii.

Frug M J 1992 *Postmodern Legal Feminism* Routledge New York.

Gatens M 1988 'Feminism, philosophy and riddles without answers' in Pateman et al 1988: 13–29.

Gatens M 1996 *Imaginary Bodies: Ethics, Power and Corporeality* Routledge London and New York.

Gatens M 2007 'The "Disciplined Imagination": Literature as "Experimental" Philosophy' *Australian Feminist Studies* 22/52: 25–34 DOI:10.1080/08164640601145020.

Genovese A 1996 'Unravelling Identities: Performance and Criticism in Australian Feminisms' *Feminist Review* 52/1: 135–153 DOI:10.1057/fr.1996.12.

Genovese A 2014 'On Australian feminist tradition: three notes on conduct, inheritance and the relations of historiography and jurisprudence' *Journal of Australian Studies* 38/4: 430–444 DOI:10.1080/14443058.2014.954137.

Genovese A 2015 'Occasions and Events: Australian Feminist Jurisprudence at 25' *Australian Feminist Law Journal* 41/1: 1–2 DOI:10.1080/13200968.2015.1045111.

Genovese A and McVeigh S 2015 'Nineteen eighty three: A jurisographic report on *Commonwealth v Tasmania*' *Griffith Law Review* 24/1: 68–88 DOI:10.1080/10383441.2015.1022891.

Goodrich P 2017 'How Strange the Change from Major to Minor' *Law Text Culture* 21: 30–53.

Grosz E A 1988a 'Part II: Women and The Humanities: Introduction' in Caine et al 1988: 55–58.

Grosz E A 1988b 'The in(ter)vention of feminist knowledges' in Caine et al 1988: 92–104.

Gunew S 1990 'Introduction' in S Gunew ed 1990 *Feminist Knowledge: Critique and Construct* Routledge London and New York: 1–12.

Huggins J 1993 'Pretty deadly tidda business' in S Gunew and A Yeatman eds 1993 *Feminism and the Politics of Difference* Routledge New York: 61–72.

Hunt A 1986 'The Theory of Critical Legal Studies' *Oxford Journal of Legal Studies* 6/1: 1–45.

Irigaray L 1978 'That Sex Which Is Not One' (first published 1977) in Foss et al 1978: 161–171.

King N 2008 '"Another way of being an intellectual": interview with Ian Hunter' *Communication, Politics and Culture* 41/1: 47–62 <http://hdl.handle.net/1959.14/80194>.

Langton M 1988 'The Getting of Power' *Australian Feminist Studies* 3/6: 1–5.

Le Dœuff M 1980 'Simone de Beauvoir and Existentialism' *Feminist Studies* 6/2: 277–289 DOI:10.2307/3177742.

Le Dœuff M 1991 *Hipparchia's Choice: An Essay Concerning Women, Philosophy, etc.* Trans T Selous Oxford Blackwell (first published 1989).

Le Dœuff M 2003 *The Sex of Knowing* Trans K Hamer and L Code Routledge London and New York.

Lewis T 2004 'Meaghan Morris and the Formation of Australian Cultural Studies: a Narrative of Intellectual Exchange and Located Transnationalism' *Cultural Studies ↔ Critical Methodologies* 4/1: 45–70 DOI:10.1177/1532708603259446.

Lyotard J F 1984 *The Postmodern Condition: A Report on Knowledge* Trans G Bennington Manchester University Press Manchester (first published 1979).

Martinis Roe A 2018 'It was about opening up the very notion that there was a particular perspective: The transdisciplinary digestion of sexual difference by a network in Sydney – including Working Papers Collective, Feminist Film Workers, and the Sydney Filmmakers Co-operative – as a practice of alliance' in A Martinis Roe ed 2018 *To Become Two: Propositions for Feminist Collective Practice* Archive Books Berlin: 93–119.

McVeigh S 2013 'Law and Postmodernism' in R Banakar and M Travers eds 2013 *Law and Social Theory* Hart Publishing Oxford (2nd edn): 233–246.

Mitchell J 1974 *Psychoanalysis and Feminism* Pantheon Books New York.

Moreton-Robinson A 2000 *Talkin' up to the white woman: Aboriginal women and feminism* University of Queensland Press St Lucia.

Moreton-Robinson A 2013 'Towards an Australian Indigenous Women's Standpoint Theory: A Methodological Tool' *Australian Feminist Studies* 28/78: 331–347 DOI:10.1080/08164649.2013.876664.

Morris M 1979 'The Pirate's Fiancée' in Morris et al 1979: 148–168.

Morris M 1984 'Identity Anecdotes' *Camera Obscura* 4/3: 41–65 DOI:10.1215/02705346-4-3_12-40.

Morris M 1988a 'Introduction: feminism, reading, postmodernism' in M Morris ed 1988 *The Pirate's Fiancée: Feminism, reading, postmodernism* Verso London and New York: 1–16.

Morris M 1988b 'Operative Reasoning: Reading Michèle Le Dœuff' in M Morris ed 1988 *The Pirate's Fiancée: Feminism, reading, postmodernism* Verso London and New York: 71–102 (first published 1981/2).

Morris M 1988c 'The Pirate's Fiancée' in M Morris ed 1988 *The Pirate's Fiancée: Feminism, reading, postmodernism* Verso London and New York: 51–69.

Morris M 1988d 'Tooth and Claw: Tales of Survival, and *Crocodile Dundee*' in M Morris ed 1988 *The Pirate's Fiancée: Feminism, reading, postmodernism* Verso London and New York: 241–269.

Morris M and Patton P eds 1979 *Michel Foucault: Power, Truth, Strategy* Feral Publications Sydney.

Muecke S 1991 'Relations of Theory: Meaghan Morris Talks with Stephen Muecke' in D Carter ed 1991 *Outside the Book: Contemporary Essays on Literary Periodicals* Local Consumption Sydney: 57–78.

O'Shane P 1976 'Is there any relevance in the women's movement for Aboriginal women?' *Refractory Girl* 12: 31–34 <http://www.womenaustralia.info/leaders/bib/WLP000178.htm>.

Pateman C 1988 *The Sexual Contract* Polity Press Cambridge.

Pateman C and Gross E eds 1988 *Feminist Challenges: Social and Political Theory* Allen & Unwin Sydney (first published 1986).

Rothfield P 1990 'Jurisprudence and Feminism: Displacing the Analytic Mise-En-Scene' *Law in Context: A Socio-Legal Journal* 8/2: 92–111.

Sheridan S ed 1988 *Grafts: Feminist Cultural Criticism* Verso London and New York.

Thornton M 1986 'Feminist Jurisprudence: Illusion or Reality?' *Australian Journal of Law and Society* 3: 5–29.

Trubek D M 1984 'Where the Action Is: Critical Legal Studies and Empiricism' *Stanford Law Review* 36/1–2: 575–622 DOI:10.2307/1228692.

Tushnet M 1986 'Critical Legal Studies: An Introduction to Its Origins and Underpinnings' *Journal of Legal Education* 36/4: 505–517.

Unger R M 1983 'The Critical Legal Studies Movement' *Harvard Law Review* 96/3: 561–675 DOI:10.2307/1341032.

van Marle K 2012 ' "We Exist, but Who Are We?" Feminism and the Power of Sociological Law' *Feminist Legal Studies* 20/2: 149–159 DOI:10.1007/s10691-012-9205-x.

Essay 6

On Conducts of Life (A Feminist Jurisography, 2022)

My Vocabulary

Why, in the end, *a jurisography*?

A vocabulary connects a person to a disciplinary lineage, and trains them in how to participate in their chosen activities and obligations. For one example, 'evidence' carries a range of contests for historians that are different than for those trained in the law. In this book, I have used certain words repeatedly: 'inherit', 'tradition', 'experience', 'persona', 'inhabit', 'relational', 'conduct', 'situated', and 'responsibility'. Essay One gave an explanation of a feminist history of necessary invention and reintroduction that attaches to that vocabulary, and I have made a conscious effort to use it throughout this collection of essays.[1] I have done so for two reasons. One is to help me place myself, and this book, into relationship with other feminists. The other is to underscore my narrative about transmission of feminist thought, and to show its influence on methods of critical jurisprudential knowledge production (rather than assume it was only ever the other way around). My vocabulary acknowledges how I have learned my crafts, and makes public the debts I have accrued. My vocabulary is also chosen to acknowledge what I am entrusted and authorised to pass on. By way of conclusion, I want to offer some notes on the conditions attached to the bequests of practice that inform my work (acknowledging it would be different for others), and how the exercise of writing this book with its particular vocabulary, over a long period, has enlivened my feminist relationships.

Partire da sé

A key idea that has informed my practice is that when we write within our disciplines (as jurisprudent, or historian), and as a feminist, we start from ourselves. What I mean is that the *persona* chosen for acting in the world with others, and one's own personal experience of that activity, are not separate (or held apart, as they are in many traditions of male writing). Drawing from the training offered by Simone de Beauvoir on this point,[2] I have explored how

DOI: 10.4324/9780429461132-6

feminists, when inhabiting disciplinary knowledges that have excluded women ontologically (and failed to recognise them institutionally), have acted with scepticism towards their disciplines' methodological orthodoxies. One consequence has been the production of transformative practices, that take embodied difference seriously, and concentrate on how to think and act relationally. In this book I have followed that lineage, making observations about my own training and experience of coming into knowledge, to tell a particular relational history, about feminist methods and jurisprudence writing, in Australia. Similar stories can be told and retold countless ways, by others, and for other places. In the Italian feminist traditions of sexual difference, for example, this way of entering into relationship is named literally and very directly, as *partire da sé*: to start from oneself. It is understood as a necessary pre-condition to recognise another, and to create together shared practices relevant for the continuously changing conditions of life that we are asked to meet, in all our capacities, as people and as scholars.

The directness of *partire da sé* as an expression is useful to work with in these final notes. It opens out for active discussion a genealogy shared by Australian and Italian feminists about conducts of life (about which I will say more in a moment), but at the same time also reminds how relational practices are attached by language and experience to the locations in which we do our work. The Italian feminist tradition of sexual difference from where *partire da sé* emerged, for example, is distinctive and radical, rather than essentialist and binary (as difference might be understood in Anglophone, especially US, feminisms). It emanates from and contributes to a specific Italian politics that seeks to reimagine the boundaries of women's experience by centralising their differences from each other, using that difference as a basis for relationship and political alliance, and conducting the transmission of knowledge and acknowledgment as explicitly matrilineal.[3] In the Australian experience, there are much older traditions of relational narrative practice taught by Indigenous feminist and Senior women knowledge holders to those that follow and inherit (as Birri-Gubba jurisprudent Nicole Watson has demonstrated in her work).[4] Non-Indigenous feminist practitioners, with a European lineage, can watch and learn a great deal, but must be cognisant that we have distinct duties to challenge the 'boundaries of the sayable and imaginable'[5] and in ways specific to conditions of life lived in the place we do. This has included interrogating the lived experience, and unjustness, of colonial violence in our own languages, and addressing how race, as well as sex, is experienced relationally.[6] Such a practice undertaken by non-Indigenous Australian feminists of this genealogical persuasion is, of course, not often successfully accomplished. But it is acknowledged, these days, as part of our responsibilities: the topics we write about, our collaborations, and the methods we use. It is important also to acknowledge how such a duty of feminist work in Australia has evolved, from the many meetings – allegorical as well as textual and literal – between

Indigenous and non-Indigenous feminists, in many disciplines, over the past 50 years.

My own experience of learning from those past meetings is one of instruction as well as conducts of participation, as what is offered is a practical wisdom. I have learned that to 'start from myself' is a question of place, as much as placement (a lesson also from Beauvoir, from 1949). An important part of my duties, as an Australian feminist jurisographer, as a result, is to historicise the ways in which institutional knowledge has shaped raced relations, as well as relations between men and women, in Australia, and to accept that Australian feminist knowledge is not exonerated in those accounts. Without starting from ourselves as a feminist community and acknowledging the complexity and complicity of the feminisms we live with and inherit, the collaborations and necessary work that that Indigenous feminist scholars invite us to shoulder in the ongoing and unfinished business of lawful relations in Australia, I think, remain limited. In this book, that has not been my central question (although it is in other current projects); however, one of my tasks here has been to show a circumscribed part of that located feminist history, and to contribute how it can be viewed as a story of methodological relations, that have implications.

This reflection on Australian conditions of scholarly life is hopefully recognisable to Australian readers, but does leave open the broader and practical question: what is required in a writing exercise (as *jurisography* certainly is) that 'starts from oneself'? What can it look like as a practical activity to join together disciplinary *personae* and personal experience, in order to draw out the themes and ideas that shape the lineage I have inherited, and have been discussing?

In Essay One, I gave an intellectual and historical answer to that question, again centring Beauvoir to do so.[7] I gave reasons for my choices of form, style, and genre in the essays that followed. These draw from the experiences of women writing before me, as well as young women writing now, at kitchen, library, and café tables: residing out of office, because the institutional world remains inhospitable, or choosing to inhabit public offices their own way to change the *status quo* of the conditions of life. But I was also advised by Australian feminist historian Ann Curthoys, who is important to me, and has given me advice about how to be a practitioner of feminist history for over 25 years, that the final section of this book could emphasise my central proposition by 'being personal', in a more conventional way.

For a long time, I speculated about how to do that well. Some of that speculation was a matter of form. Most was a matter of content. (As the Italian feminist philosopher Adriana Cavarero warns, '[p]ersonal memory is not a professional author'.)[8] Did I want to write a concluding essay about the difficulties of navigating an intellectual position (and an intellectual ambition) by using as a device some details about my life? How could I integrate the benefits of having more than one point of view without writing about my identity (my background, class, ethnicity, personal relationships), and running the risk of privileging a prescription for feminist work (my own) that homogenises and closes down other feminist experience?

How could I honour a feminist ethos of conduct of life that pays attention to fragmentation, but does not interrupt the central proposition of this project: that life and disciplinary production are not separated when asserting feminist knowledges? These kinds of worries are, gratifyingly, a central theme in much contemporary feminist fiction writing that I admire, and the writers of those texts often allude to or expressly reference their own textual inheritances (which I can recognise because they are shared).[9] Their work has been both guide and companion. But my own work is neither fiction, nor a literary essay; my decision has been to set aside the many, many notes and fragments that I have written while undertaking my project (which has gone on for a very long time) that expose my intimate view of a craft. These notes have, however, helped me. One contains a quote by a favourite writer, Natalia Ginzburg. This quote comes from her essay 'My Vocation', first published in Italian in 1949, and speaks for me (for now), on this subject:

> 'Now I no longer wanted to write like a man, because I had had children and I thought I knew a great many things about tomato sauce and even if I didn't put them into my story it helped my vocation that I knew them; in a strange, remote way these things also helped my vocation'.[10]

Other models, offered by Ann Curthoys herself, I want to emulate instead, as they offer a practical demonstration of *partire da sé*, and how it connects to the arguments I have been making and performing along the way about jurisography.

When she produced her own mediation on becoming a feminist historian in 1988, Ann's method was to include short, new introductions to her already published work, in order to explain how her practice had developed. These introductions position her thinking in its time and location, and people that thinking by recalling how it developed through conversation with friends and allies. As the feminist cultural critic Meaghan Morris notes in her foreword to Ann's 1988 book, *For and Against Feminism*, these new writings enabled a movement between

> '[A]cts of theorisation, moments of reflection, and the experience of everyday living . . . this is what was assumed or promised by the old saying "the personal is political" . . . it's a saying that is all the more appropriate to this book because it isn't a series of intimate revelations and concessions, but an intellectual journey – one that advances by making explicit connections between the author's changing social experience and her theoretical work'.[11]

So I want to take up that training, as an exercise in marking my contemporaneous experiences while finishing this collection of essays. This is to iterate a point I made in the Introduction, with reference to the work of Pierre Hadot. Hadot, as a historian of the tradition of conduct, reminds that it is not a discourse to be mastered, but a type of 'know-how' that involves continuous practical activity in order 'to change [one's] way of living and seeing the world'.[12] He goes on to note that these activities are relational in the sense that the philosopher (or in my case, feminist jurisographer) does not live outside of their work. The one who knows and writes is engaged in daily living with their discipline, as well as with others, those 'with whom [they] share temporal space, and intellectual conversation'.[13] This is an iteration of *partire da sé*. So, in what follows, I give an account of coming into relationship with the activities and work of others, that occurred while doing my own. From that position, I hope the 'I' that has appeared in this book, when I write about jurisprudence and history, clearly speaks for my public feminist relationships and intellectual experiences. I hope too that this helps make these final observations in what is an experimental project of jurisography meaningful for the here and now, by demonstrating different kinds of productive relations of disciplinary exchange, agency, and collaboration.

History Writing

In 2016, I was fortunate to spend three months in Catania, Sicily, visiting the Facoltà di Giurisprudenza, at the University of Catania. I was in Italy for many reasons. Some were to do with family, a journey of return. The more public reason was to participate with my friend, the feminist International lawyer Adriana di Stefano, in her project *Ius Migrandi: Living With Law*. Adriana's project, with colleagues from faculties across her university, made plain that contemporary migration law and policy was not only a doctrinal question for courts and state, nationally and internationally. It also has a history, and is a local concern for people in everyday life in Catania, a city with an ancient tradition of hospitality because it is central to patterns of movement across the Mediterranean that continue today. My contribution as an external collaborator was very small and came about through my experience of conducting located interdisciplinary scholarship (which in Australia can sit within Law Schools, in ways it does not in the academy of Italy). I gave a paper, toward the end of my stay, on the question of methods of disciplinary relations in my own projects of living with law. While in Catania, I was also working on these essays on feminist jurisography; and Adriana generously made connections with her feminist colleagues so I could be social in my thinking. I was extremely fortunate that my paper also made its own introductions: young women who had come along contacted me directly, and we made time to talk about resonances between my projects and theirs, between Australia and Italy. This is how I met Elena Caruso, a young graduate of the Law School, and an active member of *RivoltaPagina*, the Catanese feminist collective that had begun in 2011, in response to Berlusconi-era gendered politics, reigniting feminist collective action traditions from the 1970s and 1980s. The collective, like that of the Milan feminists of sexual difference from the North, meets in a bookshop. Members span generations, and the collective exists outside of the university and formal institutions (although membership includes many scholars and lawyers).[14]

The task of describing my jurisography project to these new friends was intellectually important, sharpening my focus on drawing out shared, inherited vocabularies, in different languages. It was also a great personal pleasure to exchange ideas on books read in common. In my case, I had been re-reading, in Catania, *Relating Narratives: Storytelling and selfhood*, by the Italian feminist philosopher Adriana Cavarero, and the (anonymous) collective work of the Milan Women's Book Store Collective, *Sexual Difference: A Theory of Social-Symbolic practice*. They were sources I had used before, for the first version of Essays One and Four in this collection.[15] I was also reading the early work of the American feminist poet and essayist Adrienne Rich, to watch how her techniques of address when thinking between institutions and experience in the 1970s, to prepare for writing Essay Four, which considers that period. These texts I had chosen to bring with me in hardcopy for my three months' stay: a luxury, when considering the restraints (and costs) of travel. But they were important instruction manuals for my writing in Catania, for the lessons they offered in what it means for woman to become the subject author, rather than the object, of her disciplinary feminist knowledge, in different times and locations. They also helped me with the difficult task of showing how writing in this tradition has historiographical foundations: it is indebted and reciprocal, yet temporally discontinuous, in the sense that its purposes and audiences are constantly renewed, and re-placed.

Here is an illustration of what I mean.

One of the essays I was reading by Rich was from 1972 and had begun its life as a talk that Rich gave at Berkeley, to the Modern Literature Association Commission on the status of women in the writing profession.[16] Rich begins her address: 'In the last few years connections have been drawn between our sexual lives and our political institutions, which are inescapable and illuminating. The sleepwalkers are coming awake, and for the first time this awakening has a collective reality'.[17] That feminist reality involved, for Rich and others, developing writing practices adequate to their own situation, by acknowledging and adapting writing techniques developed by others, in a not-too-distant past. Rich called this textual and political intimacy 'Re-vision'. She was clear that this was 'act of survival' as well as an exercise in writing a 'chapter of cultural history',[18] and exposed techniques necessary for women to join 'the energy of creation and the energy of relation' in their work.[19] This practice of re-vision could be described in other forms, and in other traditions, as a critique of formalism and of chronology. But the activity Rich is advocating is not transposable with reviewing an understood lineage of accepted texts, or even uncovering hidden ones. What Rich proposed in 1972 is made possible by, and is her own version of, Beauvoir's attitude to writing in *The Second Sex* in 1949: that the woman coming to practice her knowledge enters into relationship with all its written bequests. It involves a recognition that writing by women at other times historicises the conditions of lives lived; but also (unlike other available bequests in your discipline) guides how to take responsibility for the conduct your own life, as the one engaged in the *re-visioning*, be it as historian, philosopher, poet, or as writer, journalist, jurisprudent.

This attitude I have followed through, in my own way, in these exercises in *jurisography*. Rich's 1972 essay (like Beauvoir's 1949 book, *The Second Sex*, as I have shown) creates what it advocates. It recognises a relation between imagination and inheritance; and my chosen library for my time in Catania gave me an additional place to enter into and consider that relation. For example, from the excellent introduction to *Sexual Difference*, by the Italian feminist theorist Teresa de Lauretis, I learned that the Milan collective directly referenced the 'Re-visioning' essay by Rich (amongst other things)[20] in forming their own practices, which they called *collocazione simoblica* ('symbolic placement'). De Lauretis emphasises naming as an imaginative, political act, and explains 'symbolic placement' in a familiar vocabulary:

> 'a genealogy of women . . . that is at once discovered, invented, constructed through feminist practices of reference and address. These practices include the reading or rereading of women's writings; thinking with other women's words, thoughts, knowledges and insights as frames of reference for one's own analyses, understanding and self-definition; and trusting them to provide a symbolic mediation between oneself and others, one's subjectivity and the world'.[21]

For the conduct of reciprocal relations that is opened through those sources, the Milan Collective also gave a name of their own: *affidamento,* 'a notion of entrustment'.[22] It is a term proposed to designate coming into relationship, and 'envisions a personal and social cost, a symbolic debt';[23] where 'one woman entrusts herself symbolically to another . . . who . . . becomes her guide, mentor or point of reference. Not in spite but rather because and in full recognition of the disparity between them'.[24]

While in Catania, I started to write about my appreciation of Italian feminism of difference, and what it might offer to jurisprudence projects here. I will leave that formal exposition to the side, for now. What I want to draw out instead is how my experiences of reading and writing in Catania made possible new conversations, after my return. Some of these are taking place in Australia, with feminists who share an intellectual lineage with me, yet have different disciplinary training and obligations. They included an unexpected invitation to participate in new work by the feminist contemporary artist Alex Martinis Roe. Alex has moved between significant feminist collectives in Sydney, Milan, Barcelona, and Paris, re-introducing in multimedia, through archives and in new writing, and with others at public salons, the radical innovative practices these collectives devised, over time, to come into feminist knowledge together.[25] On her return to Australia she began a new project, in which I was pleased to be invited to participate, *The Shapes of Knowledge*. The project records how Australian feminists of different training and experience inherit their obligations of relationship, and creates public and shared discussion about how entrustment might offer new ways of undertaking our contemporary practises in a settler colony.

Other conversations are with scholars in Catania, and return full circle to where I began. One of the original members of RivoltaPagina in Catania is the feminist historian Emma Baeri. Baeri has also had a long association with feminist collective politics and intellectual projects, and a long career teaching modern history, at the University of Catania. In 1992, she wrote a book, *I Lumi e il cerchio: Una esercitazione di storia* (*The Lights and the circle: An exercise of history*). The book, on one level, tells a history of education in Catania, through analysis of traditional sources on the work of an 18th-century reformer called De Cosmi. On another level, the book is a mediation on the predicaments Baeri faced in writing it. *I Lumi e il cerchio* has become an important feminist guide for many, for its reflection on what it means for Baeri to complete a history project that 'starts from herself'. Her 'I' engages in an intensely immediate address to you, her reader, yet makes clear that the book is not the work of a memoirist, but a feminist scholar entrusted to reimagine both her relationship to feminist knowledge, and to her professional, disciplinary, activity of writing. Baeri opens these considerations by entering her historiographical mediation from the very first page, inviting her reader into her office at the University. She reflects on the fragments of sources that surround her, and considers the false starts she has made in bring this book to life (in a way that was very familiar to me):

> 'I was reading, and a constant presence would spring from between the pages: the other women, my feminist companions, interlocutors, and measures of all of this history. I attempted an interlocking of small and large events, using writing from other times irremediably consigned to a drawer, fragments of incomplete works . . . shopping lists interweaved inexorably with De Cosmi . . . appointments with the paediatrician which had interrupted faculty meetings . . . a fractured time which juxtaposed contradictory events, messing up their value. This time I wanted to understand it.'[26]

Baeri's book, in Italian, includes essay and analysis, poetry and historical narrative; her disturbance of genre illustrates how she has learned to walk between feminist methods and historical craft, to transform the very story she writes. As a reader of the book, who has a familial relationship to Italian (but it is not my mother tongue), the subtlety of Baeri's language, its poetry and play, is for me unfortunately muted. What is, however, very clear is her assertion of disciplinary freedom: to write a history that had long troubled her, and lay fragmented between what was required (as a matter of 'regular' scholarship'), and what is learned and experienced as woman, and scholar, with fidelity to the feminist projects that she participated in every day. As Baeri observes:

> 'I had contained my historical imagination . . . preventing it from passing over the boundaries of the discipline I was being taught. But later, after feminism, this prudence was betrayed as impossibility . . . it was clear to me that I had to recover the memory of myself to go further, to unravel the thread of my history to find a sense of the story'.[27]

I Lumi e il cerchio tells its own story/history (the word Baeri chooses – *storia* – is the same in Italian). It shows a contradictory time, a disturbance for history writing, and a way to contaminate the orthodox stories of knowledge without refusing them. These are important aspirations of my feminist jurisography project too, and I was very glad to meet Baeri through her book. How that happened is also important to what she, and I, are trying to say, and pass on to others.

Friendships that weave their way into the daily activities of institutional, social, and family life take their own time, and follow their own protocols; if visiting a place, that time is rarely long enough. I gave my paper to the Faculty toward the end of my stay in Catania, and met Elena a few weeks before we left. The invitation to visit RivoltaPagina was opened up by her, but I had to return to Australia, and did not have that opportunity on that occasion to meet the other members. This included Emma Baeri, from whom Elena had learned, and was learning, a great deal. In June 2018, I returned to Italy, to a different city with my family, and Elena made the time to visit and spend the day with us. She brought with her a gift: it was *I Lumi e il cerchio*, and it was inscribed to me, by Emma:

> *Recognising without ever meeting: a happy feminist paradox.*
> *We have already met, though that has not yet happened.*

My point in recording this story is to show that projects of entrustment are about relationships and relational arts, but are also intellectual interventions into the histories we tell and in which we participate, and these require serious consideration. The exchange is simple on one level: you gave me knowledge, or taught me to express a relationship of responsibility to what I know. On another it is a challenge to symbolic ordering: publicly acknowledging another person, as feminist practitioner, as intellectual accomplice, and sometimes as a friend you may not, yet, have met.

Jurisprudence Writing

How feminists come into relationship with their knowledge (the question at the centre of this book) is important at any time. But this seems particularly important in 2022, as I am finishing these notes. It has been over 70 years since Beauvoir wrote *The Second Sex*, and her innovation – to appreciate for yourself and show others that there is such a thing as feminist knowledge, in continuous renewal as a matter of everyday practice – is more valuable than ever. It offers both a genealogy of innovation in which to participate, and a repertoire of action that can equip feminists to meet the anger and uncertainty that marks the times in which we write. This sense of powerful purpose has of course been a constant for a very long time, and certainly has had different dimensions and duties since feminists began to inhabit public offices of all kinds.[28] To consider the nature of that task within the contemporary practise of jurisprudence at the university, alongside a friend, I want to introduce into these personal, final notes the Greek-British feminist jurisprudent Maria Drakopoulou.

I met Maria in December 2000 when she was a visiting scholar at Griffith Law School, in Brisbane, Australia. I remember the date very well, as I was not yet in a secure university role, and about to start maternity leave, so on the verge of experiencing a different set of conditions for life and writing. An academic at Kent Law School in England (where she still teaches), it was Maria's first visit to Australia. She had taken the time to read Australian feminist work, and asked our mutual friend, the feminist legal scholar, Rosemary Hunter, to introduce us over coffee in Sydney, where I was living and working at the time. I have been fortunate in my experiences of a feminist legal community, and grateful for the many opportunities afforded to me because of it. But from the first conversation with Maria, in part because we had read each other's work before we met in person, and because she went out of her way to meet me at a time in my life when I was struggling to pursue my projects, she has given me confidence in holding to purpose by way of example, and encouragement. What we have discussed since that first meeting is not only 'the necessity of making a feminist evaluation of our jurisprudence and of taking a jurisprudential view of feminism' (as the American feminist jurisprudent Ann Scales importantly articulated in 1981).[29] In our own ways, we also aim to treat that evaluation as a relationship of difference that requires specific historical reckoning. Feminist jurisography is my response to this provocation. Maria's iteration is different, and more publicly aligned with critical legal thought. What I want to draw out is how within the conditions of the legal academy she maintains a resolute clarity in her work about feminist intellectual expertise that captures its originality, and does so with an attitude that challenges and energises others, including me.

To put Maria's work into context, from a personal vantage point I want to return to the late 1980s and early 1990s (where I temporally landed at the end of Essay Five).[30] The institutional conditions in which feminists could do our work was then still relatively new, created by a surge of intense activity, including at law schools. Many feminist scholars I admire, and whose work I was reading as soon as it became available (in Australia, Margaret Thornton, Jenny Morgan, and Margaret Davies, for only three examples)[31] tore the fabric of law curriculum, and transformed the nature of legal participation and publication. I think those struggles, although fraught and difficult for those involved, captured a moment of institutional self-determination, but in a way that did not preclude diverse engagements. It seemed that taking up a role as a feminist in legal institutions could take many forms: as advisor to government, as empirical researcher, as advocate. But it was also capacious enough to enable the invention of the role, or persona, of the feminist scholar who was responsible for the care of legal knowledge as an intellectual task. This was something Maria began to do, in her teaching and writing, as a legal academic, at that time. In my own experience as a Postgraduate scholar, I had personal proximity to feminist innovators across disciplines. There was not yet a vast intermediary literature of 'feminist scholarship' that proscribed how to do our work, and we were encouraged to acknowledge what we learned as integral to imagining our own projects. It was an exhilarating intellectual world to inhabit. Feminist theory, including feminist legal theory, announced itself and had a certain cachet. To read it was a way for scholars of a critical persuasion, both men and women, to signify they inhabited a 'cutting edge' (in the idiom of the day), and were aware of the propositions made (whether they agreed with them or not).

But I think the purpose or responsibilities of those different roles, and their contributions, are not regarded in the same way now. The duties of feminist legal scholars are more directed, and publicly circumscribed. Addressing sexual violence, or unequal status of women (and the specificity of that question as predicated on acknowledgment of race, Indigeneity, ethnicity, class, sexual or gender identification) is urgent for feminists in 2022. It is particularly urgent for feminists at law taking up the persona of advisor, or advocate. At the same time, the institutional conditions in which to train those learning law (of any sex or gender) with the depth of feminist knowledge necessary to continuously renew these public roles becomes difficult to sustain from within the academy, a point that has been tirelessly argued by Australian feminist legal scholar Margaret Thornton, over her career.[32] This set of conditions is not aided by the fact that the feminist intellectual innovations in joining experiences and practices together, hard fought in the 1980s and 1990s, and necessary to undertake that process of renewal, are also muted in accounts of jurisprudence and legal theory, taught in law schools. They are absorbed, or seen as niche, and this affects how political projects today are conceived and carried out. This seems odd to me; a genealogical pantomime of calling out 'she's behind you', that fails to know why it should turn to the side.

One response is to be very clear about the different nature of feminist obligation, depending on the disciplinary personae we inhabit when we enter into the public world of the university. Maria, for example, exhibits an ethos of intellectual activism by the simple act of identifying herself as 'feminist jurisprudent'. I have sat with her on conference panels, where an assigned program title reveals a false assumption by the organisers that what we are collectively about to do is some haphazard amalgam of 'feminism plus history plus law', a tired exposé of bias, working within modes of historical recovery. But in resolutely insisting she is acknowledged as 'a feminist jurisprudent', Maria announces to a public audience both the traditions she carries and how she is authorized to explain the relations of difference between them, and why it matters to understand this as a serious matter of intellectual rigor, directed at and to the academy itself.

Feminist philosopher Michèle Le Dœuff pursues similar questions about the compromised view of feminist knowledge projects within the university, but in the context of her relationship to philosophy.[33] I think the comparison to jurisprudence is useful, to emphasise the shared nature of this problem for feminist work of a certain kind. In *The Sex of Knowing*, for example, Michèle Le Dœuff is exacting in her scrutiny of 'the myths or images that regulate the relationships between intellect and sex, between the sexes and the order of knowledges'.[34] Yet it is prudent, as she suggests, to pause and consider how feminist projects that undertake this work are seen and heard. As Le Dœuff observes, 'in the academic world . . . (universities, research laboratories, learned journals, union meetings and so on) [a] banality circulates casually . . . that women have a problematic relationship with . . . knowledge as such'.[35] This depends on the nature of the practice. 'Feminist knowledge', in one version, is cast simplistically as 'women's way of knowing', predicated on 'an affectionate, attentive rapport with the objects of knowledge [i.e. women 'studying' women, a simple transfer of untethered experience]'; a technical classification of exceptional women's achievement as 'honorary great men', or 'an involvement typical of the closest emotional relationship' (as intellectual wife, mistress, or fiancée, personae to which I alluded in Essay Five).[36] But if feminist knowledge is asserted in work that carries an intellectual tradition of its own but nevertheless exists in disciplinary relationship, the fate of that work can be different. It exists as a challenge, after all, to the symbolic order of things, and is susceptible to 'erasure entirely from the discussion'.[37]

Le Dœuff's project is to take seriously her own relationship with philosophy to expose and reanimate the forms of that erasure, in order to reorient them. She calls this writing activity 'reintroduction' (a term I have used throughout this book). Maria describes the same activity, in terms of her relationship with jurisprudence, as 'rehabilitation'.[38] In her long-term project, this involves close historical study of two traditions of written sources (jurisprudence and feminist knowledge) to trace specific relationships between them. 'Feminist jurisprudence' is therefore positioned and enunciated by Maria as 'an ambitious and daring undertaking wherein feminist legal scholars directly questioned the nature of law', rather than as a 'generic' engagement of 'what law does to women'.[39] From this vantage point, the formation of the world the jurisprudent inhabits (and which Maria also inhabits in her daily institutional life) is not so much permanently unknown to woman as obscured. In her books and articles, and in her collaborations and teaching, Maria moves between these two worlds to intellectually challenge that obfuscation.

I will give one example, to illustrate. In her 2013 essay, 'Revisiting Feminist Jurisprudence: A Rehabilitation', Maria delineates the genealogy of feminist jurisprudence to acknowledge its intellectual formations. But she also traces an etymological formation of jurisprudence, to remind what it enables, and to question what it refuses. Although not a seamless story of temporal continuity or static location, 'jurisprudence', as a public art obliged to care for law's forms and methods, 'remains firmly entrenched in the ethical domain'.[40] In telling this story, Maria explains that jurisprudence has not simply been a juristic science married to common law judgment. Exposed through different forms of writing (such as commentary and opinion), she shows how jurisprudence, as a body of knowledge, 'did not neglect issues concerning its own identity'.[41] It has maintained a degree of openness to other intellectual endeavours that are similarly concerned with *prudence*, or an experiential self-discipline, in the comportment of their disciplinary duties. It would seem against inherited obligation, in those terms, Maria argues, for jurisprudents to remain silent, ignorant, or forgetful about feminist knowledges that shared similar commitments and antecedents. 'Let us not forget', Maria directs, 'that despite the diverse forms of exclusion imposed on them down the years, women nevertheless have made substantial contributions to many forms of intellectual endeavour'.[42] Although properly concerned with different relationships between knowledges, 'jurisprudence' has not 'concerned itself' in these 'excavations' as it might (even though the institutional conditions to do so are now possible).

Maria's argument in this essay (and in her other work) – in content and forcefulness – is useful to others, and important. She does not proscribe that hers is the only way that feminist jurisprudence is to be done, and in fact counsels against the cataloguing down of method or form of feminist scholarship into a singular address to law. (After all, not everyone shares the same training, experience, or responsibility for the conduct of their law, as those of us who live and work in Australia are acutely aware). But through her writing, she discloses a sense of agency rather than sublimation in how a feminist might comport herself intellectually with her law. This is a continuous and central obligation of working within the contemporary academy; to rehabilitate what she knows, and to form new alliances with jurisprudence, a feminist jurisprudent has a duty to show how she is a beneficiary of her institutional belonging to law. I have tried to undertake my own iteration of those techniques in these essays, through my training in feminist historiography. In Maria's case, she began her working life as a barrister, and she advocates on the behalf of feminist jurisprudence itself:

> 'Refusing to act in the name of law it instead addresses the law as an equal, meeting it head-on; with "her" thinking challenging law's rationality, and juxtaposing a voice and a mind of "her" own to that of law's, to speak of law to law'.[43]

This seems to me an essential component of contemporary university training for lawyers who also happen to be feminists, in order to pursue their own projects, and advocate in their own ways for gender justice in courts, the parliament, the street, or the home.

Feminist Jurisography

It should be clear by now that there is never one story to be told, or told in the same ways, about a feminist's relation to their knowledge, especially if they join institutions. How you or I enter our own stories – become the ones who know and write – involves showing a technical hand about relations of difference (between the feminist practitioner and their discipline, and between those they learn from and those they work with). What can be taken up, and when, as an inheritance is already a mediated relationship, through text but also intellectual companionship and apprenticeship.

In this sense, it is important to end where I began. Jurisography has been an exercise in drawing these traditions, and conducts of life and scholarship, into relationship. It has been invented with scholars I work and talk with every day, jurisprudents Shaun McVeigh and Peter Rush. Once again, I was introduced to them through their writing before we met in person, as colleagues at Melbourne Law School. In talking and working together, we discovered we shared a certain ethos of scholarly life. Bringing our own traditions into relationship has enabled us to experiment with techniques of showing how jurisprudence is addressed and accounted for in writing at different times, but to also stage an argument about why it is a public responsibility to write about the jurisprudence that belongs to the places we live and work. Naming jurisography and experimenting with ways to write jurisprudence has enabled us to attend to the materials of law (in many diverse sources), to show not only how they order lives, and experiences, but open up a training in how to live a life with law, or conduct your own obligations to law.[44]

Working with Shaun and Peter on our jurisography projects has sustained my own thinking while writing this book. But their obligations to jurisprudence, as custodians of knowledge, and as teachers, are not identical to mine; our ways of writing are also not the same. As these essays have tried to show, one of my duties has been to historicise and make visible that there is no default feminist praxis in our own time, and to remind there are feminist traditions invested in acknowledgment of different embodied experience of knowledge, and committed to practical activities of relationship, that might be put to the test, and put to good use. Undertaking this explicit project on feminist jurisography, for example, has helped me think better about how to take up my work in discussions with my students, and in my other current projects. This includes ongoing collaborations with Indigenous and non-Indigenous historians and lawyers, both men and women, in which we take as our central topic how laws and people meet in Australia, and to return the roles, knowledge, and leadership practices of women in those meetings to the centre of collaborative production.

In the end, writing *Feminist Jurisography* has been an activity of assertion and reciprocity, to demonstrate that inhabiting a disciplinary persona is a political and intellectual act, capable of showing fields of relationships that are neither severable from self-formation as a feminist, nor from the conditions of life. One ambition has been to show how that might be done with the techniques I have inherited. The other is to show that jurisography – now it has been named – might be useful for your own writing, and for other projects of feminist reimagination.

Notes

1 See *Feminist Jurisography: Law, History Writing.*
2 See Essay One, *Feminist Jurisography.*
3 There are many examples, and sources to cite for these points. For two, written for different audiences, and produced at different points of time, see Bertolino 2008; Lauretis 1990.
4 Watson 2022. See also the work of those who generously allowed these practices to be read and witnessed over many years, importantly Watson 2014; Moreton-Robinson 2013.
5 Battersby 2000: 5.
6 Battersby 2000: 5.
7 See Essay One, *Feminist Jurisography.*
8 Cavarero 2000: 36.
9 The textual guidance and companionship during the writing of this book that I am alluding to comes from the fiction and nonfiction of Elena Ferrante, Rachel Cusk, Deborah Levy, and Natalia Ginzburg.
10 Ginzburg 2018: 101–102. This essay was first published in Italian as 'Il mio mestiere' in 1949, in *Ponte.*
11 Morris 1988: xi.
12 Hadot 2004: 274.
13 Hadot 2004: 245.
14 RivoltaPagina 2022.
15 See Essay One and Essay Four, *Feminist Jurisography.*
16 Rich 1972.
17 Rich 1972: 18.
18 Rich 1972: 18.
19 Rich 1972: 24.
20 Lauretis 1990: 3.
21 Lauretis 1990: 2.
22 Lauretis 1990: 8–9.
23 Lauretis 1990: 11.
24 Lauretis 1990: 8–9.
25 Martinis Roe 2018; Monash University Museum of Art 2019.
26 Baeri 1992: x–xi. With thanks to Elena Caruso and Cinzia Pellicciotta for correcting my translation.
27 Baeri 1992: x.
28 See Essay One *Feminist Jurisography*: 5–6, Essay Four *Feminist Jurisography*: 79–81; 86–88 and Essay Five *Feminist Jurisography*: 100–103.

29 Scales 1981: 375.
30 See Essay Five, *Feminist Jurisography*: 109–113.
31 See discussion of these texts, and influences: Hunter 2015; Genovese 2015; Graycar & Morgan 2015; Thornton & Genovese 2015; Davies 2002.
32 Thornton 1991, 1996, 2004, 2009, 2020.
33 I introduced Le Dœuff in Essay One, and read her work throughout all of the essays in this collection, as a guide to scrutinize how woman can come into relationship with knowledge in a way that does not refuse her experience. See: Le Dœuff 2003, 1991.
34 Le Dœuff 2003: xvi.
35 Le Dœuff 2003: xiii.
36 See Essay Five, *Feminist Jurisography*: 103–107.
37 Le Dœuff 2003: xiii.
38 I am working with her essay 'Revisiting Feminist Jurisprudence: A Rehabilitation' but note the practices are honed though her body of work.
39 Drakopoulou 2013: 8.
40 Drakopoulou 2013: 2.
41 Drakopoulou 2013: 3.
42 Drakopoulou 2013: 5.
43 Drakopoulou 2013: 8.
44 See Essay One, *Feminist Jurisography*.

References

Baeri E 1992 *I Lumi e il cerchio: Una esercitazione di storia* Editori Riuniti Rome.

Battersby C 2000 'Learning to Think Intercontinentally: Finding Australian Routes' *Hypatia* 15/2: 1–17 DOI: 10.1111/j.1527-2001.2000.tb00310.x.

Bertolino E 2008 'Beyond Ontology and Sexual Difference: An Interview with the Italian Feminist Philosopher Adriana Cavarero' *Differences: A Journal of Feminist Cultural Studies* 19/1: 128–167 DOI:10.1215/10407391-2007-019.

Cavarero A 2000 *Relating Narratives: Storytelling and selfhood* Trans P A Kottman Routledge London and New York (first published 1997).

Davies M 2002 'Ethics and Methodology in Legal Theory: A (Personal) Research Anti-Manifesto' *Law Text Culture* 6/1: 7–26.

Drakopoulou M 2013 'Revisiting Feminist Jurisprudence: A Rehabilitation' *feminists@law* 3/2: 1–29 DOI:10.22024/UniKent/03/fal.90.

Genovese A 2015 'Occasions and Events: Australian Feminist Jurisprudence at 25' *Australian Feminist Law Journal* 41/1: 1–2 DOI:10.1080/13200968.2015.1045111.

Ginzburg N 2018 'My Vocation' in N Ginzburg 2018 *The Little Virtues* Trans D Davis Daunt Books London (essay first published 1949): 85–109.

Graycar R and Morgan J 2015 'On *The Hidden Gender of Law*: A Public Talk' *Australian Feminist Law Journal* 41/1: 29–36 DOI:10.1080/13200968.2015.1045110.

Hadot P 2004 *What Is Ancient Philosophy?* Trans M Chase Belknap Press Cambridge (first published 1995).

Hunter R 2015 'Three Landmark Feminist Legal Texts: Personal and Political' *Australian Feminist Law Journal* 41/1: 37–42 DOI:10.1080/13200968.2015.1045114.

Lauretis T de 1990 'The Practice of Sexual Difference and Feminist Thought in Italy: An Introductory Essay' in The Milan Women's Bookstore Collective 1990 *Sexual Difference: A Theory of Social-Symbolic Practice* Trans P Cicogna and T de Lauretis Indiana University Press Bloomington (first published 1987): 1–21.

Le Dœuff M 1991 *Hipparchia's Choice: An Essay Concerning Women, Philosophy, etc.* Trans T Selous Oxford Blackwell (first published 1989).

Le Dœuff M 2003 *The Sex of Knowing* Trans K Hamer and L Code Routledge London and New York.

Martinis Roe A 2018 *To Become Two: Propositions for Feminist Collective Practice* Archive Books Berlin.

Monash University Museum of Art 2019 *Alex Martinis Roe: Our Future Network Salon* Monash University Melbourne viewed 6 February 2022 <www.monash.edu/muma/exhibitions/previous/2019/shapes-of-knowledge/shapes-of-knowledge-projects/alex-martinis-roe/related-programs/alex-martinis-roe-our-future-network-salon2>.

Moreton-Robinson A 2013 'Towards an Australian Indigenous Women's Standpoint Theory: A Methodological Tool' *Australian Feminist Studies* 28/78: 331–347 DOI:10.1080/08164649.2013.876664.

Morris M 1988 'Foreword' in A Curthoys 1988 *For and Against Feminism: A Personal Journey into Feminist Theory and History* Allen & Unwin Sydney: viii–xii.

Rich A 1972 'When We Dead Awaken: Writing as Re-Vision' *College English* 34/1: 18–30 DOI:10.2307/375215.

RivoltaPagina L 2022 'RivoltaPagina – femministe terrone a catania' *Catania* viewed 6 February 2022 <https://rivoltapaginacatania.wordpress.com/>.

Scales A C 1981 'Towards a Feminist Jurisprudence' *Indiana Law Journal* 56/3: 375–444.

The Milan Women's Bookstore Collective 1990 *Sexual Difference: A Theory of Social-Symbolic Practice* Trans P Cicogna and T de Lauretis Indiana University Press Bloomington (first published 1987).

Thornton M 1991 'Portia Lost in the Groves of Academe Wondering What to Do About Legal Education' *Law in Context: A Socio-Legal Journal* 9/2: 9–26.

Thornton M 1996 *Dissonance and Distrust: Women in the Legal Profession* Oxford University Press Melbourne.

Thornton M 2004 'Neoliberal Melancholia: The Case of Feminist Legal Scholarship' *Australian Feminist Law Journal* 20/1: 7–22 DOI:10.1080/13200968.2004.10854321.

Thornton M 2009 'Universities Upside Down: The Impact of the New Knowledge Economy' *Canadian Journal of Women and the Law* 21/2: 375–394 DOI:10.1353/jwl.0.0045.

Thornton M 2020 'Postscript: Feminist Legal Theory in the 21st Century' *Laws* 9/3: 16–19 DOI:10.3390/laws9030016.

Thornton M and Genovese A 2015 'On *The Liberal Promise*: A Conversation' *Australian Feminist Law Journal* 41/1: 3–18 DOI:10.1080/13200968.2015.1045113.

Watson I 2014 'First Nations Stories, Grandmother's Law: Too Many Stories to Tell' in H Douglas, F Bartlett, T Luker and R Hunter eds 2014 *Australian Feminist Judgements: Righting and Rewriting Law* Hart Publishing Oxford: 46–53.

Watson N 2022 *Aboriginal Women, Law and Critical Race Theory: Storytelling from the Margins* Palgrave Macmillan Cham.

Index

Note: Page numbers followed by an "n" indicate a note on the corresponding page.

Milton Keynes UK
Ingram Content Group UK Ltd.
UKHW051822220624
444418UK00011B/226

9 781032 420431